# Mastering NetBeans

Master building complex applications with NetBeans to become a more proficient programmer

**David Salter**

BIRMINGHAM - MUMBAI

# Mastering NetBeans

First published: August 2015

Production reference: 1250815

Published by Packt Publishing Ltd.
Livery Place
35 Livery Street
Birmingham B3 2PB, UK.

ISBN 978-1-78528-264-5

www.packtpub.com

# Credits

**Author**
David Salter

**Reviewers**
Michel Graciano
Halil Karaköse
Mario Pérez Madueño

**Commissioning Editor**
Nadeem Bagban

**Acquisition Editor**
Larissa Pinto

**Content Development Editor**
Anand Singh

**Technical Editor**
Ankita Thakur

**Copy Editor**
Swati Priya

**Project Coordinator**
Vijay Kushlani

**Proofreader**
Safis Editing

**Indexer**
Monica Ajmera Mehta

**Production Coordinator**
Arvindkumar Gupta

**Cover Work**
Arvindkumar Gupta

# About the Author

**David Salter** is an enterprise software developer and architect who has been developing software professionally since 1991. His relationship with Java goes right back to the beginning, when he used Java 1.0 to write desktop applications and applets for interactive websites. He has been developing enterprise Java applications using both Java EE (and J2EE) and open source solutions since 2001. He has also written *NetBeans IDE 8 Cookbook* and *Seam 2.x Web Development* and coauthored *Building SOA-Based Composite Applications Using NetBeans IDE 6*, all by Packt Publishing.

First and foremost, I would like to thank my wife and family for putting up with my many hours at the computer while writing this book. Special thanks and love to my wife for all her encouragement and support.

I'd also like to say thanks to all the people at Packt Publishing for helping me with this book. Thank you, Larissa, for your encouragement from the beginning. I would also like to thank Anand and Ankita for their hard work in helping me complete this book.

Finally, thanks to everyone who has worked on NetBeans, making it the product it is today. Without you all, this book would not exist.

# About the Reviewers

**Michel Graciano** is highly familiar with development techniques, such as object- and component-oriented programming, design patterns' applicability, and software analysis. An expert in application development with open source software, he is currently working as an instructor at Código Efetivo, a training company in Brazil.

He is actively involved with open source projects, such as NetBeans, and has delivered talks at JustJava, The Developer's Conference, and JavaOne conferences.

His longtime contributions to NetBeans started with the Portuguese translation project and continued through his participation in the NetFIX and NetCAT programs, leading to him becoming a NetBeans Dream Team member.

> I would like to thank my wife for all her encouragement and support, in this and the other projects I get involved in.

**Halil Karaköse** is a freelance software architect who graduated from Işik University Computer Engineering Department in 2005.

He worked in the telecommunications industry as a software developer and software architect for 10 years, including companies such as Turkcell and Ericsson. In 2014, he quit Ericsson to establish his own software consultancy company, `kodfarki.com`.

He has keen interest in Java tools, which speed up development, such as NetBeans and Intellij IDEA. He loves mouseless driven development.

**Mario Pérez Madueño** graduated in computer engineering from the Open University of Catalonia (UOC), Spain, in 2010. He is an early adopter of Java tech and advocates agile development methodologies. He has been a member of the NetBeans Community Acceptance Testing (NetCAT) program for many years. He has also contributed as a technical reviewer to *Building SOA-Based Composite Applications Using NetBeans IDE 6* and *Java EE 7 Development with NetBeans 8*, both by Packt Publishing.

I would like to thank my wife, María, for her unconditional help and support in all the projects I get involved in. I would also like to thank Martín and Matías for giving me the strength to go ahead.

# www.PacktPub.com

## Support files, eBooks, discount offers, and more

For support files and downloads related to your book, please visit `www.PacktPub.com`.

Did you know that Packt offers eBook versions of every book published, with PDF and ePub files available? You can upgrade to the eBook version at `www.PacktPub.com` and as a print book customer, you are entitled to a discount on the eBook copy. Get in touch with us at `service@packtpub.com` for more details.

At `www.PacktPub.com`, you can also read a collection of free technical articles, sign up for a range of free newsletters and receive exclusive discounts and offers on Packt books and eBooks.

https://www2.packtpub.com/books/subscription/packtlib

Do you need instant solutions to your IT questions? PacktLib is Packt's online digital book library. Here, you can search, access, and read Packt's entire library of books.

## Why subscribe?

- Fully searchable across every book published by Packt
- Copy and paste, print, and bookmark content
- On demand and accessible via a web browser

## Free access for Packt account holders

If you have an account with Packt at `www.PacktPub.com`, you can use this to access PacktLib today and view 9 entirely free books. Simply use your login credentials for immediate access.

# Table of Contents

# Preface

NetBeans is the only IDE that can be downloaded with Java itself. It provides developers with many cutting-edge features that are not available with all the other IDEs.

This book will teach you how to master the NetBeans IDE. You will learn how to utilize and master the NetBeans IDE to become a proficient developer.

This book is packed with many hints, tips, and time-saving techniques. Reading this book will teach you about the features provided by NetBeans that newcomers to the IDE are not aware of and experienced programmers make extensive use of on a day-to-day basis.

## What this book covers

*Chapter 1, Getting Started with NetBeans*, describes the different versions of NetBeans that are available to download and shows you how to install NetBeans from an installable package or from the source code.

*Chapter 2, Editing Files and Projects*, teaches you about the many different facilities available while editing files. You will learn about macros, project groups, the NetBeans windowing system, and much more.

*Chapter 3, The NetBeans Developer's Life Cycle*, explains how NetBeans helps with the tasks that every developer does on a daily basis—running, debugging, testing, and profiling applications.

*Chapter 4, Managing Services*, shows you how NetBeans manages external services such as Maven repositories, PaaS, and continuous integration systems.

*Chapter 5, Database Persistence*, describes the features that NetBeans provides to help write database applications, from both a code-first and data-first perspective.

*Chapter 6, Desktop Development*, describes the excellent features provided by NetBeans for developing desktop Swing applications.

*Chapter 7, Creating the Business Layer*, teaches you the tools provided to help developers write the business layers of applications, describing subjects such as EJBs and bean validation.

*Chapter 8, Creating the Web Tier*, explains the different features available for Java web developers, including details of creating Spring web applications and using CSS preprocessors.

*Chapter 9, Creating and Consuming Web Services*, explains how NetBeans makes it straightforward to create and consume both RESTful and SOAP-based web services.

*Chapter 10, Extending NetBeans*, describes how to create NetBeans plugins for those situations where you need to customize the IDE along with the details of how to start using NetBeans as the platform for desktop applications.

# What you need for this book

To use this book, you need to download and install the NetBeans IDE on either Windows, Mac OS X, or Linux.

You also need to have a modern version of Java (preferably, Java 8). To benefit the most when learning about web services and EJB-related technologies, a Java EE application server is required. The enterprise download bundle of NetBeans is supplied with full support for GlassFish 4 Open Source edition.

# Who this book is for

This book is written for Java developers of all the levels who want to gain more knowledge about how their IDE works and learn new techniques to enable them to become more productive when using NetBeans.

A reasonable level of Java and Java EE knowledge is assumed.

# Conventions

In this book, you will find a number of text styles that distinguish between different kinds of information. Here are some examples of these styles and an explanation of their meaning.

Code words in text, database table names, folder names, filenames, file extensions, pathnames, dummy URLs, user input, and Twitter handles are shown as follows: "From there, double-click on the included NetBeans xxx.mpkg file to start the installation (the exact names of the .dmg and .mpkg files varies, depending upon the version and bundle downloaded)."

A block of code is set as follows:

```
public class Main {
    public static void main(String args[]) {
        Greeter greeter = new Greeter();

        System.out.println(greeter.greet("David"));
    }
}
```

When we wish to draw your attention to a particular part of a code block, the relevant lines or items are set in bold:

```
<#assign licenseFirst = "/*">
<#assign licensePrefix = " * ">
<#assign licenseLast = " */">
<#include "${project.licensePath}">

<#if package?? && package != "">
package ${package};

</#if>
/**
 * Project: ${project.name}
 * ${url}
 *
 * @author ${user}
 */
public class ${name} {

}
```

Any command-line input or output is written as follows:

```
chmod +x netbeans-<xxx>-linux.sh
```

**New terms** and **important words** are shown in bold. Words that you see on the screen, for example, in menus or dialog boxes, appear in the text like this: "From here, we can customize NetBeans by clicking on the **Customize** button."

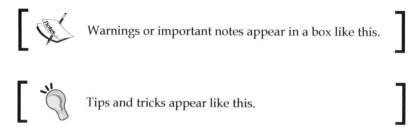

Warnings or important notes appear in a box like this.

Tips and tricks appear like this.

# Reader feedback

Feedback from our readers is always welcome. Let us know what you think about this book—what you liked or disliked. Reader feedback is important for us as it helps us develop titles that you will really get the most out of.

To send us general feedback, simply e-mail feedback@packtpub.com, and mention the book's title in the subject of your message.

If there is a topic that you have expertise in and you are interested in either writing or contributing to a book, see our author guide at www.packtpub.com/authors.

# Customer support

Now that you are the proud owner of a Packt book, we have a number of things to help you to get the most from your purchase.

# Downloading the example code

You can download the example code files from your account at http://www.packtpub.com for all the Packt Publishing books you have purchased. If you purchased this book elsewhere, you can visit http://www.packtpub.com/support and register to have the files e-mailed directly to you.

# Downloading the color images of this book

We also provide you with a PDF file that has color images of the screenshots/diagrams used in this book. The color images will help you better understand the changes in the output. You can download this file from: https://www.packtpub.com/sites/default/files/downloads/26450S_ColorImages.pdf.

# Errata

Although we have taken every care to ensure the accuracy of our content, mistakes do happen. If you find a mistake in one of our books—maybe a mistake in the text or the code—we would be grateful if you could report this to us. By doing so, you can save other readers from frustration and help us improve subsequent versions of this book. If you find any errata, please report them by visiting `http://www.packtpub.com/submit-errata`, selecting your book, clicking on the **Errata Submission Form** link, and entering the details of your errata. Once your errata are verified, your submission will be accepted and the errata will be uploaded to our website or added to any list of existing errata under the Errata section of that title.

To view the previously submitted errata, go to `https://www.packtpub.com/books/content/support` and enter the name of the book in the search field. The required information will appear under the **Errata** section.

# Piracy

Piracy of copyrighted material on the Internet is an ongoing problem across all media. At Packt, we take the protection of our copyright and licenses very seriously. If you come across any illegal copies of our works in any form on the Internet, please provide us with the location address or website name immediately so that we can pursue a remedy.

Please contact us at `copyright@packtpub.com` with a link to the suspected pirated material.

We appreciate your help in protecting our authors and our ability to bring you valuable content.

# Questions

If you have a problem with any aspect of this book, you can contact us at `questions@packtpub.com`, and we will do our best to address the problem.

# 1
# Getting Started with NetBeans

NetBeans IDE 8 is the official IDE for Java 8, and the only IDE that can be downloaded with official distributions of Java 8.

The latest version, NetBeans IDE 8.0.2, provides tools to allow developers to create desktop, mobile, and web applications using all of the latest Java specifications such as Java SE 8, Java ME 8, and Java EE 7.

This chapter will cover the following topics:

- Choosing a download bundle of NetBeans
- Downloading and installing NetBeans
- Updating NetBeans to the latest version
- Downloading NetBeans source code from Mercurial
- Building NetBeans
- NetBeans configuration

## Choosing a download bundle of NetBeans

There are three different installation bundles of NetBeans (which can be downloaded from the NetBeans site) that are relevant to Java developers:

- Java SE
- Java EE
- All

In addition to these three bundles, C/C++ and HTML5 & PHP bundles are also available for download. These bundles are not targeted at Java developers though, so they will not be discussed further in this book.

The Java SE bundle provides the standard NetBeans Platform SDK along with support for Java SE and Java FX developers.

The Java EE bundle contains everything that the SE bundle includes, but adds support for Java EE and HTML5 developers. GlassFish Server Open Source Edition 4.1 and Apache Tomcat 8.0.15 are also included with the Java EE bundle.

The All bundle contains everything that the EE bundle includes, but adds support for C/C++, Groovy, and PHP developers.

| | NetBeans IDE Download Bundles | | | | |
|---|---|---|---|---|---|
| Supported technologies * | Java SE | Java EE | C/C++ | HTML5 & PHP | All |
| NetBeans Platform SDK | • | • | | | • |
| Java SE | • | • | | | • |
| Java FX | • | • | | | • |
| Java EE | | • | | | • |
| Java ME | | | | | – |
| HTML5 | | • | | • | • |
| Java Card™ 3 Connected | | | | | – |
| C/C++ | | | • | | • |
| Groovy | | | | | • |
| PHP | | | | • | • |
| **Bundled servers** | | | | | |
| GlassFish Server Open Source Edition 4.1 | | • | | | • |
| Apache Tomcat 8.0.15 | | • | | | • |
| | Download | Download | Download | Download | Download |
| | Free, 105 MB | Free, 222 MB | Free, 72 MB | Free, 72 MB | Free, 243 MB |

# Downloading and installing NetBeans

Downloading an installation of NetBeans (Java SE, Java EE, or All) is achieved by selecting the bundle to download and then clicking on the **Download** button for that bundle, as shown in the preceding screenshot.

All of the examples and screenshots in this book have been created with the Java EE bundle of NetBeans. It is recommended that you use the Java EE download bundle of NetBeans to adhere as closely as possible to the examples in this book.

 To install any version of NetBeans 8, the Java JDK Version 7 Update 10 or later, or Java JDK 8 or later, is required. These can be downloaded, if not already installed on your target system, from http://www.oracle.com/technetwork/java/javase/downloads.

Having downloaded the appropriate NetBeans bundle installer for your operating system, you can install NetBeans on your development system. The installation procedure differs slightly for the three main operating systems NetBeans is available for.

For Windows, simply launch the NetBeans installer by double-clicking on the file, `netbeans-<xxx>-windows.exe` (the exact filename differs depending upon the version and bundle downloaded).

For Mac OS X, double-click on the downloaded file, `netbeans-<xxx>-macosx.dmg`, to mount the installation device. From there, double-click on the included NetBeans `xxx.mpkg` file to start the installation (the exact names of the `.dmg` and `.mpkg` files vary, depending upon the version and bundle downloaded).

For Linux, NetBeans is installed via a command-line script, so first we must change the permissions of the downloaded file to be executable. From a terminal window, execute the following command:

```
chmod +x netbeans-<xxx>-linux.sh
```

**Downloading the example code**

You can download the example code files from your account at `http://www.packtpub.com` for all the Packt Publishing books you have purchased. If you purchased this book elsewhere, you can visit `http://www.packtpub.com/support` and register to have the files e-mailed directly to you. You can also download the code samples from `https://github.com/doobrie/masteringnb`.

To continue with the installation on Linux, we must now execute the downloaded installer. From a terminal window, execute the following command:

```
./netbeans-xxx-linux.sh
```

The installation of the JDK can sometimes be complex on some Linux distributions. Fortunately, NetBeans can be easily executed with an unpacked JDK. If installation of the JDK is complex, simply unpack the JDK files into a `<jdk_folder>` folder and then execute the installer with the `–javahome` argument passing in the JDK folder, for example, `/netbeans-xxx-linux.sh –javahome <jdk_folder>`.

On all of the major operating systems (Windows, Mac OS X, and Linux), the procedure for installing NetBeans is now very similar. After launching the setup procedure, the installer takes you through the several steps in a wizard style to install NetBeans.

Having agreed to the NetBeans license and selected a folder for installation, the installer displays the **Installation Type** window:

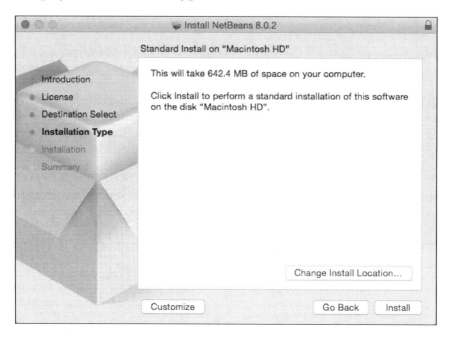

From here, we can customize NetBeans by clicking on the **Customize** button.

>  On Windows and Linux, the preceding screenshot will differ slightly, showing the different application servers that can be installed with NetBeans.

The next screenshot shows the customization options for the Java EE bundle. The options may differ depending upon which bundle you choose to download. For the Java EE bundle, different base components of the NetBeans Platform can be installed, namely **Base IDE, Java SE, HTML5**, and **Java EE**.

The Java EE bundle (and also the All bundle) gives the option of installing GlassFish Open Source Edition and Tomcat 8. If either GlassFish or Tomcat is chosen for installation, NetBeans will automatically configure them as servers within the IDE.

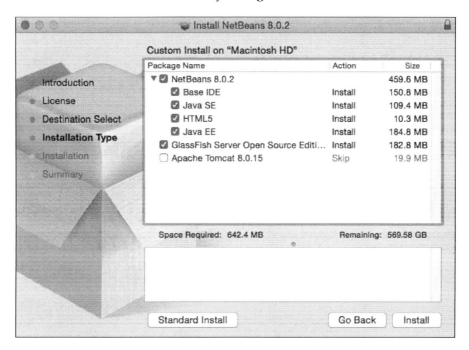

# Installing other versions of NetBeans

Usually, installing the latest released version of NetBeans is the best course of action. With NetBeans, however, it is possible to download and install the previous versions or even daily builds.

Be careful with daily builds; they have not been through the rigorous testing procedure that the full release builds had, and may contain bugs!

To download the previous released versions of NetBeans, browse to the NetBeans download page at http://www.netbeans.org/downloads and click on the **Archive** link in the top-right corner of the page, as shown in the following screenshot:

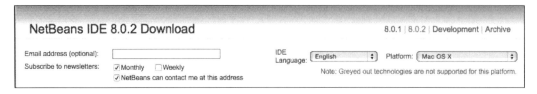

 For easy access, the previous version of NetBeans is available for downloading by clicking on the appropriate link at the top of the page (version 8.0.1 in the preceding screenshot) rather than clicking on the **Archive** link and manually selecting a version to install.

From the resultant page, select the previous release you wish to download (for example, NetBeans 7.3) and then click on the **Continue** button. From here, you can choose whether to download the Java SE, Java EE, or All distributions of NetBeans. The following screenshot shows the previous versions of NetBeans that are currently available for download:

To download the latest daily build of NetBeans, simply click on the **Development** link in the top-right corner of the NetBeans download page. Again, from the resulting page, select the download bundle (Java SE, Java EE, or All) you require and follow the standard NetBeans installation procedure for your operating system, as outlined previously.

# NetBeans user directory

When installing NetBeans, a special directory is created on your computer that stores all the user configuration data for NetBeans; this folder is referred to as a `userdir` or `user` directory. This folder contains information on what plugins you have activated in NetBeans, what editor settings you've configured, and much more data. In fact, everything that makes your instance of NetBeans unique to you is stored in this folder.

On Mac OS X, the user directory is located at `~/Library/Application Support/NetBeans`.

On Windows, it is located at `c:\Users\<user>\AppData\Roaming\NetBeans`.

On Linux, the user directory is located at `~/.netbeans`.

In the user directory are the separate directories for each different version of NetBeans that you have installed. With this technique, it is therefore possible to have different configurations for different versions of NetBeans that are installed.

In addition to a user directory, NetBeans also makes use of a hidden cache directory, often referred to as a `cachedir`. The cache directory contains large amount of cache data and thus, it can become a large directory. Due to the information that's written into the cache directory, it must be stored in a different location to the user directory. The contents of the cache directory can be deleted without any settings being lost; it will be recreated the next time NetBeans is executed.

On Mac OS X, the cache directory is located at `~/Library/Caches/NetBeans`.

On Windows, the cache directory is located at `c:\Users\<user>\AppData\Local\NetBeans\Cache`.

On Linux, the cache directory is located at `~/.cache/netbeans`.

An easy way to find out the location of the user and cache directories is to display the NetBeans **About** dialog. In this dialog, the location of these directories is given along with the information about the version of NetBeans and Java that are in use:

> **Product Version:** NetBeans IDE 8.0.2 (Build 201411181905)
> **Updates:** NetBeans IDE is updated to version <u>NetBeans 8.0.2 Patch 2</u>
> **Java:** 1.8.0_40; Java HotSpot(TM) 64-Bit Server VM 25.40-b25
> **Runtime:** Java(TM) SE Runtime Environment 1.8.0_40-b25
> **System:** Mac OS X version 10.10.4 running on x86_64; UTF-8; en_US (nb)
> **User directory:** /Users/david/Library/Application Support/NetBeans/8.0.2
> **Cache directory:** /Users/david/Library/Caches/NetBeans/8.0.2

# Updating NetBeans to the latest version

When new versions of NetBeans are released, one simple way to upgrade to the latest version is to download the new version and install it, as shown previously.

When you install NetBeans this way and already have an installation of NetBeans on your computer, NetBeans will ask whether you wish to use the settings from the previous version:

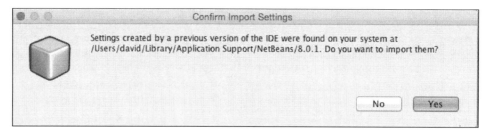

Selecting **Yes** to this option will import all of the user directory settings from the previous version of NetBeans into the newly installed version. Selecting **No** will start NetBeans with a clean and empty user directory.

 After installing a new version of NetBeans, it's always a good idea to check whether there are any updates to plugins by going to the plugin manager and selecting **Check for Updates**.

# Obtaining the NetBeans source code

The source code for NetBeans itself is available under the **Common Development and Distribution License (CDDL)** v1.0 and GNU **General Public License (GPL)** v2.

It's possible to obtain the source for NetBeans either as a `.zip` file, containing the entire source for a specific release, by cloning the code from the NetBeans Mercurial repository or by viewing the files from within a browser.

# Downloading a zipped archive of the NetBeans source code

If you just want to look at the NetBeans source code and aren't interested in making changes, you can download the source as a `.zip` archive from the relevant download page for any release. At the bottom of each download page, there is a link to download the source in the ZIP file format, as shown in the following screenshot:

> \* You can add or remove packs later using the IDE's Plugin Manager (Tools | Plugins).
>
> Java 7 and later versions are required for installing and running the PHP and C/C++ NetBeans Bundles. You can download the latest Java at java.com.
>
> JDK 7 and later versions are required for installing and running the Java SE, Java EE and All NetBeans Bundles. You can download standalone JDK or download the latest JDK with NetBeans IDE Java SE bundle.
>
> You can start developing applications based on the NetBeans Platform using the NetBeans IDE for Java SE. Learn more about the NetBeans Platform. NetBeans source code and binary builds without bundled runtimes are also available in zip file format. See also instructions on how to build the IDE from sources or installation instructions.

# Cloning the NetBeans source code from Mercurial

The alternative to downloading a ZIP archive of the NetBeans source code is to clone the code from the NetBeans Mercurial repository. To perform this operation, you must have the Mercurial client installed on your computer. It can be downloaded for Windows and Mac OS X. For Linux and Mac OS X, it can be installed via the operating system's appropriate package manager, for example, `apt-get` on Ubuntu or `yum install` on Fedora. The Mercurial site at `http://mercurial.selenic.com` provides all the details on how to install Mercurial.

The NetBeans source code can be cloned from Mercurial from either the command line or from within NetBeans. Let's first look at how to achieve this using the command line.

Having installed Mercurial, we are in a good position to clone the NetBeans source code using the `hg clone` operation.

The NetBeans source code is stored within several branches and tags in the Mercurial repository. The main development for the next version of NetBeans is performed within `main-silver` branch. This branch contains the latest development that has been picked up by the latest automatic stable build of NetBeans.

To check out this branch, execute the following command from within a terminal or command prompt:

```
hg clone http://hg.netbeans.org/main-silver
```

If this is your first check out of a branch, Mercurial may take a long time to clone the repository. Depending on your computer and network connection, this may take several hours.

Due to the way Mercurial works, hidden files are created on the local filesystem during the first phase of a Mercurial `clone` operation. No console output is provided during the checkout phase either, so it may appear that the `clone` operation is not working correctly as there is no visible feedback that the sources are being cloned.

It's possible to tell Mercurial to output status information so that you can see that all is working correctly. This can be especially useful on the first clone of a branch, which can be a lengthy operation. To clone a branch and get status updates output to the console, we must add the `--debug` parameter onto the `clone` operation:

```
hg --debug clone http://hg.netbeans.org/main-silver/
```

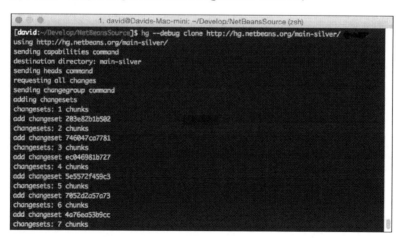

After cloning the NetBeans source files from the Mercurial repository, we have many subdirectories within the `main-silver` directory, as shown in the following screenshot:

| Name | ^ | Date Modified |
| --- | --- | --- |
| ▼ main-silver | | Today 14:32 |
| ▶ ant.browsetask | | Today 14:33 |
| ▶ ant.debugger | | Today 14:33 |
| ▶ ant.freeform | | Today 14:33 |
| ▶ ant.grammar | | Today 14:33 |
| ▶ ant.kit | | Today 14:33 |
| ▶ api.annotations.common | | Today 14:33 |
| ▶ api.debugger | | Today 14:33 |
| ▶ api.debugger.jpda | | Today 14:33 |
| ▶ api.htmlui | | Today 14:33 |
| ▶ api.intent | | Today 14:33 |
| ▶ api.io | | Today 14:33 |
| ▶ api.java | | Today 14:33 |
| ▶ api.java.classpath | | Today 14:33 |
| ▶ api.java.classpath.nb | | Today 14:33 |
| ▶ api.maven | | Today 14:33 |
| ▶ api.mobility | | Today 14:33 |
| ▶ api.progress | | Today 14:33 |
| ▶ api.progress.compat8 | | Today 14:33 |

# Cloning specific versions of NetBeans

In the previous section, we showed how to clone the `main-silver` branch from the NetBeans Mercurial repository. What if we don't want the latest cutting edge development, but want to look at the source code for a specific version of NetBeans?

Fortunately, each release of NetBeans has the source code tagged in the Mercurial repository, so it's possible to check out any older release going back to December 1999 (this is the first tagged release within Mercurial).

The complete list of tagged releases is available at `http://hg.netbeans.org/releases/tags`, as shown in the following screenshot:

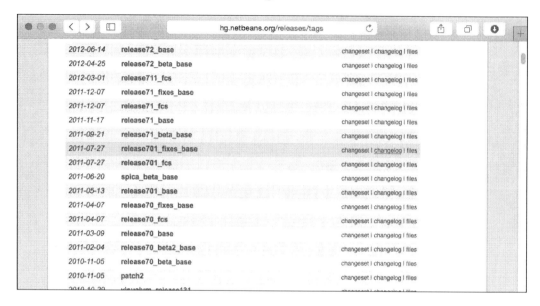

To view any of these tagged releases, simply check out the **releases** branch and then change to the specified folder for the requested release.

# Cloning the NetBeans source code from within NetBeans

To enable us to use Mercurial from within NetBeans, we must first ensure that NetBeans is configured with the location of the Mercurial executable—`hg.exe` on Windows and `hg` on Mac OS X and Linux.

To configure Mercurial within NetBeans, perform the following steps:

1. Open the NetBeans **Options** dialog. On Windows and Linux, this is achieved by selecting **Tools** and then **Options** from the main menu. On Mac OS X, clicking on **NetBeans** and then **Preferences** from the application menu opens the **Options** dialog.

2. In the **Options** dialog, click on the **Team** option and then choose the **Versioning** tab.

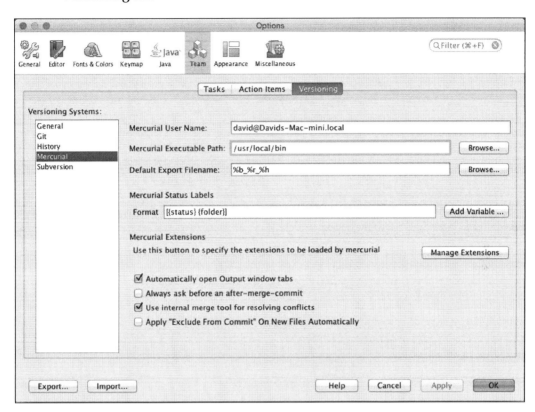

3. On the **Versioning** tab, ensure that the **Mercurial Executable Path** field is set as appropriate for your operating system. In the preceding screenshot, you can see that it is set to /usr/local/bin, which is the folder that contains the hg executable on my computer.

Once we've configured the Mercurial support within NetBeans, we can clone the source code repository by performing the following steps:

1. Open the **Clone External Repository** wizard by clicking on **Team** and then **Mercurial** and eventually, **Clone Other...** from the application menu.

2. Enter the repository URL as `http://hg.netbeans.org/main-silver`.

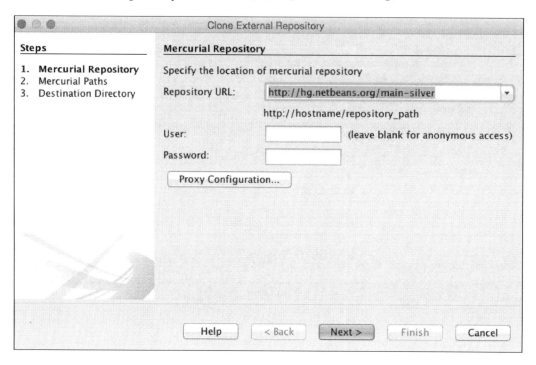

3. Continue on through the wizard until the **Destination Directory** stage is displayed. On this page, enter the parent directory into which the NetBeans source code will be cloned and ensure that the **Scan for NetBeans Projects after Clone** option is checked. With this option checked, NetBeans will automatically open the cloned project after the repository is cloned.

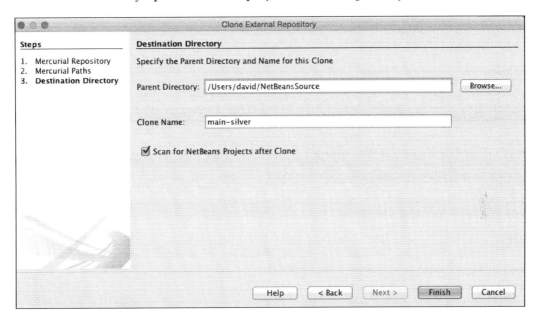

4. Click on the **Finish** button to commence the cloning process.

Cloning the NetBeans source code in this way via NetBeans does not provide any visual feedback on the progress of the cloning operation. If you wish to see visual feedback so that you know something is happening, consider cloning the repository via the command line, as described earlier.

# Browsing the NetBeans source code online

The NetBeans source code is available to browse online at `http://hg.netbeans.org/main/file`. Viewing the source code this way can be very useful for the casual observer who wants to see how something is done within the NetBeans source code, but does not want to download the entire source code to their computer.

The following screenshot shows the top level of the NetBeans source code in a browser window:

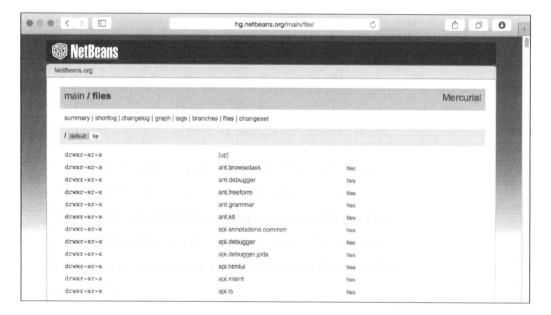

# Building NetBeans

Once we've downloaded the source code for NetBeans, we can build it either using the command line or via NetBeans.

To build the NetBeans IDE from the source code, we need to have the following software installed first:

- JDK 7
- Apache Ant

 NetBeans can be built with JDK 8, but additional steps are required for this; we'll see what these are shortly!

# Building NetBeans via the command line

To build NetBeans via the command line, open up a terminal or command prompt
and change the directory to the directory containing the source code. Executing the
`ant` command will build the source code, downloading any external dependencies
that are required:

```
[david:~/Develop/NetBeans/main-silver]$ ant
```

If you are running JDK 8 instead of 7, you will be presented with an error when
attempting to build the source code stating that builds are forbidden when using
JDK 8. This error is presented so as not to introduce any Java 8 features into the
source code.

If you wish to use JDK 8 to build the code, you can set the `permit.jdk8.builds`
property to `true`:

```
[david:~/Develop/NetBeans/main-silver]$ ant –Dpermit.jdk8.builds=true
```

Alternatively, if you have both JDK 7 and 8 installed, you can set the `nbjdk.home`
property to point to a valid JDK 7 installation and the build will then complete using
the specified JDK 7 instead of JDK 8.

Once you have successfully build NetBeans, you can execute the freshly built
instance by executing the `ant tryme` task:

```
[david:~/Develop/NetBeans/main-silver]$ ant tryme
```

This will execute the instance of NetBeans that you have just built using `<build-location>/nbbuild/testuserdir` as the user directory. The actual instance of NetBeans is stored within the `<build-location>/nbbuild/netbeans` folder.

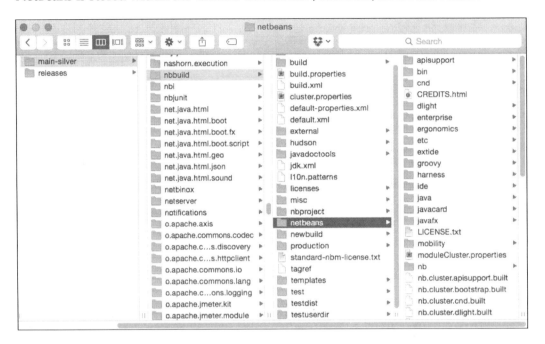

Alternatively, you can also start the freshly-built instance of NetBeans by executing the `netbeans` or `netbeans.exe` commands from within the `<build-location>/nbbuild/netbeans/bin` directory, either from the command line of Windows / Linux explorer or Mac OSX Finder.

# Building NetBeans from within NetBeans

Now that we've seen how to build NetBeans via the command line, let's see how we can build it from within NetBeans itself.

If you cloned the NetBeans source code via the team support in NetBeans, then the **NetBeans Build System** project will already be opened within NetBeans, ready for building, as shown in the following screenshot:

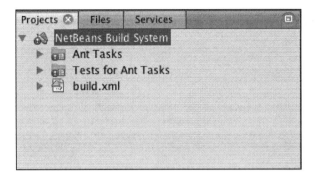

If you cloned NetBeans via the command line, you will need to open the **NetBeans Build System** project located within the `main-silver/nbbuild` directory.

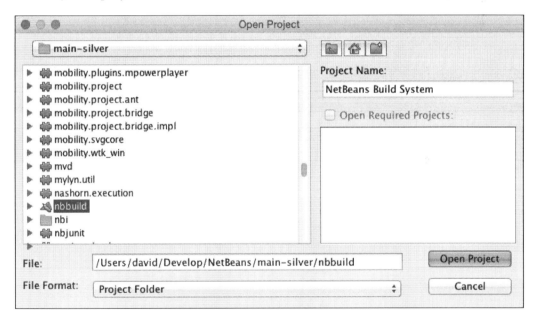

After opening the project, you will see that there are error badges shown against the **Ant Tasks** and **Tests for Ant Tasks** project nodes within the **Projects** window. These errors simply indicate that artifacts needed for the build haven't been downloaded yet; the build process will download the necessary files, and once built, these error badges will no longer appear.

To start building NetBeans, we must first build the necessary Ant tasks that the full build process relies on. To perform this, right-click on the **NetBeans Build System** project and select the **Build** option:

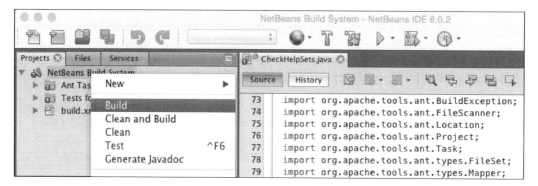

Once the build system is completed with no errors (you will see several warnings displayed during the build process, but these can be safely ignored), you can build NetBeans by right-clicking on the **NetBeans Build System** project and selecting the **Build IDE (No ZIP File)** option:

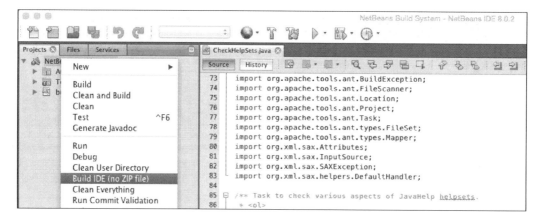

If you are using JDK 7, you will see that NetBeans is built correctly after a few minutes of activity.

If you are using JDK 8, you will see a failure message in the NetBeans output window, indicating that the project cannot be built using JDK 8, as shown in the following screenshot:

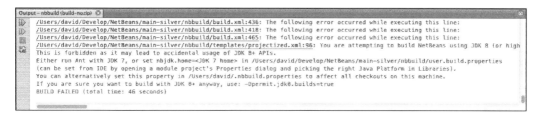

Since NetBeans provides its own installation of Ant to build projects, if we wish to use JDK 8 to build NetBeans, we must configure the `permit.jdk8.builds` property before attempting to build.

To configure the Ant properties from within NetBeans, perform the following steps:

1. Open the NetBeans **Options** dialog. On Windows and Linux, this is achieved by selecting **Tools** and then **Options** from the main menu. On Mac OS X, clicking on **NetBeans** and then **Preferences** from the application menu opens the **Options** dialog.

2. In the **Options** dialog, click on the **Java** option and then choose the **Ant** tab.

3. Within the **Ant** tab, append the `permit.jdk8.builds=true` line into the **Properties** edit box:

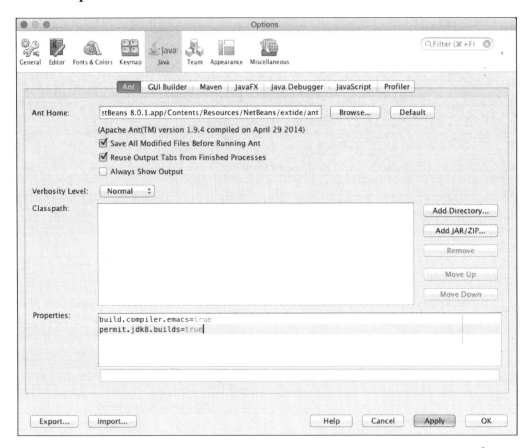

4. Click on the **OK** button to save the configuration changes.

Now that we've configured the `permit.jdk8.builds` property for the internal instance of Ant, we can build the project successfully using JDK 8. This is achieved by right-clicking on the **NetBeans Build System** project within the **Projects** window and selecting the **Build IDE (No ZIP File)** option.

# NetBeans configuration

In the previous sections of this chapter, we saw how to choose an installation of NetBeans and install it. We also saw how to download and build NetBeans from its Java source code.

Let's now take a look at the different options that are used to start NetBeans and see how these can be configured.

The configuration options used to start NetBeans are defined as command-line arguments in the `netbeans.conf` file supplied with a NetBeans distribution.

On Windows and Linux, this file is located within the NetBeans installation directory at `<NetBeans Install Dir>/etc/netbeans.conf`.

On Mac OS X, this file is hidden due to the way Mac OS X packages are deployed. To view and edit the `netbeans.conf` file on OS X, right-click on the `NetBeans.app` executable file and select the **Show Package Contents** menu option:

The contents of the `NetBeans.app` package will then be displayed. The `netbeans.conf` file is located at `Contents/Resources.NetBeans/etc/netbeans.conf` within the package contents.

This configuration is a simple text file and can be opened with any text editor. In the file, we can see several configuration properties that can be modified to suit your requirements. Let's go through these now and see what options are available.

# User and cache directories

Earlier in this chapter, we discussed the NetBeans user and cache directories and what information is stored within them. If you wish to change the user directory for a specific instance of NetBeans (for example, you may want to use a completely fresh user directory or a user directory from a previous installation of NetBeans), this can be achieved by specifying the `netbeans_default_userdir` parameter. Similarly, the cache directory can be changed by specifying the `netbeans_default_cachedir` parameter:

```
netbeans_default_userdir="${DEFAULT_USERDIR_ROOT}/8.0.2"

netbeans_default_cachedir="${DEFAULT_CACHEDIR_ROOT}/8.0.2"
```

 Unless you have a specific reason, you're probably not going to need to change the user and cache directories for NetBeans.

# NetBeans default options

The NetBeans default startup options are probably the most likely of the command-line arguments that you'll need to change for NetBeans. These options are specified by the `netbeans_default_options` parameter:

```
netbeans_default_options="-J-client -J-Xss2m -J-Xms32m -J-XX:PermSize=32m
-J-Dapple.laf.useScreenMenuBar=true -J-Dapple.awt.graphics.UseQuartz=true
-J-Dsun.java2d.noddraw=true -J-Dsun.java2d.dpiaware=true -J-Dsun.zip.disa
bleMemoryMapping=true""true"
```

The preceding example options are from a Mac OS X installation of NetBeans 8.0.2.

The first option (`-J-client`) specifies that the JVM for NetBeans will run as a client VM instead of server VM. The client VM is essentially useful for applications requiring fast startup or small footprints. The server VM is typically used where performance is more important.

 For more information on client and server configurations, check out `http://www.oracle.com/technetwork/java/hotspotfaq-138619.html#compiler_types`.

The second set of options (`-J-Xss2m -J-Xms32m -J-XX:PermSize=32m`) define the default memory allocation sizes used by the JVM running NetBeans (the thread stack size, initial memory allocation pool size, and size of the permanent generation, respectively). These options are specific for different version of the JDK, and all of them may not apply to the version of the JDK you are using.

For more information on the Java 7 and Java 8 command-line parameters, refer to `https://docs.oracle.com/javase/7/docs/technotes/tools/windows/java.html` and `https://docs.oracle.com/javase/8/docs/technotes/tools/windows/java.html`.

The final parameters specified in the default options ensure that certain optimizations are performed on the JVM to make it more stable and perform better. Some of these parameters are operating system-specific and may not exist on configuration files for different operating system.

# NetBeans JDK

By default, NetBeans uses the system-defined JDK to run the IDE (you'll remember this can be overridden using the `--javahome` argument to the NetBeans installer, as discussed earlier in this chapter). This can be overridden in the `netbeans.conf` file by defining the `netbeans_jdkhome` property to specify the base directory of a different JDK installation:

```
netbeans_jdkhome="/path/to/jdk"
```

It's not usually necessary to change the JDK that NetBeans uses as this is set at the time of installation. However, if you wish to use a newer (or older) JDK than the one used when you installed NetBeans, it can be configured with this variable.

If you wish to run NetBeans as a one-off instance and do not wish to edit the `netbeans.conf` file, you can pass the `--jdkhome <jdk_home>` parameter on the command line instead when launching NetBeans.

# Additional module clusters

A NetBeans cluster is a directory on disk that contains a set of modules such as the NetBeans Platform or the Java EE support within the NetBeans IDE. Additional clusters can be configured within NetBeans by adding the directory in which the cluster resides onto the `netbeans_extraclusters` parameter:

```
netbeans_extraclusters="/absolute/path/to/cluster1:/absolute/path/to/
cluster2""cluster2"
```

It is most likely that you will not need to define the additional module clusters to be loaded at the startup unless you are developing NetBeans **rich client platform (RCP)** applications.

Installing additional module clusters is not to be confused with installing NetBeans plugins. Plugins are installed into the IDE directly within the IDE itself.

# Further options

Several other NetBeans command-line arguments are available that provide more control over the NetBeans user experience.

To run NetBeans in a locale different from that of the operating system, the `--locale` option can be used. For example, `--locale en:GB` runs NetBeans with the `en:GB` locale.

If you wish to increase the base font size of NetBeans, the `--fontsize` option allows this to be achieved. For example, `--fontsize 20` increases the base font size to 20px. This can be useful when demoing code or showing NetBeans to larger audiences.

The full list of different command-line options that are available within NetBeans is provided at `http://wiki.netbeans.org/FaqStartupParameters`.

# Summary

In this chapter, we took a look at the different bundles of NetBeans that can be downloaded for Java developers. We saw that there are three main bundles for Java developers, namely the Java SE, Java EE, and All bundles. We looked at the differences between those bundles, and saw how to configure the installation of NetBeans for the Java EE and All bundles.

Having seen how to install NetBeans, we also learned how to upgrade an existing NetBeans installation keeping the user directory so that all the configuration data from previous versions of NetBeans is kept.

We then discussed the source code for NetBeans and saw how we can view it online, download zipped distributions of it, and even cloned it from the NetBeans Mercurial repository. We followed this up by learning how to build the NetBeans IDE, both from the command line and from within NetBeans itself.

Finally, we looked at the different command-line options available to NetBeans, and saw how we can change these to change how NetBeans operates.

In the next chapter, we'll look at creating projects and editing within NetBeans, and see how we can become more productive using the IDE.

# 2
# Editing Files and Projects

NetBeans is an excellent **integrated development environment (IDE)**, providing many of the features that a modern Java developer requires. NetBeans provides templates for many different types of projects, all the way from mobile to desktop to enterprise projects. NetBeans also offers many features for editing these projects and the files within them.

We don't give a second thought to some of these features, such as the Java source code editor, as we would expect even a basic text editor to provide this functionality. In this chapter, we'll see many of the features that NetBeans provides to make editing projects and files a much quicker and efficient task.

In this chapter, we will cover the following topics:

- The NetBeans screen layout
- Specifying default templates for files
- Code templates and code snippets
- Macro recording and playback
- Splitting windows
- Code folds
- Project groups

# The NetBeans screen layout

Upon running NetBeans for the first time, NetBeans **Start Page** is displayed, as shown in the following screenshot. This page acts as a welcome to NetBeans, providing links to demos, tutorial, the NetBeans community, and much more content related to NetBeans. Control over whether this page is displayed when NetBeans is started comes from the **Show On Startup** checkbox in the top-right corner of the window. The default for this option is checked so that the start page is displayed when NetBeans starts up.

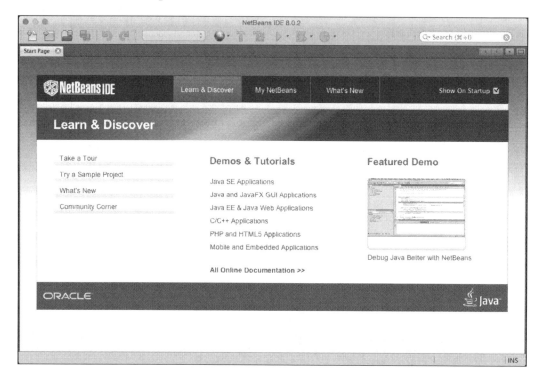

After reading the **Start Page** and creating a project, the standard NetBeans screen layout is displayed. This consists of several windows, which can be rearranged. The basic NetBeans screen layout is shown in the following screenshot:

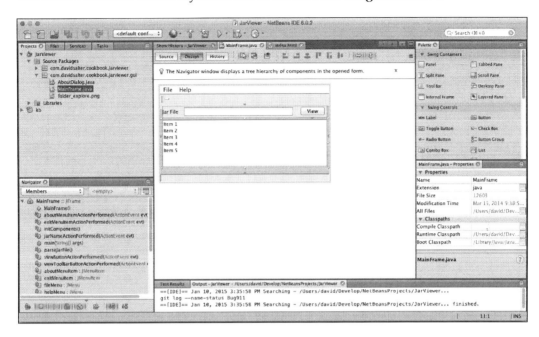

The main screen is broken down into six main areas:

- The explorer style windows (**Projects**, **Files**, **Services**, and so on)
- The **Navigator** window
- The source code editor window
- The **Palette** window
- The **Properties** window
- The **Output** window

# The explorer style windows

The explorer style windows are displayed at the top-left of the main NetBeans window. This window displays tabs for browsing through projects, files, and services.

The explorer style windows are used for showing hierarchical data. The first of these windows is the **Projects** window, which displays all the currently open projects within NetBeans. Next, we have the **Files** window, which shows similar data to the **Projects** window, but concentrates on the viewpoint of the files within the local filesystem rather than the files used by a project. Finally, we have the **Services** window, which displays different services such as databases, servers, or web services that your application can interact with.

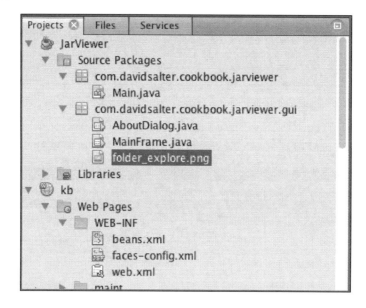

# The Favorites window

The **Favorites** window is where we can list all our favorite files irrespective of whether they are in the currently open project or not.

At the top of the **Favorites** window is a folder representing the user's home directory on the computer. Expanding this folder allows access to all the files within the user's home directory. Right-clicking on any of the files or folders within this hierarchy and selecting the **Tools** and then **Add to Favorites...** menu options will add the entry into the **Favorites** window. This is, therefore, a very useful window if you have many files that you constantly refer to as it allows them to be easily grouped together in one accessible window.

Files and folders (including Java packages) can also be added to the **Favorites** window from within both the **Projects** and **Files** windows by right-clicking and selecting the **Tools** and then **Add to Favorites...** menu options.

If the **Favorites** window is not open, selecting the **Favorites** menu option from the main **Window** menu will open it.

# The Navigator window

Next, we have the **Navigator** window. This is displayed directly underneath the explorer style windows. The **Navigator** window shows an outline of what is selected for editing in the main editor window. So, for example, if a Swing form is being edited, a hierarchy of the Swing controls will be displayed in the **Navigator** window. If an HTML page is being edited in the main editor window, the DOM for the page will be displayed in the **Navigator** window.

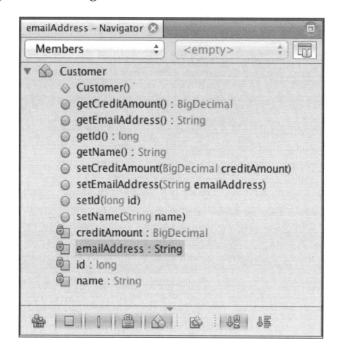

# The source code editor window

In the middle of the NetBeans main window, we find the source code editor window. The exact contents of this window changes depending upon the type of file that is being edited. For example, when editing a Java source code file, the contents of the file are displayed, as you would expect with a standard text editor. Or, when editing Swing components, a graphical representation of the component being edited is displayed.

NetBeans watches the files that you have open in the source code editor window for external changes. If you make changes to, say, a Java source code file outside of NetBeans, the file within NetBeans will be refreshed as soon as any external changes are saved.

In the source code editor window, there are many different keyboard shortcuts that can be used to aid productivity. To become a proficient developer, it can be very useful to memorize some of these shortcuts. Some of the more common shortcuts that you will find useful when editing files are shown in the following table:

| | |
|---|---|
| *Alt + Insert / Ctrl + I* | Insert code |
| *Ctrl + Shift + I / Cmd + Shift + I* | Fix import statements |
| *Alt + Shift + S / Ctrl + Shift + S* | Reformat the selected code |
| *Ctrl* + click / *Cmd* + click | Go to the definition of the object that was clicked |

The shortcut keys that are assigned to different options can be configured in the **Keymap** tab of the NetBeans **Options** dialog:

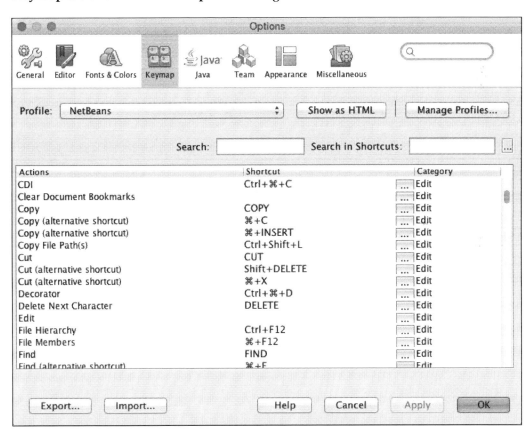

Within the **Keymap** options, each of the different keyboard shortcuts for NetBeans is broken down into different categories (such as **Build**, **Debug**, **Edit**, and others). For each action, the shortcut key can be defined or reset back to its original value.

It's worth looking through all the keyboard shortcuts to establish which ones you use most often in your daily routine. The shortcut keys that you use regularly may not be the same as the ones that another developer uses, so learning your shortcut keys can make a huge difference.

# The History view

When editing files, it is very common to see at the minimum, buttons for editing the **Source** and for viewing the **History** of the file at the top of the code editor window. This is shown in the following screenshot with the editor for HTML files:

```
Show History – JarViewer      MainFrame.java      index.html      faces-config.xml

Source    History

 1    <!DOCTYPE html>
 2    <html>
 3        <head>
 4            <title>Start Page</title>
 5            <meta http-equiv="Content-Type" content="text/html; charset=UTF-8">
 6        </head>
 7        <body>
 8            <h1>Hello World!</h1>
 9        </body>
10    </html>
```

The file's **History** window shows a complete set of local file changes for a file. This can be especially useful when comparing the history of a file that has not been checked into source control and the source control history is, therefore, not available. The default setting is for the history for local files to be capped to 7 days, but this can be configured to any number of days or even switched off completely so that the local history is never reset. The configuration for the local history can be changed in the NetBeans **Options** window on the **Versioning** tab within the **Team** options:

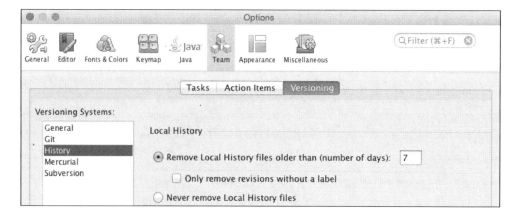

When viewing the history of a file, all the edits are listed in the top half of the **History** window. Each of these entries corresponds to when the file in question was last saved. In the following screenshot, the file was created on October 28, 2014, and then edited twice at 2:49:44 pm and 2:50:27 pm:

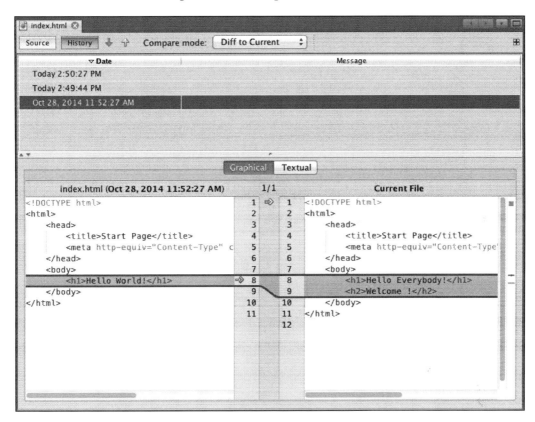

Clicking on any of the history items at the top of the window causes NetBeans to compare the file at that point in time with the current version of the file. The earlier instance of the file is shown on the left-hand side pane and the latest revision of the file is shown on the right-hand side pane.

# e Palette window

ie right-hand side of the main NetBeans window, we can see the **Palette**
ow. In a similar fashion to the **Navigator** window, the **Palette** window is
context-sensitive and shows the components that are relevant to the file type that
is currently being edited. So, for example, when editing a Swing file, the **Palette**
shows different Swing components such as labels and buttons that can be dragged
onto the main editing window. For HTML files, the **Palette** displays a set of HTML
components such as tables and buttons that can be dragged into the HTML page. The
purpose of the **Palette** window is to allow predefined components to be dragged into
the main editor window to make editing more fluid. Of course, if the main editor
window is displaying information that does not support the dragging and dropping
of components onto it, the **Palette** window is not displayed.

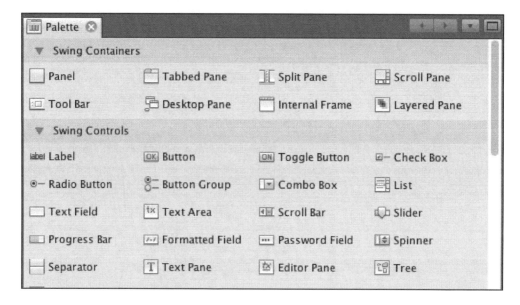

If the **Palette** window is not open, selecting the **IDE Tools** and then **Palette** menu
options in the main **Window** menu will open it.

# The Properties window

Again, on the right-hand side of the main NetBeans window, underneath the **Palette** is the **Properties** window. As with the **Palette** window, the **Properties** window is only shown when appropriate. In this case, the **Properties** window is displayed when something is selected in the main editor window that has properties that can be edited. For example, when editing a Swing component, the **Properties** window is displayed to show the properties (and events, bindings, and custom code) for the Swing component that is currently selected:

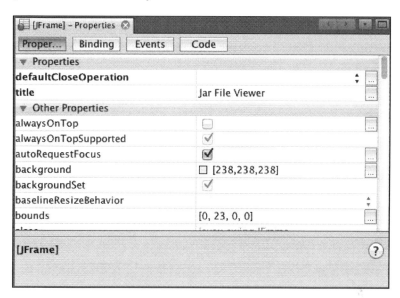

# The Output window

Finally, towards the bottom of the main NetBeans window is the **Output** window. This window shows any output from the actions that are being performed from within NetBeans. So, for example, output from a running application (such as that generated by System.out.println) or output from checking out a file from Git, or even the result of running unit tests is shown in this window.

# Window management

Of course, within NetBeans, there are many other windows that can be opened in the application. However, these windows are generally grouped into one of the six locations we've detailed earlier:

- Top-left (for example, the **Projects** window)
- Bottom-left (for example, the **Navigator** window)
- Central (for example, the main editor window)
- Top-right (for example, the **Palette** window)
- Bottom-right (for example, the **Properties** window)
- Bottom (for example, the **Output** window).

A list of all the different windows that can be laid out within NetBeans is accessible from the main **Window** menu option.

Some developers prefer to use keyboard shortcuts over mouse shortcuts as this can offer a productivity boost. On the main **Window** menu, each window has a shortcut that can be used for selecting and opening a window (if it is not already opened). Learning these shortcuts can be a worthwhile exercise.

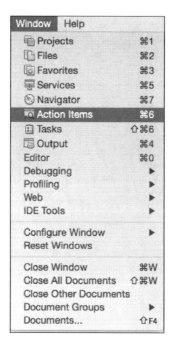

This layout of the different windows within NetBeans is just the default layout and can be changed to suit a particular developer's needs. Each of these groups can be minimized so that they are only displayed when required. To minimize a window, right-click on the required window and select either the **Minimize** or **Minimize Group** menu options. The window will then be minimized to the side of the main NetBeans window, providing more space for the main central editor window.

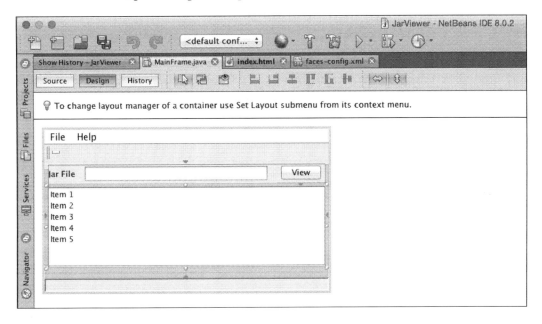

All the windows can be minimized to the side of the main NetBeans window apart from the code editor window, which cannot be minimized.

 The **Minimize** option is displayed when there is more than one window at a specified location. The **Minimize Group** option is displayed every time irrespective of the number of windows at a specific location.

Once a window has been minimized, moving the mouse over the window's name or clicking on the window's name (for example, **Projects** in the preceding screenshot) will cause the window to be displayed in a floating fashion, as shown in the following screenshot:

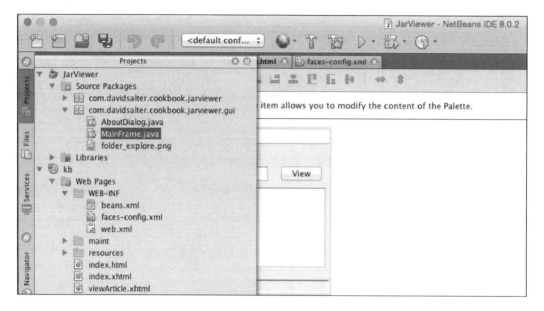

When a window is floating, clicking anywhere outside the window will cause it to be minimized again. To restore the window back to its docked state, click on the dock button (  ) at the top-right of the window.

Individual windows can be maximized as well as minimized. To maximize a window, right-click on it and select the **Maximize** option. This can be particularly useful for the main editor window so that when maximized, more code can be seen without distraction from other windows.

> A quick way to maximize a window is to double-click on the window's title. For example, double-clicking on the filename of the file being edited in the main editor window will maximize the editor window.

In addition to minimizing and maximizing windows, they can be floated away from the main IDE and subsequently docked back into the IDE main window. To float a window or window group, right-click on the window and select **Float** or **Float Group** as appropriate. The following screenshot gives an example of floating windows within NetBeans:

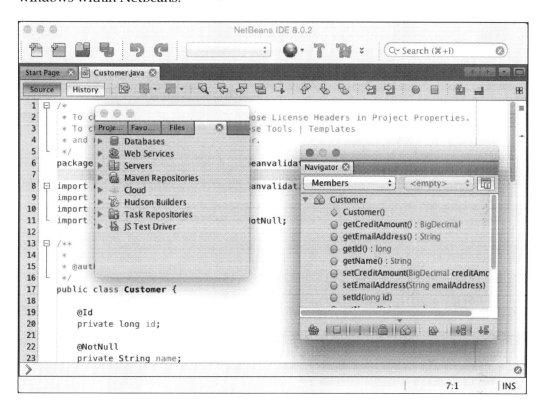

Once windows have been floated within NetBeans, they can be docked back into the main NetBeans window by right-clicking on them and selecting the **Dock** or **Dock Group** options.

Finally, if we don't like the position of windows within NetBeans, we can move them to different docked locations by dragging the title bar to a different location in the NetBeans main window. For example, we can drag the **Navigator** window from the left-hand side of the NetBeans window and drop it on the right-hand side of the NetBeans main window.

Now that we've seen how we can arrange the layout of the main NetBeans window, let's take a look at how NetBeans can help us edit files and projects.

# Specifying default templates for files

One of the first things we do within the editing component of NetBeans is to create new files. NetBeans supports many different file formats that can be created by selecting the **File** and then **New File** menu options.

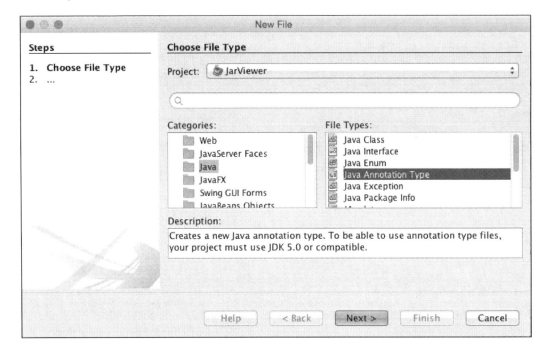

Within NetBeans, FreeMarker (http://www.freemarker.org) is used as the template engine when creating different file types. It's not important to understand FreeMarker fully to edit NetBeans templates; however, if you wish to create templates from scratch, a better understanding of FreeMarker would be beneficial.

To view all the templates that are currently defined within NetBeans for new file types, select the **Tools** and **Templates** menu options. The **Template Manager** dialog is then displayed, as shown in the following screenshot:

Down the left-hand side of the **Template Manager** dialog, we can see all the templates that are currently defined within NetBeans. These templates are all grouped into a hierarchy to categorize them and make them easier to find.

We can add existing FreeMarker templates by clicking on the **Add...** button or duplicate the existing templates by the **Duplicate** button. New folders can be added to the template hierarchy by the **New Folder** button, and templates can be moved up and down the hierarchy using the **Move Up** and **Move Down** buttons. Templates and folders can be deleted and renamed by using the **Delete** and **Rename** buttons. Finally, if we want to remove all the customization we've added, we can click on **Revert to Default** to return the templates to the state they were in from a fresh installation of NetBeans.

Once a template has been selected in the **Template Manager** dialog, clicking on the **Open in Editor** button will cause the selected FreeMarker template to be opened for editing.

When editing a FreeMarker template, several predefined variables are available. Entering any of these in to a template will cause the corresponding value to be used when the file for the template is created. The following predefined variables are available:

| Variable | Description |
|---|---|
| ${date} | The current date |
| ${encoding} | The default encoding for the file |
| ${name} | The name of the file |
| ${nameAndExt} | The name and extension of the file |
| ${package} | The package the file is created in |
| ${time} | The current time |
| ${project.license} | The license header |
| ${project.name} | The project's name |
| ${project.displayName} | The project's display name |

In addition to these predefined variables, custom variables can be created. Clicking on the **Settings** button in the **Template Manager** dialog opens up the User.properties file into which any user-specific variables can be set. This file is located in the User directory (see *Chapter 1, Getting Started with NetBeans*, for a description of the User directory and where it is located) at:

**<User Directory>\config\Templates\Properties\User.properties**

In a fresh installation of NetBeans, the User.properties file has no variables defined within it. NetBeans, however, makes extensive use of the ${user} variable to insert the user's name into source files. As this is not defined in a fresh installation of NetBeans, it is important to define this variable.

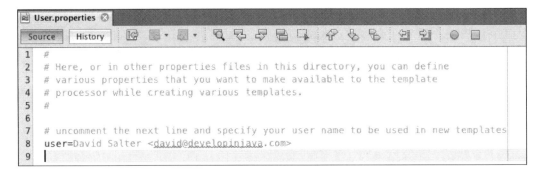

Now that we've seen the predefined variables used in the NetBeans templates and how to define custom variables, let's take a look at creating a template for a new file type. Let's assume that we want to alter the default **New Class** template to include the name of the project the class belongs to and also add a URL to a resource for the project. We could edit the existing **New Class** template, but let's create a copy of this so that we can see how the new template appears in the **New File** wizard. To do this, perform the following steps:

1.  Open the **Template Manager** window by selecting **Tools** and then **Templates** from the main NetBeans menu.

2.  In the **Template Manager** window, click on the **Settings** button to open the `User.properties` file.

3.  In the `User.properties` file, add a new variable:

    `url=http://www.packtpub.com`

4.  Open the **Template Manager** window again (it automatically closes after step 2) and locate the **Java Class** template.

5.  Press the **Duplicate** button to create a copy of the **Java Class** template and then rename it to be called `Java Class With Project Info`. The **Template Manager** screen should now look similar to the following screenshot:

6. Click on the **Open in Editor** button to open the template for editing and add the project name and URL into the template, as shown in the following code:

```
<#assign licenseFirst = "/*">
<#assign licensePrefix = " * ">
<#assign licenseLast = " */">
<#include "${project.licensePath}">

<#if package?? && package != "">
package ${package};

</#if>
/**
 * Project: ${project.name}
 * ${url}
 *
 * @author ${user}
 */
public class ${name} {

}
```

7. Save the template and invoke the **New File** wizard by selecting **File** and then **New File** from the main NetBeans menu. If we select the Java category, we can see that our new file type, **Java Class With Project Info**, is available in the list of **File Types**, as shown in the following screenshot:

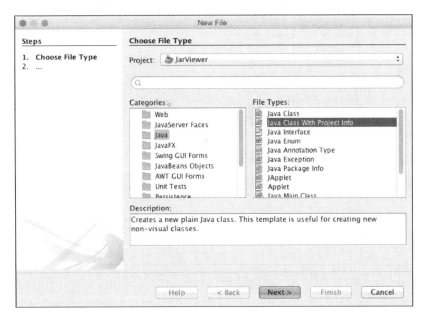

8. Upon completing the **New File** wizard, we can see that the project name and the project-specific URL have been automatically added into the new class file along with our name and e-mail address, as defined by the template:

```java
package com.davidsalter.cookbook.jarviewer;

/**
 * Project: JarViewer
 * http://www.packtpub.com
 *
 * @author David Salter <david@developinjava.com>
 */
public class FooFactory {

}
```

# Code templates and code snippets

In the previous section, we saw how to create and customize templates for different file types. This can be very useful when creating new files.

NetBeans takes automatic code creation even further, however, with the ability to define both code templates and code snippets. Code templates allow a short piece of code to be entered within the main source code editor that is expanded into a larger template upon pressing the *Tab* key.

# Inserting code using code templates

First, let's take a look at code templates. NetBeans provides over 100 code templates for the Java language and many more for JavaScript, HTML, and others. Some of the more common code templates are shown in the following table:

| Code template | Description |
| --- | --- |
| pf | Expands to public final |
| do | Expands into a do ... while loop |
| fori | Expands to a for loop |
| log | Expands to a Logger class to output a log entry |
| serr | Expands to System.err.println(""); |
| sout | Expands to System.out.println(""); |
| trycatch | Expands into a try ... catch statement |

Code templates are managed from within the **Editor** section in the NetBeans **Options** window, as shown in the following screenshot:

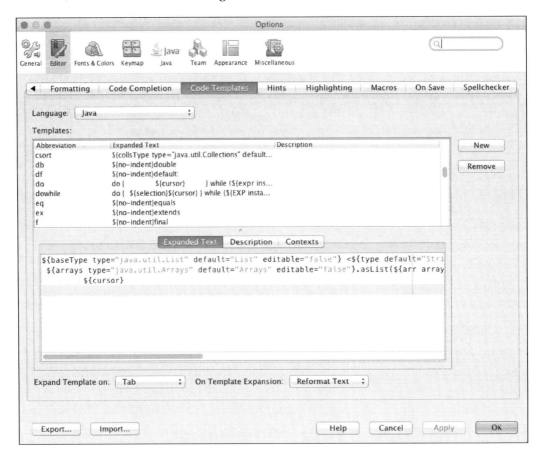

In the **Code Templates** window, the language for the code templates can be defined. A list of templates for each language is displayed into which new templates can be added, or existing templates can be created.

The final two options in the **Code Templates** window are the keys that cause the template to be expanded and show what happens to the file upon expansion of the template. The default key to expand templates is the **Tab** key, but this can be changed to **space**, **Shift + space**, or **Enter**. Upon expansion of the template, the file can be reformatted, reindented, or left as it is.

To see the code templates in use, open a Java source code file and type in psvm and then press the *Tab* key. NetBeans will expand the psvm template into a public static void main() {} statement.

Learning the different NetBeans code templates can be a very effective way of increasing your productivity with NetBeans. It's worth spending some time looking at the different templates, and see which ones are important to you.

# Code snippets – the NetBeans Palette window

Now that we've looked at code templates, let's take a look at how code snippets can also help increase a developer's productivity.

Code snippets are stored in the **Palette** window and can be dragged and dropped onto the code editor window to allow code to be quickly built up. As we've seen earlier in this chapter, the **Palette** window is not applicable to all the file types; for example, it does not contain any entries for Java source code. However, the **Palette** window is extremely useful when you develop HTML files.

When editing HTML files, new entries can be added into the **Palette** window by simply highlighting the required HTML code to create a palette entry and then dragging this onto the palette.

When the selected code is dragged onto the palette, the **Add to Palette** dialog is displayed, as shown in the following screenshot:

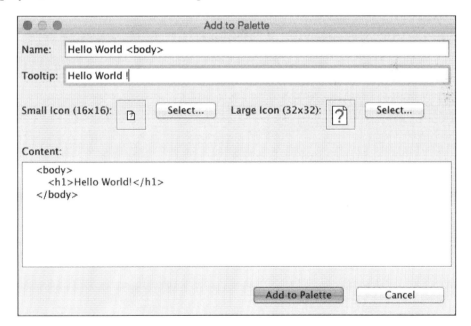

In the **Add to Palette** dialog, a name and a tooltip can be supplied for the palette entry. The entry can be edited within the **Content** editor before clicking on the **Add to Palette** button to create the new palette entry. Unfortunately, once an entry has been added into the palette, there is no easy way to edit it. We'll see shortly how editing and deleting palette entries can be performed though.

Once we've added an entry into the palette, it is available instantly for dragging and dropping anywhere in another HTML file:

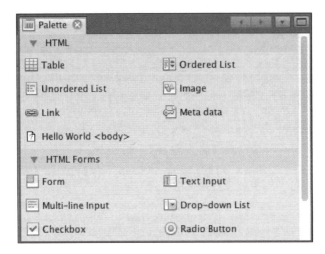

## Deleting palette items – the Palette Manager

Using the **Palette Manager**, we can arrange items on the palette and create new groups into which we can store the individual palette items. To access the **Palette Manager** dialog, right-click anywhere in the **Palette** window and select the **Palette Manager** menu option.

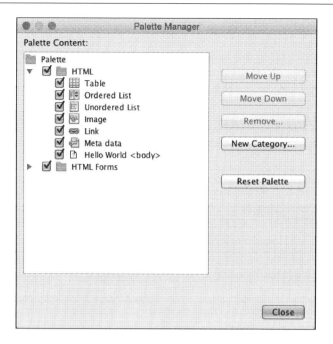

In the **Palette Manager** dialog, we can move items up and down within their respective categories, remove items and categories, and create new categories. Finally, we can also reset the palette to the original state provided by NetBeans when it was downloaded. This will remove all our customizations, so check thoroughly before proceeding to do this!

It's important to note that we can move items up and down within a category in the **Palette Manager** dialog using the **Move Up** and **Move Down** buttons. However, if we wish to move an item from one category to another (for example, if we wish to move an item from the **HTML** to the **HTML Forms** category, as shown in the preceding screenshot), this can be accomplished by dragging the item from one category to another.

# Editing palette items

In the previous section, we stated that there is no easy way to edit items in the NetBeans **Palette** window. Unfortunately, the current version of NetBeans (8.0) doesn't provide a GUI for editing palette entries.

A simple way to edit items in the palette is to delete them and then re-add the updated content. This, however, can be error prone, and isn't necessarily ideal. A better solution is to edit the palette directly outside NetBeans.

All the custom palette entries, that is to say, the ones that you have created, are stored in an XML file inside the User directory for NetBeans. Within the User directory, palette entries for each category are stored in the config\HTMLPalette directory with a subdirectory for each category. Within the category folders is the XML file that holds the palette custom items:

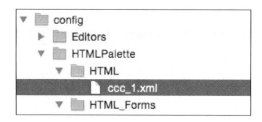

These custom palette item XML files can be opened with any text editor, modified to update the palette item and then saved again over the original file. When NetBeans is reloaded, the palette item will effectively have been edited. Understandably, this isn't an ideal situation, but is the best solution for editing palette entries until this feature is added into NetBeans.

An example custom palette XML file looks similar to the following:

```
<?xml version="1.0" encoding="UTF-8"?>
<!DOCTYPE editor_palette_item PUBLIC "-//NetBeans//Editor Palette Item
1.1//EN" "http://www.netbeans.org/dtds/editor-palette-item-1_1.dtd">

<editor_palette_item version="1.0">
    <body>
        <![CDATA[
    <body>
        <h1>Hello World!</h1>
    </body>
        ]]>
    </body>
    <icon16 urlvalue =
```

```
        "org/netbeans/modules/palette/resources/unknown16.gif" />
    <icon32 urlvalue =
        "org/netbeans/modules/palette/resources/unknown32.gif" />
    <inline-description>
        <display-name>Hello World &lt;body></display-name>
        <tooltip>Hello World !</tooltip>
    </inline-description>
</editor_palette_item>
```

In the XML file, we can see that there are several important elements that hold information about the palette entry:

- `<body>`: This holds the code snippet that will be inserted into the HTML document

- `<icon16>`: This holds the path to a small icon for displaying in the **Palette** window

- `<icon32>`: This holds the path to a large icon for displaying in the **Palette** window

- `<inline-description>`: This holds the display name and tooltip for the palette entry within the `<display-name>` and `<tooltip>` subelements

# Macro recording and playback

In the previous sections, we've seen how to quickly insert stock code into a source code file via both code templates and dragging and dropping palette items. The next technique for modifying or inserting new code into a file that we will look at is macros.

Within NetBeans, macros allow us to capture screen recording and then assign the recording to a keyboard shortcut, which, when selected, will playback the recorded keystrokes. This can be very useful for performing automated tasks against a source code file or indeed, any editable file.

A basic installation of NetBeans is supplied with three existing macros. To view the macros that are stored within NetBeans, access the NetBeans **Options** menu (select **Tools** and then **Options** from the main menu on Windows and Linux or select **NetBeans** and then **Preferences...** from the menu on a Mac). In the **Options** dialog, select the **Editor** option and then the **Macros** tab to see how macros are defined within NetBeans:

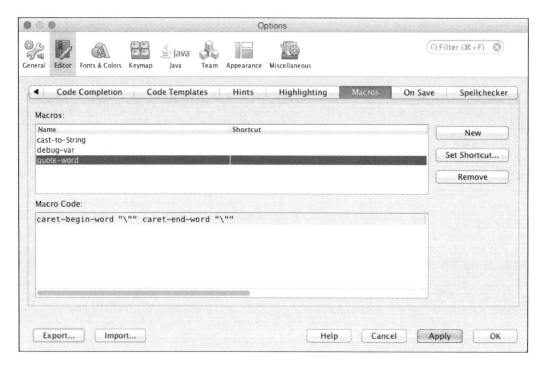

As can be seen in the preceding screenshot, there are three macros that are provided with a fresh installation of NetBeans:

- `cast-to-String`: This casts the selected variable to a String
- `debug-var`: This adds a debug statement into Java code for a specified variable
- `quote-word`: This places quote marks around the selected word

Let's take a look at the `quote-word` macro and see how it can be used.

# Assigning shortcuts for macro playback

To run a macro, we need to assign a shortcut key to it. This is performed in the **Macros** options screen, as shown earlier. Select the **quote-word** macro from the list of macros and press the **Set Shortcut...** button. This will cause the **Add Shortcut** dialog to be displayed, in which we can define the shortcut key for the macro:

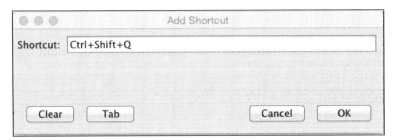

To define a shortcut key for a macro, we simply press the combination of keys that we wish to use to invoke the macro. Since the `quote-word` macro begins with the letter "Q", it makes sense to add a memorable shortcut. In this example, you can see that I've assigned the keyboard shortcut *Ctrl + Shift + Q* to this macro.

Once a key for a macro has been defined, we can close the **Add Shortcut** dialog by pressing the **OK** button. Closing the **Options** dialog will then return us to the NetBeans editor window so that we can try out the keyboard shortcut for the macro.

 The **Clear** button in the **Add Shortcut** dialog clears the currently selected shortcut, while the *Tab* button inserts the tab character into the shortcut sequence.

Once back in the NetBeans editor, we can place the cursor inside a piece of text that we wish to add quotes around:

```
String world = Hello;
```

Then, by simply pressing the shortcut key we defined (*Ctrl + Shift + Q*), the selected text will become quoted:

```
String world = "Hello";
```

Now that we've seen how to playback macros defined within NetBeans, let's see how to record new macros.

# Recording new macros

Macro recording simply records all the keystrokes entered by the user so that they can be played back at a later date.

To start NetBeans recording macros, select the **Edit** and then **Start Macro Recording** menu items from the main NetBeans menu. NetBeans will then indicate that it is recording macros by showing the **Recording** text at the bottom-left of the main IDE window.

To record a macro, we simply now enter the key strokes that we wish to record. For example, to record a macro similar to the `quote-word` macro we just looked at, we could record the following key strokes:

- Move to the beginning of the current word
- Insert quote mark
- Move to the end of the current word
- Insert quote mark

Once we've finished recording a macro, we select the **Edit** and **Stop Macro Recording** menu options. This stops the recording and displays the **New Macro** dialog, allowing us to name the newly recorded macro:

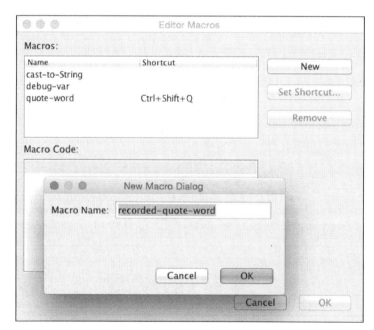

From here, we can add a name to the macro and then assign a shortcut key for subsequent use.

Shortcut buttons for recording and finishing recording macros are available in the editor window toolbar. To start recording, press the record button (⬤) and to finish, press the finish button (⬛).

# Splitting windows

When editing a file, such as a Java source code file or an HTML file, it can sometimes be necessary to view two parts of the file at the same time. How many times have you found yourself having to scroll to the top of a file to check something and then having to scroll to the bottom of the file again to type some code?

In NetBeans, we can split a file horizontally so that we can see the top and bottom of a file or vertically to see the left- and right-hand sides of a file, all at the same time.

So, how do we split views so that we can simultaneously view different aspects of the file?

At the top-right of an editor window that supports file splitting is a small cross (⊞). To split a file vertically, drag this cross left so that the file is split vertically into the correct proportions. To split it horizontally, drag this cross down until the view is split as required.

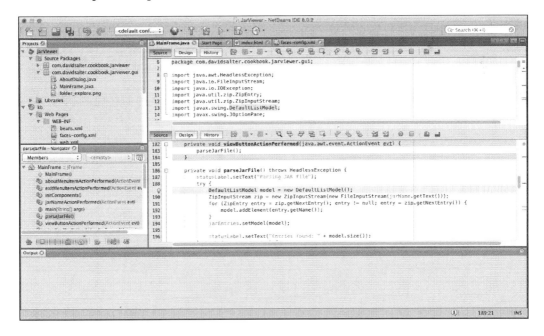

After splitting the view onto a file, the file can be edited within either pane or the split view. That is to say none of the panes are read-only. As a result of this, any changes that are made within one pane are automatically displayed in the second pane—both panes are just two different views onto the same file. Similarly, when selecting a piece of code within one pane, this causes all the corresponding pieces of code to be highlighted in the other pane. For example, if we highlight a Java variable within one pane, all the visible instances of the variable will be highlighted in the other pane as well as in the original pane.

Once the view onto a file has been split, it can be repositioned by simply dragging the splitter bar left/right or up/down as required.

To close the splitter view and only display a single view onto a file, drag the splitter window fully to any of the edges of the editor window. So, for example, to close the splitter view on a horizontally split window, drag the splitter bar either fully to the top or bottom of the window that is split.

# Code folds

Splitting windows either horizontally or vertically is an excellent way to utilize screen space when it is necessary to compare two sections of a file. Using code folds is another excellent technique for "folding" or "collapsing" sections of code, thus helping to provide more screen space. With a code fold, pressing the + or – buttons on the left-hand side margin expands or collapses the code and can, therefore, be used to get more code onto the current view of a file.

Creating a code fold is simply a matter of placing an especially formatted comment around the piece of code that requires folding, as shown in the following code snippet:

```
// <editor-fold desc="Variable definitions">
int foo;
String bar;
// </editor-fold>
```

```
// <editor-fold desc="Variable definitions">
int foo;
String bar;
// </editor-fold>

Variable definitions
```

The `<editor-fold>` XML defines that the enclosed code will be available within NetBeans as a code fold and has several attributes, all of which are optional:

- `desc`: It is the description that is displayed within the NetBeans code editor when the code fold is collapsed

- `defaultState`: It takes the value of "collapsed" to indicate that, by default, the code fold will be collapsed

In addition to custom code folds, as defined by the `<editor-fold>` code comments, NetBeans automatically adds a code fold wherever the scope of code changes, for example, whenever new classes or new methods are created.

Whether these code folds are collapsed by default is defined in the NetBeans **Folding** options. This is accessed within the **Folding** tab in the **Editor** options:

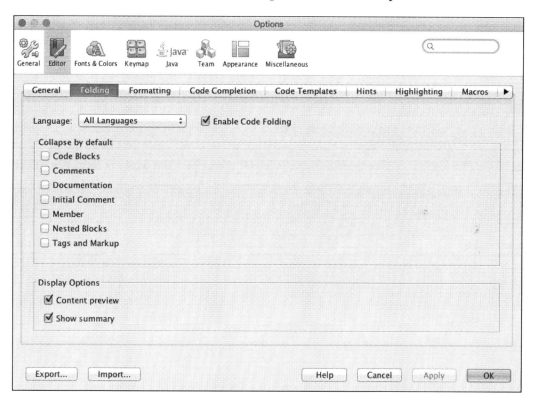

# Project groups

So far in this chapter, we've looked at the layout of NetBeans and how to configure and use different windows within the IDE. We've also looked at different shortcuts for generating or altering code within a project. With large projects, it can be useful to organize the projects themselves as well as the code within them. In this section, we're going to see how we can organize projects into project groups.

In the **Projects** window, we are shown a list of all the currently open projects in NetBeans, and can drill down into the project's hierarchy to see all the files and resources used by the project. With a large project, it can be useful to organize projects into the following categories, for example:

- Data repository projects
- Web projects
- Mobile projects
- Client projects

NetBeans allows us to group projects together and shows only the projects from the currently open group within the **Projects** window.

To create a project group, click on the **File** and then **Project Groups...** menu items. This causes the **Manage Groups** dialog to be shown, which lists all the defined groups, in addition to facilitating new group creation and group editing.

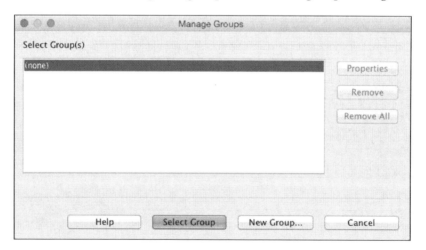

Initially, when NetBeans starts up, there are no groups defined (you could say that there is one group called **none**). To create a new group, click on the **New Group...** button. This opens up the **Create New Group** dialog where we can define which projects belong to the group.

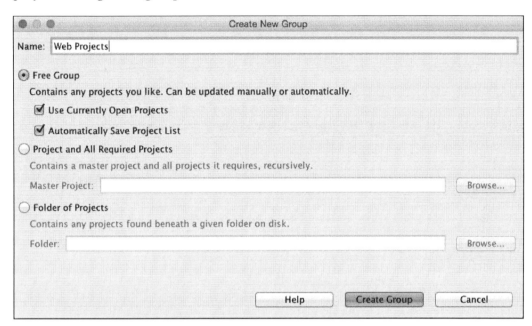

In the **Create New Group** dialog, we can specify the name of the new group along with these three options for defining which projects belong to the newly created group:

- **Free Group**: This group is managed by the user and can have whatever projects in it that are required. These can be manually selected after the group is created or the **Use Currently Open Projects** checkbox can be checked to create the group and populate it with all the currently open projects.

- **Project and All Required Projects**: This group is defined by selecting a master project. Any subprojects used by the master project will be added to the group along with the master project.

- **Folder of Projects**: This group is defined by any NetBeans projects that are stored in the specified folder on the filesystem.

Upon defining the group and clicking on the **Create Group** button, NetBeans will open the group. The title of the **Projects** window will be changed to append the group name as an indicator of which group is currently open:

If we have created a free group, we can add and remove projects into the group from the **Projects** window as we see fit. If we have created either of the remaining project group types, the projects in the group will be automatically updated according to the group's criteria.

To view a different group of projects, simply invoke the **Manage Groups** dialog by selecting **File** and then **Project Groups** from the NetBeans **File** menu. From here, select the required project group and click on the **Select Group** button.

# Summary

In this chapter, we looked at the layout of NetBeans and the different windows (and their content) that are available to help us develop applications. We saw how we can rearrange the windows, including docking them to the main NetBeans window and floating them away from it.

We looked at shortcuts to generating and amending code, learning about file templates, code templates, and code drag and drop. We also saw how to create and playback macros for those situations where we want to record keystrokes and then play them back at a later date.

Finally, we saw how to manage project groups so that we can efficiently organize large projects.

In the next chapter, we'll look at the NetBeans developer's lifecycle, taking a look at running, testing, profiling, and debugging applications. We'll see how NetBeans can aid developers in these areas.

# 3
# The NetBeans Developer's Life Cycle

On a day-to-day basis, developers spend much of their time writing and running applications. While writing applications, they typically debug, test, and profile them to ensure that they provide the best possible application to customers. Running, debugging, profiling, and testing are all integral parts of the development life cycle, and NetBeans provides excellent tooling to help us in all these areas.

In this chapter, we will cover the following topics:

- Running applications
- Debugging applications
- Profiling applications
- Testing applications
- Introducing **test-driven development (TDD)** with NetBeans

## Running applications

Executing applications from within NetBeans is as simple as either pressing the *F6* button on the keyboard or selecting the **Run** menu item or **Project Context** menu item. Choosing either of these options will launch your application without specifying any additional Java command-line parameters using the default platform JDK that NetBeans is currently using.

Sometimes we want to change the options that are used for launching applications. NetBeans allows these options to be easily specified by a project's properties.

Right-clicking on a project in the **Projects** window and selecting the **Properties** menu option opens the **Project Properties** dialog. Selecting the **Run** category allows the configuration options to be defined for launching an application.

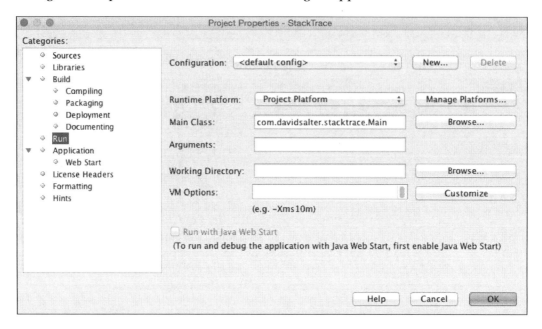

From this dialog, we can define and select multiple run configurations for the project via the **Configuration** dropdown. Selecting the **New...** button to the right of the **Configuration** dropdown allows us to enter a name for a new configuration. Once a new configuration is created, it is automatically selected as the active configuration. The **Delete** button can be used for removing any unwanted configurations.

The preceding screenshot shows the **Project Properties** dialog for a standard Java project. Different project types (for example, web or mobile projects) have different options in the **Project Properties** window.

 The source code for the StackTrace example application, shown in the preceding screenshot, is provided as a part of the code bundle for this chapter, which can be downloaded from this book's web page (https://www.packtpub.com/books/content/support/22286).

As can be seen from the preceding **Project Properties** dialog, several pieces of information can be defined for a standard Java project, which together make up the launch configuration for a project:

- **Runtime Platform**: This option allows us to define which Java platform we will use when launching the application. From here, we can select from all the Java platforms that are configured within NetBeans. Selecting the **Manage Platforms...** button opens the **Java Platform Manager** dialog, allowing full configuration of the different Java platforms available (both Java Standard Edition and Remote Java Standard Edition). Selecting this button has the same effect as selecting the **Tools** and then **Java Platforms** menu options.

- **Main Class**: This option defines the main class that is used to launch the application. If the project has more than one main class, selecting the **Browse...** button will cause the **Browse Main Classes** dialog to be displayed, listing all the main classes defined in the project.

- **Arguments**: Different command-line arguments can be passed to the main class as defined in this option.

- **Working Directory**: This option allows the working directory for the application to be specified.

- **VM Options**: If different VM options (such as heap size) require setting, they can be specified by this option. Selecting the **Customize** button displays a dialog listing the different standard VM options available which can be selected (ticked) as required. Custom VM properties can also be defined in the dialog.

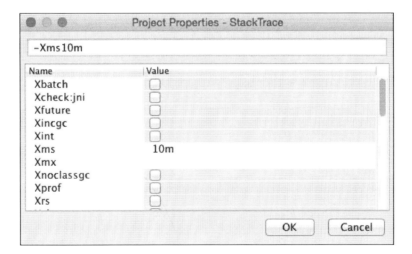

For more information on the different VM properties for Java, check out http://www.oracle.com/technetwork/java/ javase/tech/vmoptions-jsp-140102.html. From here, the VM properties for Java 7 (and earlier versions) and Java 8 for Windows, Solaris, Linux, and Mac OS X can be referenced.

- **Run with Java Web Start**: Selecting this option allows the application to be executed using Java Web Start technologies. This option is only available if Web Start is enabled in the **Application | Web Start** category.

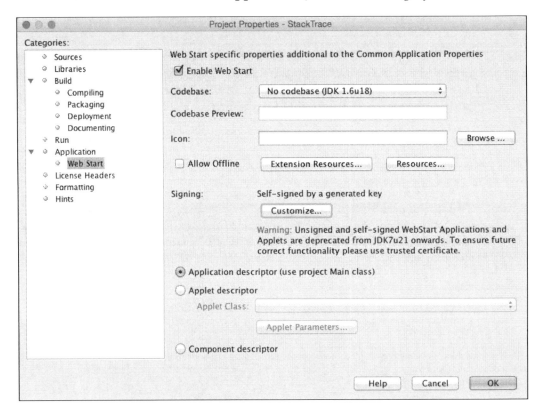

 For more information on Java Web Start technology, check out http://www.oracle.com/technetwork/ java/javase/javawebstart/index.html.

When running a web application, the project properties are different from those of a standalone Java application. In fact, the project properties for a Maven web application are different from those of a standard NetBeans web application. The following screenshot shows the properties for a Maven-based web application; as discussed previously, Maven is the standard project management tool for Java applications, and the recommended tool for creating and managing web applications:

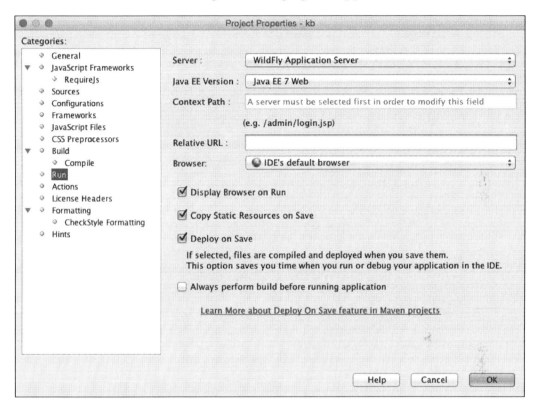

We will learn more about the **Run** properties for web projects in *Chapter 8, Creating the Web Tier*.

# Debugging applications

In the previous section, we saw how NetBeans provides the easy-to-use features to allow developers to launch their applications, but then it also provides more powerful additional features. The same is true for debugging applications.

For simple debugging, NetBeans provides the standard facilities you would expect, such as stepping into or over methods, setting line breakpoints, and monitoring the values of variables. For more details on these features, refer to my book, *NetBeans IDE 8 Cookbook, Packt Publishing*.

When debugging applications, NetBeans provides several different windows, enabling different types of information to be displayed and manipulated by the developer:

- Breakpoints
- Variables
- Call stack
- Loaded classes
- Sessions
- Threads
- Sources
- Debugging
- Analyze stack

All of these windows are accessible from the **Window** and then **Debugging** main menu within NetBeans.

# Breakpoints

NetBeans provides a simple approach to set breakpoints and a more comprehensive approach that provides many more useful features.

Breakpoints can be easily added into Java source code by clicking on the gutter on the left-hand side of a line of Java source code. When a breakpoint is set, a small pink square is shown in the gutter and the entire line of source code is also highlighted in the same color. Clicking on the breakpoint square in the gutter toggles the breakpoint on and off.

```
 9    /**
10     *
11     * @author David Salter <david@developinjava.com>
12     */
13    public class FaultyImplementation {
14        public void doUntestedOperation() {
           throw new NullPointerException();
16        }
17    }
18
```

Once a breakpoint has been created, instead of removing it altogether, it can be disabled by right-clicking on the bookmark in the gutter and selecting the **Breakpoint** and then **Enabled** menu options. This has the effect of keeping the breakpoint within your codebase, but execution of the application does not stop when the breakpoint is hit.

Creating a simple breakpoint like this can be a very powerful way of debugging applications. It allows you to stop the execution of an application when a line of code is hit.

If we want to add a bit more control onto a simple breakpoint, we can edit the breakpoint's properties by right-clicking on the breakpoint in the gutter and selecting the **Breakpoint** and then **Properties** menu options. This causes the **Breakpoint Properties** dialog to be displayed:

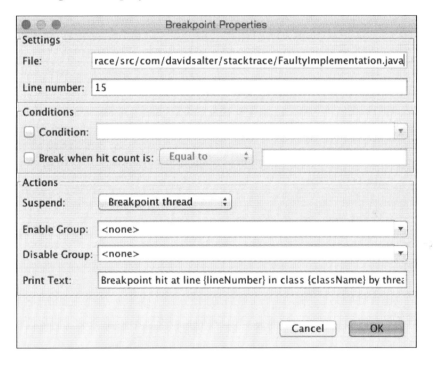

In this dialog, we can see the line number and the file that the breakpoint belongs to. The line number can be edited to move the breakpoint if it has been created on the wrong line. However, what's more interesting is the conditions that we can apply to the breakpoint.

The **Condition** entry allows us to define a condition that has to be met for the breakpoint to stop the code execution. For example, we can stop the code when the variable `i` is equal to 20 by adding a condition, `i==20`.

When we add conditions to a breakpoint, the breakpoint becomes known as a **conditional breakpoint**, and the icon in the gutter changes to a square with the lower-right quadrant removed, as shown in the following screenshot:

```
 9    /**
10     *
11     * @author David Salter <david@developinjava.com>
12     */
13    public class FaultyImplementation {
14        public void doUntestedOperation() {
          throw new NullPointerException();
16        }
17    }
18
```

We can also cause the execution of the application to halt at a breakpoint when the breakpoint has been hit a certain number of times. The **Break when hit count is** condition can be set to **Equal to**, **Greater than**, or **Multiple of** to halt the execution of the application when the breakpoint has been hit the requisite number of times.

Finally, we can specify what actions occur when a breakpoint is hit. The **Suspend** dropdown allows us to define what threads are suspended when a breakpoint is hit. NetBeans can suspend All threads, Breakpoint thread, or no threads at all. The text that is displayed in the **Output** window can be defined via the **Print Text** edit box and different breakpoint groups can be enabled or disabled via the **Enable Group** and **Disable Group** drop-down boxes. But what exactly is a breakpoint group?

Simply put, a breakpoint group is a collection of breakpoints that can all be set or unset at the same time. It is a way of categorizing breakpoints into similar collections, for example, all the breakpoints in a particular file, or all the breakpoints relating to exceptions or unit tests.

Breakpoint groups are created in the **Breakpoints** window. This is accessible by selecting the **Debugging** and then **Breakpoints** menu options from within the main NetBeans **Window** menu.

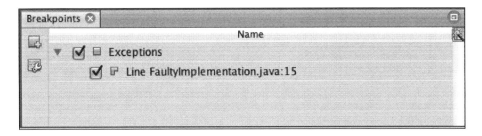

To create a new breakpoint group, simply right-click on an existing breakpoint in the **Breakpoints** window and select the **Move Into Group...** and then **New...** menu options.

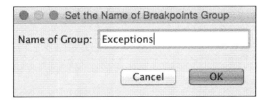

The **Set the Name of Breakpoints Group** dialog is displayed in which the name of the new breakpoint group can be entered.

After creating a breakpoint group and assigning one or more breakpoints into it, the entire group of breakpoints can be enabled or disabled, or even deleted by right-clicking on the group in the **Breakpoints** window and selecting the appropriate option.

Any newly created breakpoint groups will also be available in the **Breakpoint Properties** window.

So far, we've seen how to create breakpoints that stop on a single line of code, and also how to create conditional breakpoints so that we can cause an application to stop when certain conditions occur for a breakpoint. These are excellent techniques to help debug applications. NetBeans, however, also provides the ability to create more advanced breakpoints so that we can get even more control of when the execution of applications is halted by breakpoints.

So, how do we create these breakpoints? These different types of breakpoints are all created from in the **Breakpoints** window by right-clicking and selecting the **New Breakpoint...** menu option.

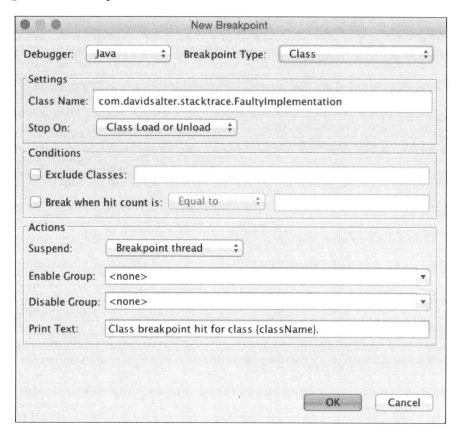

In the **New Breakpoint** dialog, we can create different types of breakpoints by selecting the appropriate entry from the **Breakpoint Type** drop-down list. The preceding screenshot shows an example of creating a **Class** breakpoint. The following types of breakpoints can be created:

- **Class**: This creates a breakpoint that halts execution when a class is loaded, unloaded, or either event occurs.

- **Exception**: This stops execution when the specified exception is caught, uncaught, or either event occurs.

- **Field**: This creates a breakpoint that halts execution when a field on a class is accessed, modified, or either event occurs.

- **Line**: This stops execution when the specified line of code is executed. It acts the same way as creating a breakpoint by clicking on the gutter of the Java source code editor window.

- **Method**: This creates a breakpoint that halts execution when a method is entered, exited, or when either event occurs. Optionally, the breakpoint can be created for all methods inside a specified class rather than a single method.

- **Thread**: This creates a breakpoint that stops execution when a thread is started, finished, or either event occurs.

- **AWT/Swing Component**: This creates a breakpoint that stops execution when a GUI component is accessed.

For each of these different types of breakpoints, conditions and actions can be specified in the same way as on simple line-based breakpoints.

# The Variables debug window

The **Variables** debug window lists all the variables that are currently within the scope of execution of the application. This is therefore thread-specific, so if multiple threads are running at one time, the **Variables** window will only display variables in scope for the currently selected thread.

In the **Variables** window, we can see the variables currently in scope for the selected thread, their type, and value, as shown in the following screenshot:

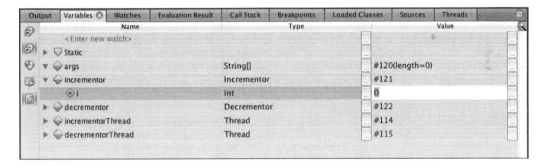

This screenshot is taken while debugging the MultiThread application that is included as part of the code bundle for this chapter. To gain a better understanding of the debugging process, it is recommended to download this application and experiment with setting breakpoints and examining the different debug windows.

To display variables for a different thread to that currently selected, we must select an alternative thread via the **Debugging** window.

Using the triangle button to the left of each variable, we can expand variables and drill down into the properties within them.

When a variable is a simple primitive (for example, integers or strings), we can modify it or any property within it by altering the value in the **Value** column in the Variables window. The variable's value will then be changed within the running application to the newly entered value.

By default, the **Variables** window shows three columns (**Name**, **Type**, and **Value**), as shown in the preceding screenshot. We can modify which columns are visible by pressing the selection icon (▨) at the top-right of the window.

Selecting this displays the **Change Visible Columns** dialog, from which we can select from the **Name**, **String value**, **Type**, and **Value** columns:

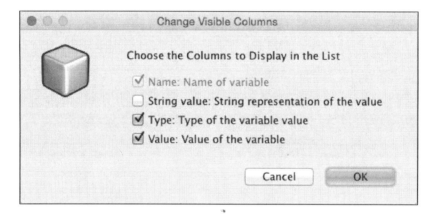

## The Watches window

The **Watches** window allows us to see the contents of variables and expressions during a debugging session, as can be seen in the following screenshot:

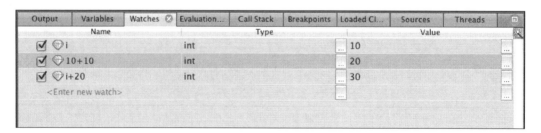

In this screenshot, we can see that the variable i is being displayed along with the expressions 10+10 and i+20.

New expressions can be watched by clicking on the **<Enter new watch>** option or by right-clicking on the Java source code editor and selecting the **New Watch...** menu option.

# Evaluating expressions

In addition to watching variables in a debugging session, NetBeans also provides the facility to evaluate expressions. Expressions can contain any Java code that is valid for the running scope of the application. So, for example, local variables, class variables, or new instances of classes can be evaluated.

To evaluate variables, open the **Evaluate Expression** window by selecting the **Debug** and then **Evaluate Expression** menu options.

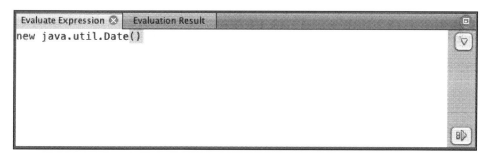

Enter an expression to be evaluated in this window and press the **Evaluate Code Fragment** button at the bottom-right corner of the window. As a shortcut, pressing the *Ctrl + Enter* keys will also evaluate the code fragment.

Once an expression has been evaluated, it is shown in the **Evaluation Result** window:

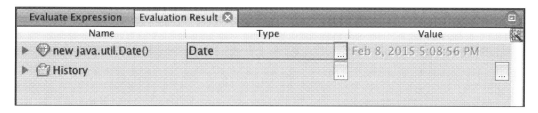

The **Evaluation Result** window shows a history of each expression that has previously been evaluated. Expressions can be added to the list of watched variables by right-clicking on the expression and selecting the **Create Fixed Watch** expression.

# The Call Stack window

The **Call Stack** window displays the call stack for the currently executing thread:

The call stack is displayed from top to bottom with the currently executing frame at the top of the list. Double-clicking on any entry in the call stack opens up the corresponding source code in the Java editor within NetBeans.

Right-clicking on an entry in the call stack displays a pop-up menu with the choice to:

- **Make Current**: This makes the selected thread the current thread
- **Pop To Here**: This pops the execution of the call stack to the selected location
- **Go To Source**: This displays the selected code within the Java source editor
- **Copy Stack**: This copies the stack trace to the clipboard for use elsewhere

When debugging, it can be useful to change the stack frame of the currently executing thread by selecting the **Pop To Here** option from within the stack trace window. Imagine the following code:

```
// Get some magic
int magic = getSomeMagicNumber();
// Perform calculation
performCalculation(magic);
```

During a debugging session, if after stepping over the getSomeMagicNumber() method, we decided that the method has not worked as expected, our course of action would probably be to debug into the getSomeMagicNumber() method. But, we've just stepped over the method, so what can we do? Well, we can stop the debugging session and start again or repeat the operation that called this section of code and hope there are no changes to the application state that affect the method we want to debug.

A better solution, however, would be to select the line of code that calls the getSomeMagicNumber() method and pop the stack frame using the **Pop To Here** option. This would have the effect of rewinding the code execution so that we can then step into the method and see what is happening inside it.

As well as using the **Pop To Here** functionality, NetBeans also offers several menu options for manipulating the stack frame, namely:

- **Make Callee Current**: This makes the callee of the current method the currently executing stack frame

- **Make Caller Current**: This makes the caller of the current method the currently executing stack frame

- **Pop Topmost Call**: This pops one stack frame, making the calling method the currently executing stack frame

When moving around the call stack using these techniques, any operations performed by the currently executing method are not undone. So, for example, strange results may be seen if global or class-based variables are altered within a method and then an entry is popped from the call stack. Popping entries in the call stack is safest when no state changes are made within a method.

The call stack displayed in the **Debugging** window for each thread behaves in the same way as in the **Call Stack** window itself.

# The Loaded Classes window

The **Loaded Classes** window displays a list of all the classes that are currently loaded, showing how many instances there are of each class as a number and as a percentage of the total number of classes loaded:

Depending upon the number of external libraries (including the standard Java runtime libraries) being used, you may find it difficult to locate instances of your own classes in this window. Fortunately, the filter at the bottom of the window allows the list of classes to be filtered, based upon an entered string. So, for example, entering the filter `String` will show all the classes with `String` in the fully qualified class name that are currently loaded, including **java.lang.String** and **java.lang. StringBuffer**. Since the filter works on the fully qualified name of a class, entering a package name will show all the classes listed in that package and subpackages. So, for example, entering a filter value as **com.davidsalter.multithread** would show only the classes listed in that package and subpackages.

## The Sessions window

Within NetBeans, it is possible to perform multiple debugging sessions where either one project is being debugged multiple times, or more commonly, multiple projects are being debugged at the same time, where one is acting as a client application and the other is acting as a server application.

The **Sessions** window displays a list of the currently running debug sessions, allowing the developer control over which one is the current session:

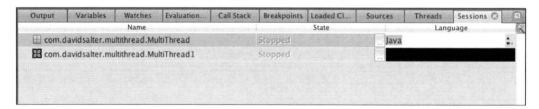

Right-clicking on any of the sessions listed in the window provides the following options:

- **Make Current**: This makes the selected session the currently active debugging session
- **Scope**: This debugs the current thread or all the threads in the selected session
- **Language**: This options shows the language of the application being debugged—Java
- **Finish**: This finishes the selected debugging session
- **Finish All**: This finishes all the debugging sessions

The **Sessions** window shows the name of the debug session (for example the main class being executed), its state (whether the application is **Stopped** or **Running**) and language being debugged. Clicking the selection icon (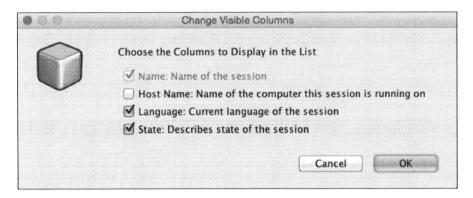) at the top-right of the window allows the user to choose which columns are displayed in the window.

The default choice is to display all columns except for the **Host Name** column, which displays the name of the computer the session is running on.

# The Threads window

The **Threads** window displays a hierarchical list of threads in use by the application currently being debugged, as shown in the following screenshot:

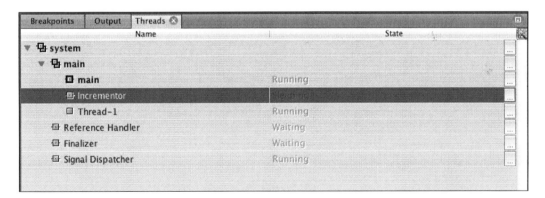

The current thread is displayed in bold. Double-clicking on any of the threads in the hierarchy makes the thread current. Similar to the **Debugging** window, threads can be made current, suspended, or interrupted by right-clicking on the thread and selecting the appropriate option.

The default display for the **Threads** window is to show the thread's name and its state (**Running, Waiting,** or **Sleeping**). Clicking the selection icon (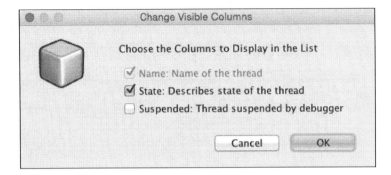) at the top-right of the window allows the user to choose which columns are displayed in the window.

# The Sources window

The **Sources** window simply lists all of the source roots that NetBeans considers for the selected project. These are the only locations that NetBeans will search when looking for source code while debugging an application. If you find that you are debugging an application, and you cannot step into code, the most likely scenario is that the source root for the code you wish to debug is not included in the **Sources** window. To add a new source root, right-click in the **Sources** window and select the **Add Source Root** option.

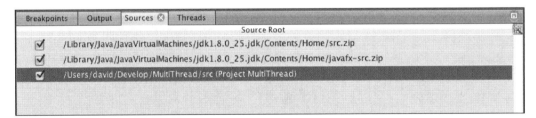

# The Debugging window

The **Debugging** window allows us to see which threads are running while debugging our application. This window is, therefore, particularly useful when debugging multithreaded applications.

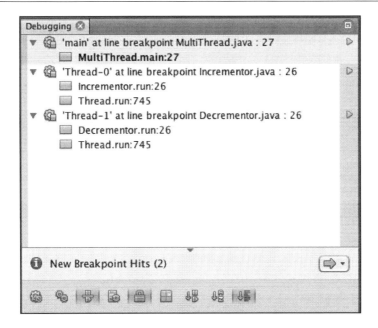

In this window, we can see the different threads that are running within our application. For each thread, we can see the name of the thread and the call stack leading to the breakpoint. The current thread is highlighted with a green band along the left-hand side edge of the window. Other threads created within our application are denoted with a yellow band along the left-hand side edge of the window. System threads are denoted with a gray band.

We can make any of the threads the current thread by right-clicking on it and selecting the **Make Current** menu option. When we do this, the **Variables** and **Call Stack** windows are updated to show new information for the selected thread.

 The current thread can also be selected by clicking on the **Debug** and then **Set Current Thread...** menu options. Upon selecting this, a list of running threads is shown from which the current thread can be selected.

Right-clicking on a thread and selecting the **Resume** option will cause the selected thread to continue execution until it hits another breakpoint.

For each thread that is running, we can also **Suspend**, **Interrupt**, and **Resume** the thread by right-clicking on the thread and choosing the appropriate action.

In each thread listing, the current methods call stack is displayed for each thread. This can be manipulated in the same way as from the **Call Stack** window.

When debugging multithreaded applications, new breakpoints can be hit within different threads at any time. NetBeans helps us with multithreaded debugging by not automatically switching the user interface to a different thread when a breakpoint is hit on the non-current thread. When a breakpoint is hit on any thread other than the current thread, an indication is displayed at the bottom of the **Debugging** window, stating **New Breakpoint Hit** (an example of this can be seen in the previous window). Clicking on the icon to the right of the message shows all the breakpoints that have been hit together with the thread name in which they occur. Selecting the alternate thread will cause the relevant breakpoint to be opened within NetBeans and highlighted in the appropriate Java source code file.

NetBeans provides several filters on the **Debugging** window so that we can show more/less information as appropriate.

From left to right, these images allow us to:

- Show less (suspended and current threads only)
- Show thread groups
- Show suspend/resume table
- Show system threads
- Show monitors
- Show qualified names
- Sort by suspended/resumed state
- Sort by name
- Sort by default

 Debugging multithreaded applications can be a lot easier if you give your threads names. The thread's name is displayed in the **Debugging** window, and it's a lot easier to understand what a thread with a proper name is doing as opposed to a thread called **Thread-1**.

# Deadlock detection

When debugging multithreaded applications, one of the problems that we can see is that a deadlock occurs between executing threads. A deadlock occurs when two or more threads become blocked forever because they are both waiting for a shared resource to become available. In Java, this typically occurs when the synchronized keyword is used.

 For more information on synchronization and concurrency, check out the Java tutorial at `http://docs.oracle.com/javase/tutorial/essential/concurrency/index.html`.

NetBeans allows us to easily check for deadlocks using the **Check for Deadlock** tool available on the **Debug** menu.

When a deadlock is detected using this tool, the state of the deadlocked threads is set to **On Monitor** in the **Threads** window. Additionally, the threads are marked as deadlocked in the **Debugging** window. Each deadlocked thread is displayed with a red band on the left-hand side border and the **Deadlock detected** warning message is displayed:

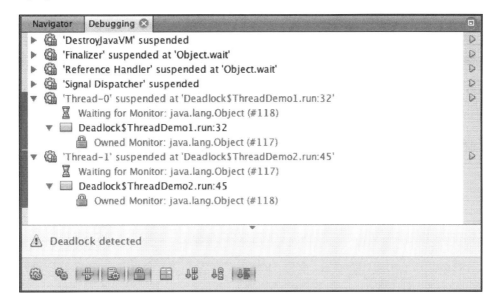

The preceding screenshot is taken from the Deadlock application that is included as part of the code bundle for this chapter. It is recommended that you download this example application and examine its source and how it runs to gain a wider knowledge of deadlock detection in NetBeans.

## Analyze Stack Window

When running an application within NetBeans, if an exception is thrown and not caught, the stack trace will be displayed in the **Output** window, allowing the developer to see exactly where errors have occurred. From the following screenshot, we can easily see that a NullPointerException was thrown from within the FaultyImplementation class in the doUntestedOperation() method at line 16. Looking before this in the stack trace (that is the entry underneath), we can see that the doUntestedOperation() method was called from within the main() method of the Main class at line 21:

```
Output - StackTrace (run)
run:
Exception in thread "main" java.lang.NullPointerException
        at com.davidsalter.stacktrace.FaultyImplementation.doUntestedOperation(FaultyImplementation.java:16)
        at com.davidsalter.stacktrace.Main.main(Main.java:21)
Java Result: 1
BUILD SUCCESSFUL (total time: 0 seconds)
```

In the preceding example, the FaultyImplementation class is defined as follows:

```
public class FaultyImplementation {
    public void doUntestedOperation() {
        throw new NullPointerException();
    }
}
```

The full source code for this example is provided within the StackTrace application that is available in the code bundle for this chapter.

Java is providing an invaluable feature to developers, allowing us to easily see where exceptions are thrown and what the sequence of events was that led to the exception being thrown. NetBeans, however, enhances the display of the stack traces by making the class and line numbers clickable hyperlinks which, when clicked on, will navigate to the appropriate line in the code. This allows us to easily delve into a stack trace and view the code at all the levels of the stack trace. In the previous screenshot, we can click on the hyperlinks FaultyImplementation.java:16 and Main.java:21 to take us to the appropriate line in the appropriate Java file.

This is an excellent time-saving feature when developing applications, but what do we do when someone e-mails us a stack trace to look at an error in a production system? How do we manage stack traces that are stored in log files?

Fortunately, NetBeans provides an easy way to allow a stack trace to be turned into clickable hyperlinks so that we can browse through the stack trace without running the application.

To load and manage stack traces into NetBeans, the first step is to copy the stack trace onto the system clipboard. Once the stack trace has been copied onto the clipboard, **Analyze Stack Window** can be opened within NetBeans by selecting the **Window** and then **Debugging** and then **Analyze Stack** menu options (the default installation for NetBeans has no keyboard shortcut assigned to this operation).

**Analyze Stack Window** will default to showing the stack trace that is currently in the system clipboard. If no stack trace is in the clipboard, or any other data is in the system's clipboard, **Analyze Stack Window** will be displayed with no contents. To populate the window, copy a stack trace into the system's clipboard and select the **Insert StackTrace From Clipboard** button.

Once a stack trace has been displayed in **Analyze Stack Window**, clicking on the hyperlinks in it will navigate to the appropriate location in the Java source files just as it does from the **Output** window when an exception is thrown from a running application.

 You can only navigate to source code from a stack trace if the project containing the relevant source code is open in the selected project group.

# Variable formatters

When debugging an application, the NetBeans debugger can display the values of simple primitives in the **Variables** window. As we saw previously, we can also display the `toString()` representation of a variable if we select the appropriate columns to display in the window.

Sometimes when debugging, however, the `toString()` representation is not the best way to display formatted information in the **Variables** window, as can be seen in the following screenshot:

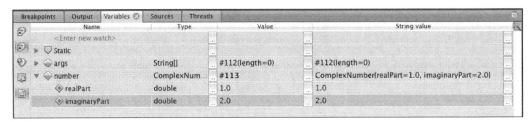

In this window, we are showing the value of a complex number class that we have used in high school math. The `ComplexNumber` class being debugged in this example is defined as:

```java
public class ComplexNumber {

    private double realPart;
    private double imaginaryPart;

    public ComplexNumber(double realPart, double imaginaryPart) {
        this.realPart = realPart;
        this.imaginaryPart = imaginaryPart;
    }

    @Override
    public String toString() {
        return "ComplexNumber{" + "realPart=" + realPart + ",
imaginaryPart=" + imaginaryPart + '}';
    }

    // Getters and Setters omitted for brevity…

}
```

The complete source code for this example is provided within the `VariableFormatters` application that is included as part of the code bundle for this chapter. It's recommended that you download this sample application and examine it in NetBeans in order to aid your understanding of variable formatters.

Looking at this class, we can see that it essentially holds two members—`realPart` and `imaginaryPart`. The `toString()` method outputs a string, detailing the name of the object and its parameters which would be very useful when writing ComplexNumbers to log files, for example:

```
ComplexNumber{realPart=1.0, imaginaryPart=2.0}
```

When debugging, however, this is a fairly complicated string to look at and comprehend—particularly, when there is a lot of debugging information being displayed.

NetBeans, however, allows us to define custom formatters for classes that detail how an object will be displayed in the **Variables** window when being debugged.

To define a custom formatter, select the **Java** option from the NetBeans **Options** dialog and then select the **Java Debugger** tab. From this tab, select the **Variable Formatters** category, as shown in the following screenshot:

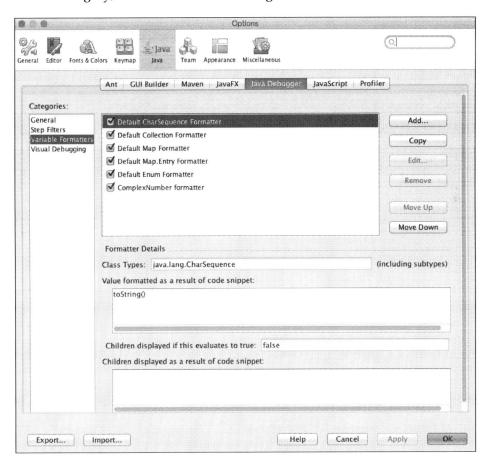

On this screen, all the variable formatters that are defined within NetBeans are shown. To create a new variable formatter, select the **Add...** button to display the **Add Variable Formatter** dialog.

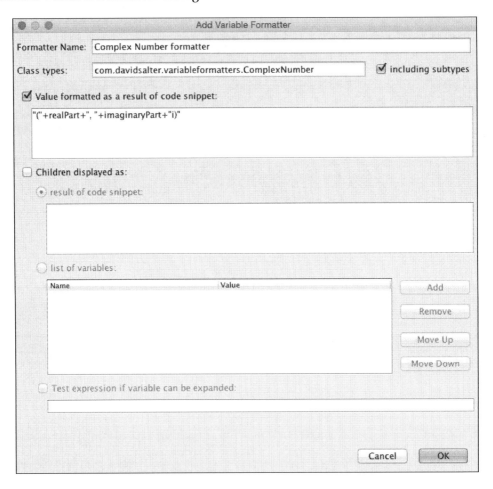

In the **Add Variable Formatter** dialog, we need to enter **Formatter Name** and a list of **Class types** that NetBeans will apply the formatting to when displaying values in the debugger. To apply the formatter to multiple classes, enter the different classes, separated by commas.

The value that is to be formatted is entered in the **Value formatted as a result of code snippet** field. This field takes the scope of the object being debugged. So, for example, to output the ComplexNumber class, we can enter the custom formatter as:

```
"("+realPart+", "+imaginaryPart+"i)"
```

We can see that the formatter is built up from concatenating static strings and the values of the members `realPart` and `imaginaryPart`.

We can see the results of debugging variables using custom formatters in the following screenshot:

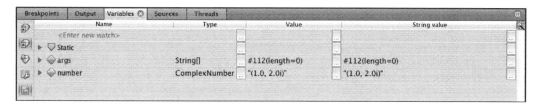

# Debugging remote applications

The NetBeans debugger provides rapid access for debugging local applications that are executing within the same JVM as NetBeans.

What happens though when we want to debug a remote application? A remote application isn't necessarily hosted on a separate server to your development machine, but is defined as any application running outside of the local JVM (that is the one that is running NetBeans).

To debug a remote application, the NetBeans debugger can be "attached" to the remote application. Then, to all intents, the application can be debugged in exactly the same way as a local application is debugged, as described in the previous sections of this chapter.

To attach to a remote application, select the **Debug** and then **Attach Debugger...** menu options.

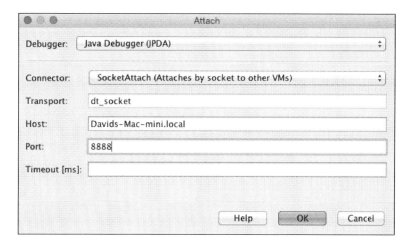

On the **Attach** dialog, the connector (**SocketAttach**, **ProcessAttach**, or **SocketListen**) must be specified to connect to the remote application. The appropriate connection details must then be entered to attach the debugger. For example, the process ID must be entered for the **ProcessAttach** connector and the host and port must be specified for the **SocketAttach** connector.

For more information on debugging "remote" application, check out `http://docs.oracle.com/javase/7/docs/technotes/guides/jpda/conninv.html`.

# Profiling applications

Learning how to debug applications is an essential technique in software development. Another essential technique that is often overlooked is profiling applications.

Profiling applications involves measuring various metrics such as the amount of heap memory used or the number of loaded classes or running threads. By profiling applications, we can gain an understanding of what our applications are actually doing and as such we can optimize them and make them function better. NetBeans provides first class profiling tools that are easy to use and provide results that are easy to interpret. The NetBeans profiler allows us to profile three specific areas:

- Application monitoring
- Performance monitoring
- Memory monitoring

Each of these monitoring tools is accessible from the **Profile** menu within NetBeans. To commence profiling, select the **Profile** and then **Profile Project** menu options. After instructing NetBeans to profile a project, the profiler starts providing the choice of the type of profiling to perform.

In this section, the `Factorial` and `MultiThread` applications from the code bundle for this chapter are used to demonstrate profiling.

# Application monitoring

Application monitoring provides us with three different views on the running state of an application. To commence application monitoring, select the **Monitor** option on the **Profile** dialog and then select the **Run** button. For each type of profiling, NetBeans displays an indication of the overhead the profiling will have on the performance of the running application. For application monitoring, the overhead is negligible.

Once profiling has commenced, the **Profiler** window is automatically opened showing the status of the running application and also providing basic telemetry, such as the number of threads currently executing, the amount of memory in use, and the time spent in garbage collecting.

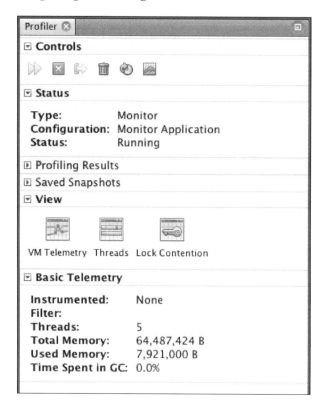

In this window, we can see that there are three options to display different views on the profiling data:

- **VM Telemetry**: This view displays a window showing the heap memory used within the application, the surviving generations, and relative time spent in garbage control.

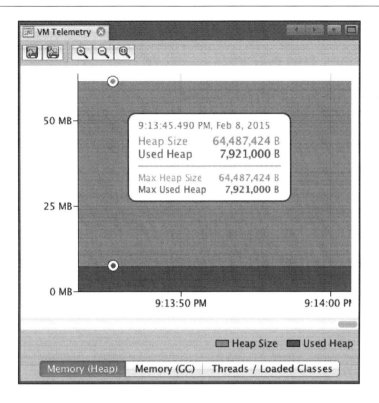

- **Threads**: This view displays the threads that have been instantiated within the application and the state of the threads (**Running, Sleeping, Wait, Park,** or **Monitor**). For each thread, the amount of time running is given as a percentage and as a length of time in milliseconds.

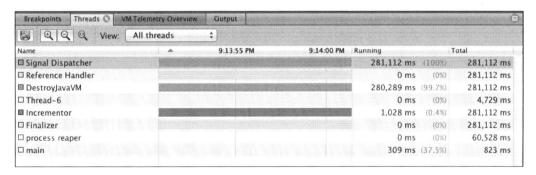

- **Lock Contention**: Finally, if lock contention monitoring has been selected (the default option is to not monitor this), any locks within the threads are profiled and displayed in the **Lock Contention** window.

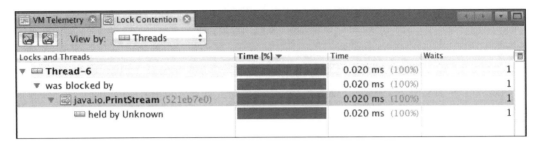

While profiling an application, NetBeans provides facilities to dump the heap from the currently running program by selecting the **Dump Heap** button from within the **Profiler** window. Once the heap has been dumped, it can be opened in the **Heap Walker** window. This allows us to view the state of the heap at a specific moment in time. Information such as the number of bytes used, number of classes loaded, and basic thread information can be obtained from the **Heap Walker** window. Details of the biggest objects by retained size are also available. If several heap files have been saved, they can be compared to give an indication of how the heap of the application has changed over time.

Outside of a profiling session, heap dumps can be loaded by selecting the **Profile** and then **Load Heap Dump...** menu options.

# Performance monitoring

To begin performance monitoring of an application, select the CPU button on the main **Profile** dialog.

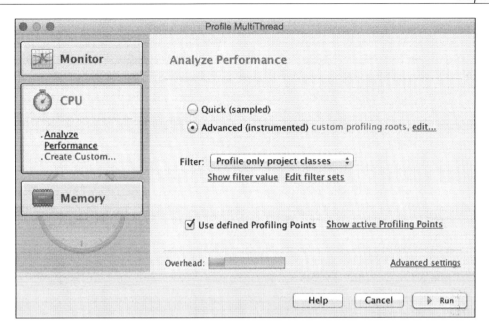

For performance monitoring, the user is given the option of performing either quick or advanced profiling. Quick profiling samples the application periodically, taking a stack trace at set intervals. As the application is not monitored constantly, this has a lower overhead than advanced profiling, but is less accurate. Advanced profiling works by instrumenting the methods of the application and therefore is more accurate (method invocations cannot be missed between samples) but has a higher overhead. When performing advanced performance monitoring, NetBeans allows the developer to choose which classes will be instrumented. With more classes being instrumented, there will be a higher performance overhead against a profiled application, so it's a good idea to only instrument the classes that you wish to monitor.

When profiling performance of an application, the **Live Results** button is available to show the method hot spots within the application. This window shows the amount of time spent within the methods in the application together with the number of invocations of each method.

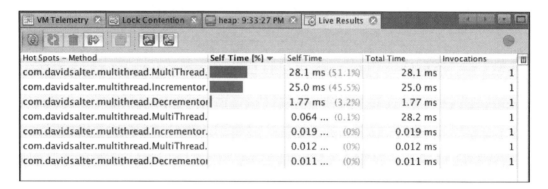

## Memory monitoring

Memory profiling displays the allocated objects used within an application and for each one shows the number of bytes and objects allocated.

When running memory profiling, we again have the options of **Quick and Advanced** profiling, similar to what we had for the CPU monitoring. Quick profiling samples the application at predetermined intervals, whereas advanced instruments all the classes that are loaded in the JVM. As quick profiling only samples the application at the predefined intervals, it can only provide data on the live objects, whereas advanced profiling can provide data about all the objects that are allocated during the applications lifetime.

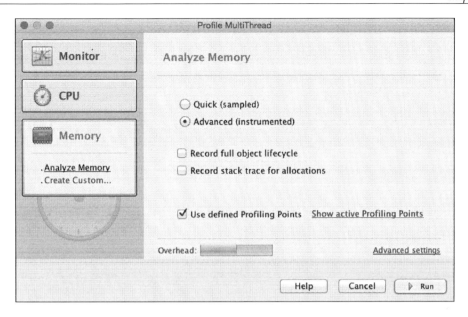

When configuring memory profiling we have the option to record the full object life cycle and stack trace for allocations. Recording the full life cycle of objects allows profiling to record all the information about an object, including the number of generations survived. Recording the full stack trace for object allocations allows the call stack to be viewed from saved memory snapshots.

The **Live Results** window shows the memory allocations used within the application while memory profiling is being performed, as shown in the following screenshot:

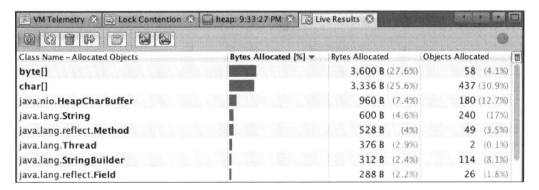

While profiling an application, NetBeans allows us to take snapshots of the state of the running application. These snapshots can then be compared at a later date so that we can gain some understanding of performance/degradation of our applications.

Prior to performing profiling for the first time, NetBeans will display a dialog stating that it needs to calibrate itself so that it can provide accurate results. Calibration is performed once for each JDK used for profiling. It basically performs some self-timings so that NetBeans knows how much time to take of the timing results that it displays during profiling.

# Testing applications

Writing tests for applications is probably one of the most important aspects of modern software development. NetBeans provides the facility to write and run both JUnit and TestNG tests and test suites. In this section, we'll provide details on how NetBeans allows us to write and run these types of tests, but we'll assume that you have some knowledge of either JUnit or TestNG.

For more information on JUnit, check out `http://junit.org`. You can read more about TestNG at `http://testng.org`.

TestNG support is provided by default with NetBeans, however, due to license concerns, JUnit may not have been installed when you installed NetBeans. If JUnit support is not installed, it can easily be added through the NetBeans Plugins system.

In a project, NetBeans creates two separate source roots: one for application sources and the other for test sources. This allows us to keep tests separate from application source code so that when we ship applications, we do not need to ship tests with them.

Some customers require that we ship tests with applications as part of acceptance testing. If this is the case, we can still ship an application as a set of one or more archives, and a test suite as a set of one or more archives.

This separation of application source code and test source code enables us to write better tests and have less coupling between tests and applications. The best situation is for the test source root to have a dependency on application classes and the application classes to have no dependency on the tests that we have written.

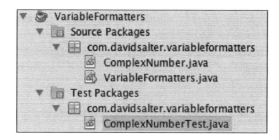

To write a test, we must first have a project. Any type of Java project can have tests added into it. To add tests into a project, we can use the **New File** wizard. In the **Unit Tests** category, there are templates for:

- **JUnit Tests**
- **Tests for Existing Class** (this is for JUnit tests)
- **Test Suite** (this is for JUnit tests)
- **TestNG Test Case**
- **TestNG Test Suite**

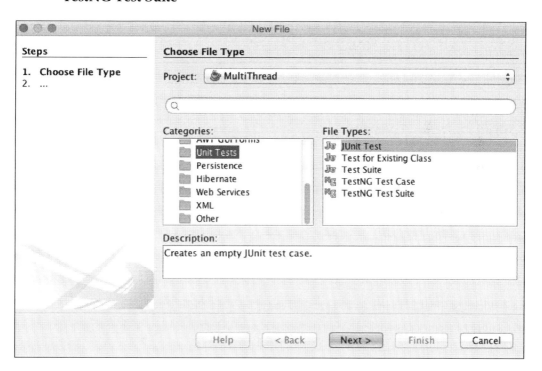

When creating classes for these types of tests, NetBeans provides the option to automatically generate code; this is usually a good starting point for writing classes.

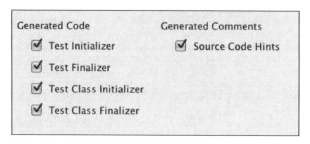

When executing tests, NetBeans iterates through the test packages in a project looking for the classes that are suffixed with the word `Test`. It is therefore essential to properly name tests to ensure they are executed correctly.

Once tests have been created, NetBeans provides several methods for running the tests. The first method is to run all the tests that we have defined for an application. Selecting the **Run** and then **Test Project** menu options runs all of the tests defined for a project. The type of the project doesn't matter (Java SE or Java EE), nor whether a project uses Maven or the NetBeans project build system (Ant projects are even supported if they have a valid test activity), all tests for the project will be run when selecting this option.

After running the tests, the **Test Results** window will be displayed, highlighting successful tests in green and failed tests in red.

The screenshots shown in this section are taken from the kb application—a simple `Knowledge Base` application that is included as part of the code bundle for this chapter. This application provides a good example of unit testing and code coverage. It is recommended that you download this example application and browse the source code to see how NetBeans can help with application testing.

In the **Test Results** window, we have several options to help categorize and manage the tests:

- **Rerun all of the tests**
- **Rerun the failed tests**
- **Show only the passed tests**
- **Show only the failed tests**
- **Show errors**
- **Show aborted tests**
- **Show skipped tests**
- **Locate previous failure**
- **Locate next failure**
- **Always open test result window**
- **Always open test results in a new tab**

The second option within NetBeans for running tests it to run all the tests in a package or class. To perform these operations, simply right-click on a package in the **Projects** window and select **Test Package** or right-click on a Java class in the **Projects** window and select **Test File**.

The final option for running tests it to execute a single test in a class. To perform this operation, right-click on a test in the Java source code editor and select the **Run Focussed Test Method** menu option.

 Just like application source code, unit tests can be debugged to see where they are going wrong. To debug tests, choose the debug variant of the options described in this section, for example, **Debug Focussed Test Method** or **Debug Package**.

After creating tests, how do we keep them up to date when we add new methods to application code? We can keep tests suites up to date by manually editing them and adding new methods corresponding to new application code or we can use the **Create/Update Tests** menu. Selecting the **Tools** and then **Create/Update Tests** menu options displays the **Create Tests** dialog that allows us to edit the existing test classes and add new methods into them, based upon the existing application classes.

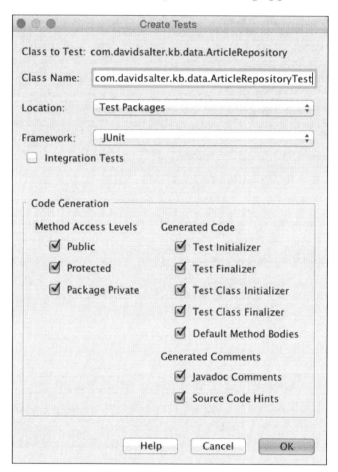

# Code coverage

In some organizations, code coverage is an important metric to show how many tests are available for application source code. Whether the actual level of code coverage is useful is a debatable point. However, viewing the code coverage for an application certainly helps a developer see what parts of an application aren't covered by tests.

NetBeans has built-in support for the JaCoCo code coverage engine.

For more information on JaCoCo, check out
http://www.eclemma.org/jacoco/.

To enable code coverage on a Maven project, the project's pom.xml needs to have some minor modifications to allow JaCoCo to run. Add the following into your application's pom.xml to enable code coverage:

```
<build>
    <plugins>

        <plugin>
            <groupId>org.jacoco</groupId>
            <artifactId>jacoco-maven-plugin</artifactId>
            <version>0.7.2.201409121644</version>
            <executions>
                <execution>
                    <id>default-prepare-agent</id>
                    <goals>
                        <goal>prepare-agent</goal>
                    </goals>
                </execution>
                <execution>
                    <id>default-report</id>
                    <phase>prepare-package</phase>
                    <goals>
                        <goal>report</goal>
                    </goals>
                </execution>
                <execution>
                    <id>default-check</id>
                    <goals>
                        <goal>check</goal>
                    </goals>
                    <configuration>
                        <rules>

                        </rules>
                    </configuration>
                </execution>
            </executions>
        </plugin>
    </plugins>
</build>
```

Once this has been entered into the project's `pom.xml` file, a **Code Coverage** menu option will be available when one right-clicks on a project in the **Projects** window. This menu has the following options:

- **Collect and Display Coverage**: When this option is selected, NetBeans will automatically perform code coverage analysis whenever unit tests are run
- **Clear Results**: This option clears the stored code coverage results
- **Show Report**: This displays the **Code Coverage** report
- **Show Editor Bar**: This option displays the code coverage status bar at the bottom of source code windows

To perform code coverage analysis, all we need to do is run our tests, and NetBeans and JaCoCo take care of everything else. If we decide that we do not want to gather code coverage information, we can stop the collection by unchecking the **Collect and Display Coverage** option.

When code coverage analysis has been run, a window is opened within NetBeans, showing how much coverage each class in the project has, as shown in the following screenshot:

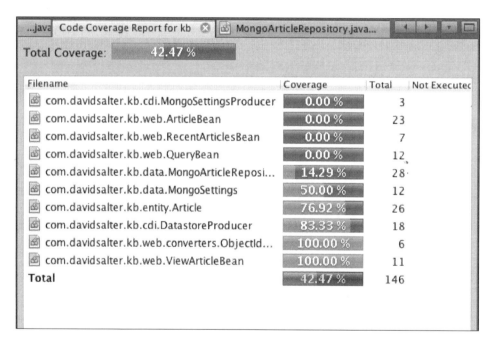

Double-clicking on any of the entries in the **Code Coverage** report will open the corresponding Java source code file. When code coverage data is being collected and displayed, source code files are highlighted to show which lines have been tested and which have not. Any source code that has been tested in a unit test is displayed with a green background color, whereas any code that has not been executed as part of a unit test is displayed with a red background color, as shown in the following screenshot:

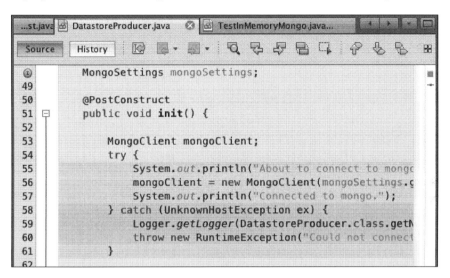

Along the bottom of the application source code windows is the code coverage toolbar. This shows the percentage of the file that has been covered by unit tests along with the buttons to run the tests for the particular class, run all tests, clear the coverage reports, show the coverage reports, or disable code coverage analysis.

# Performing TDD within NetBeans

Now that we've seen all the different aspects of the development life cycle, let's pull it all together and give a brief demonstration of how to use these techniques to perform **TDD** within NetBeans.

TDD is a software development process where the developer writes a test for a piece of functionality before writing the functionality itself. The test will obviously fail at this point as the implementation has not been written. The next stage is to write just enough of the implementation to get the test to succeed. Subsequently, the developer needs to take stock of their code and refactor it to remove any unnecessary code.

Due to the way that tests initially fail, then are fixed and then refactored, the TDD cycle is often referred to as the **Red-Green-Refactor cycle**.

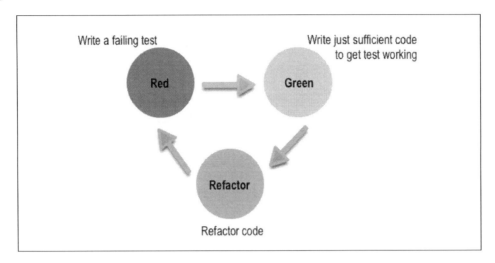

 For more information about TDD, check out http://en.wikipedia. org/wiki/Test-driven_development.

To give an overview of how to perform TDD within NetBeans, let's use TDD to write a method that calculates the factorial of an integer. The factorial of a number is described as the product of all positive integers less than or equal to the number. One additional rule is that the factorial of 1 is 0. Let's see how we can apply these rules with TDD to develop some code.

 The sample application, Factorial, that is generated to show TDD concepts is included as part of the code bundle for this chapter.

The first stage is to create a NetBeans project. Use the **New Project** wizard and create a Java Class Library called Factorial. At this stage, we should have no source code in the library project and no tests.

Remembering that the first stage of TDD is to write a failing test, let's create a blank new JUnit Test class called `com.davidsalter.masteringnb.factorial.FactorialTest`, as shown in the following screenshot (if NetBeans should ask what version of JUnit to use, select JUnit 4.x as this provides a richer API for modern development):

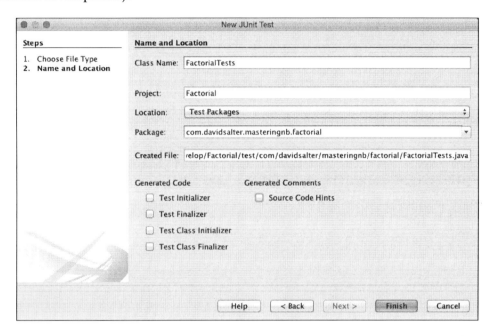

Let's now create our first failing test. Looking at our description of the problem, we know that the factorial of 0 is 1, so the corresponding test would be:

```
@Test
public void factorialOfZeroIsOne() {
    Factorial factorial = new Factorial();
    int result = factorial.calculate(0);
    assertEquals("0! should equal 1", 1, result);
}
```

Using the NetBeans code completion tools, we can create the first instance of our `Factorial` class as:

```
public class Factorial {

  public int calculate(int i) {
    throw new UnsupportedOperationException("Not written yet");
  }
}
```

We've now completed the first phase in the TDD cycle—we've written a test, which we expect to fail as we've not written any application functionality yet. Sure enough, if we press *Shift + F6* to test the application, we get a failed test, just as expected.

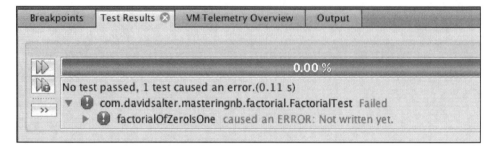

The next step in the TDD cycle is to write just the minimum amount to get the test working. In this instance, let's change the `Factorial` class so that it returns the correct value for 0, as shown in the following code fragment:

```
public int calculate(int i) {

    if (0 == i) {
        return 1;
    }
    throw new UnsupportedOperationException("Not written yet.");
}
```

If we now press *Shift + F6* to run the tests again, we can see that our singular test has passed.

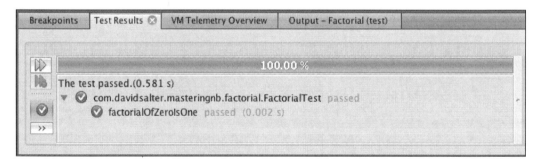

We've now completed the second phase of the TDD cycle—we've made our tests go from red to green.

The next phase is to look at our code and say, "Do I like what I've written? Can I make the code better?" It's important not to go overboard here and add new features though as the functionality of the code should remain constant. In our simple example, there's not much refactoring we could do here, so we go back to the red phase of the TDD cycle and write another failing test.

The next test that we could write is to verify that results are only returned from the `calculate` method if a positive integer is passed into the method. Again, we need to write a failing test first before writing code to make the test pass. We can therefore write the following test:

```
@Test
public void factorialOfNegativeNumberIsZero() {
   Factorial factorial = new Factorial();
   int result = factorial.calculate(-10);
   assertEquals("Factorial of -ve number should be 0.", 0, result);
}
```

You get the procedure now. We've written a test that fails when we run it, so we see red test results in the **Test Results** window. We will now need to write some application code to fix the failing test. Again, we must be wary not to implement too much functionality. We only want to write sufficient application code to make our failing test work (ensuring that our other tests don't fail in the process). Our application code can therefore be updated to the following (this fixes the failing test but doesn't add any new functionality):

```
public int calculate(int i) {

    if (0 == i) {
        return 1;
    }

    if (i < 0 ) {
        return 0;
    }
    throw new UnsupportedOperationException("Not written yet.");
}
```

Running the tests for the project again at this stage should produce two successful tests and no failing tests.

At this point, we should be fairly happy that we're writing good code, but we need to look at refactoring the code again. We need to see whether there's anything we can improve before moving on to the red phase of the TDD cycle—writing another failing test.

We've looked at a couple of cycles of the Red-Green-Refactor loop for TDD, so I'll leave it as an exercise to complete the development of the `Factorial` class. For those who want to check their results or simply to see the complete solution, the complete project is available as part of the code bundle for this book.

# Summary

In this chapter, we looked at the typical tasks that a developer does on a day-to-day basis when writing applications. We saw how NetBeans can help us to run and debug applications and how to profile applications and write tests for them. Finally, we took a brief look at TDD, and saw how the Red-Green-Refactor cycle can be used to help us develop more stable applications.

In the next chapter, we'll look at managing services within NetBeans and see how we can manage and interact with them all from within the NetBeans IDE.

# 4
# Managing Services

Historically, developers used to write monolithic applications that ran on a single machine without interacting with any other systems. Of course, that was long time ago (in terms of software development), and now, developers write all sorts of applications that can run on a wide range of devices such as mobile telephones, desktop computers, or remote servers that provide **Platforms as a Service (PaaS)**.

In addition to running our applications on a range of devices, as developers, we also consume a lot of different services—some within our applications, and some purely to make our development easier and more robust. For example, we all use bug-tracking systems, and many of us use continuous integration systems or remote databases. Even something as ubiquitous as Maven is a service that we need to manage effectively while using it.

In this chapter, we'll be looking at the different services that a Java developer will typically use from within NetBeans and see how NetBeans can enhance our effectiveness using these services. We'll be looking at the following services:

- Databases
- Web Services
- Application Servers
- Maven Repositories
- Cloud services
- Hudson Builders
- Task Repositories

# Databases

Many applications require databases to store information, ranging from embedded data using tools such as Apache Derby to large enterprise databases such as Oracle. Java does not only provide many different APIs to access these databases, such as JDBC and JPA, but also provides the facilities for managing databases, whether they are local to the developer's machine or hosted remotely. We'll look at developing against databases in the next chapter, but first, let's take a look at how we can manage databases from within NetBeans.

The first entry in the **Services** window in NetBeans (on a fresh installation with no additional plugins installed) is the **Databases** explorer:

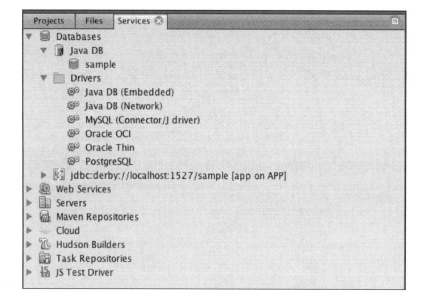

Expanding the **Databases** node in the **Services** window allows us to see what databases we have registered along with the database drivers that are installed within NetBeans and any connections that we have made to the databases.

# Connecting to Java DB

NetBeans provides native support for Java DB (Apache Derby) and MySQL. Connections to other databases can be made by JDBC connections. The preceding screenshot shows an example of the default Java DB connection that is provided with NetBeans; here, we can see that there is one connection to the sample database. The default Java DB connection is to a Java DB instance that is provided with your JDK. We can see and modify the connection details for the Java DB connection by right-clicking on the **Java DB** node and selecting **Properties**.

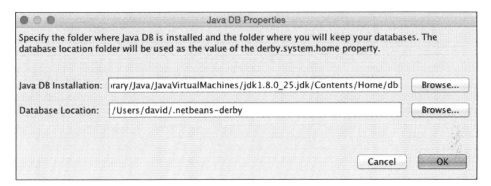

The **Java DB Properties** dialog allows the Java DB installation folder (the location for the `.Jar` files containing Java DB) to be specified along with the database location (the location of the data files that make up the database).

We can start and stop the configured Java DB by right-clicking on the **Java DB** node and selecting the **Start Server** and **Stop Server** options, respectively.

Finally, we can create new databases within the configured Java DB by right-clicking on the **Java DB** node and selecting the **Create Database...** option.

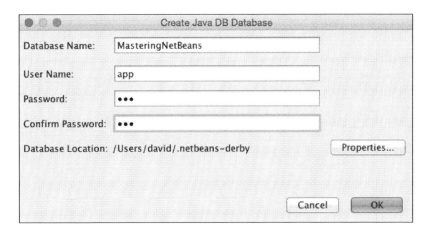

When creating a database, we can gain access to the Java DB properties (the location of the Java DB .Jar files and the location where the data files associated with the database are stored) by clicking on the **Properties...** button.

After clicking on the **OK** button to create a database, the Java DB instance will be started if it is not already running, and the database will be created. The newly created database will then be displayed within the **Java DB** node in the **Services** window and a connection to the new database will be made, as shown in the following screenshot:

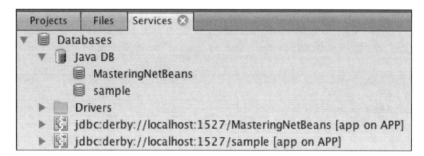

We'll take a look at how to use these connections in a moment, but first, let's see how we can make connections to MySQL and other databases.

# Connecting to MySQL

In addition to providing native support for Java DB, NetBeans provides native built-in support for MySQL. By this, we mean that no additional drivers need to be downloaded to connect to MySQL databases; everything is provided as standard with NetBeans.

To create a connection to a MySQL database, right-click on the **Databases** node in the **Services** window and select the **Register MySQL Server...** menu option. Selecting this opens the **MySQL Server Properties** dialog, allowing both the basic and admin properties to be specified:

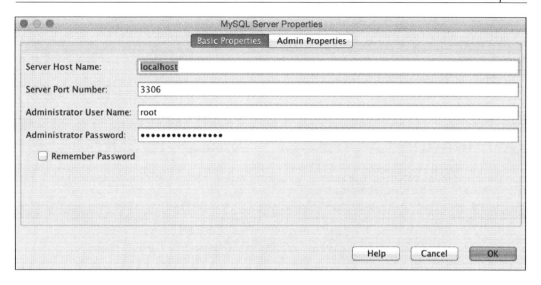

The basic properties are where the connection details for the MySQL Server instance are specified. These include the server host, port number, and administrator username and password.

The admin properties allow us to specify the commands and their arguments to start and stop the MySQL Server if these are being managed from within NetBeans. The path to the MySQL administration tool (for example, MySQL Workbench) can also be specified on the **Admin Properties** page. If you are using web-based management tools for MySQL (such as PhpMyAdmin), this can also be specified here instead of the path to the executable administration tool. The specified administration tool for MySQL can be launched from within NetBeans by right-clicking on the MySQL Server instance within the **Databases** node of the **Services** window and selecting the **Run Administration Tool** menu option. The database properties for MySQL can be accessed after a connection to the MySQL Server has been defined by right-clicking on the MySQL Server instance and selecting the **Properties...** menu option.

Upon expanding the MySQL Server node, a list of the databases in the server is displayed. Any of these can be connected to and managed by right-clicking and selecting the **Connect...** menu option. In a similar fashion to using Java DB, once a connection is made to a database, it is displayed after the **Drivers** node in the **Services** window.

Since MySQL allows multiple databases to be created within a single server, NetBeans provides an option to perform this task as well. Right-clicking on the MySQL Server instance in the **Services** window provides the **Create Database...** menu option. From here, we can create new databases within the MySQL Server.

This functionality can also be performed by running the MySQL administration tool discussed earlier; however, when databases are created via the **Create Database...** menu option, connections to them are automatically established in the **Services** window for the ease of use.

# Connecting to other databases via JDBC

Although NetBeans provides built-in native support for Java DB and MySQL, we can connect to any database from within NetBeans if an appropriate JDBC driver is available. The list of the recognized JDBC drivers is displayed within the **Drivers** node:

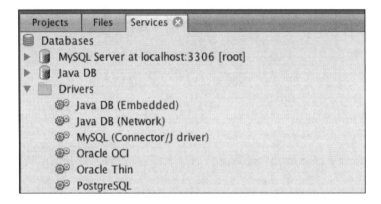

Although the **Drivers** list only shows the available JDBC drivers for Java DB, MySQL, Oracle, and PostgreSQL, any database with a JDBC driver can be accessed from within NetBeans. To register a new driver, simply right-click on the **Drivers** node and select the **New Driver...** menu option.

In the **New JDBC Driver** dialog, we can specify the path to the .Jar file(s) that implement the JDBC driver together with the driver class and the name that we wish to reference the driver by. The following screenshot shows an example of the details required to register a Microsoft SQL Server JDBC driver:

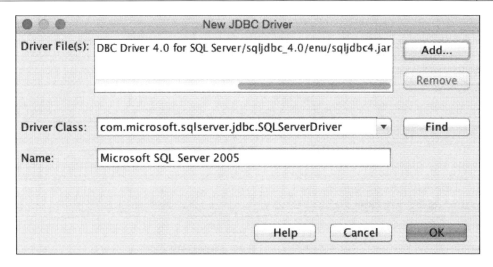

 Note that although Oracle is listed in the **Drivers** node of the **Services** window, the actual Oracle JDBC drivers are not supplied with NetBeans as this is not permitted by the Oracle license. To connect to an Oracle database, the JDBC drivers need to be downloaded either from `http://oracle.com` or used from within your Oracle database installation.

For any registered JDBC drivers, a connection can be made to the specified database by right-clicking on the driver and selecting the **Connect Using...** menu option. Upon selecting this menu option, a dialog is displayed, asking for the connection details to the database (username, host, password, and others). Once these have been entered, a connection will be established and opened.

All of the connections within NetBeans to databases, irrespective of whether they are to the Java DB, MySQL, or JDBC databases, are actually made by JDBC and are listed after **Drivers** in the **Services** window, as shown in the following screenshot:

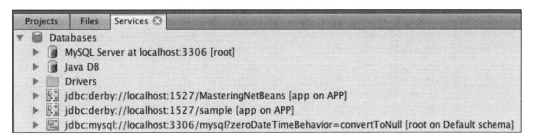

Open connections are shown with the symbol, (▣), whereas closed connections are shown with the same symbol but with a tear down the middle of it (▣).

Right-clicking on a database connection provides the option to either **Connect** or **Disconnect** to the specified database.

# Managing databases

Once we have connected to a database, we can execute SQL commands against it by right-clicking on the connection and selecting the **Execute Command...** menu option. Selecting this menu option opens a SQL editor window within the main part of the NetBeans IDE into which we can type and execute SQL statements against the database.

In the SQL editor window, we can perform multiple database operations:

- **Run SQL**: This executes all the SQL statements in the SQL window

- **Run Statement**: This executes only the currently selected statement in the SQL window

- **Select Connection In Services**: This selects the current JDBC connection in the **Services** window

- **SQL History**: This displays the previously executed SQL statements

After executing a SQL statement, the results of the statement are displayed in the **Output** window. This output will state whether the execution of the statement was successful, how many rows were affected, and the time it took to perform the operation. If a SQL statement returned data (such as a `select` statement), the result set will be displayed in a paginated list at the bottom of the SQL window. When executing statements in the SQL editor, NetBeans uses an auto commit feature so that a database commit operation is performed after each statement or batch of statements is executed.

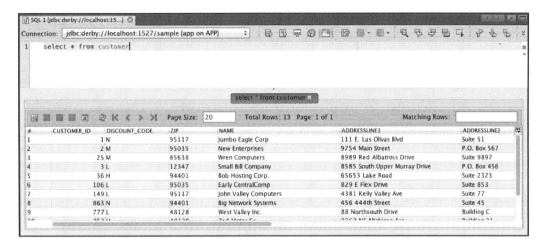

From within this window, we can perform much more than simply looking at the results returned from the SQL operation. Right-clicking within the results pane allows us to:

- **Insert record**: A dialog is displayed allowing us to enter data for the specific table being viewed

- **Delete selected record**: This lets us delete the selected record from the database

- **Commit Selected Record(s)**: This feature commits any edited records into the database

- **Cancel Edits Selected Record(s)**: This cancels any changes made to the existing records

- **Truncate Table**: This removes all the data in the selected table

- **Copy Cell Values**: This copies the selected cell values to the clipboard

- **Copy Row Values**: This copies the selected row values to the clipboard

- **Copy Row Values (With Header)**: This copies the selected row values with header to the clipboard

- **Show SQL Script for CREATE**: This displays a SQL script for creating the selected table

- **Show SQL Script for INSERT**: This displays a SQL script for inserting the selected entries

- **Show SQL Script for DELETE**: This displays a SQL script for deleting the selected entries

- **Show SQL Script for UPDATE**: This displays a SQL script for updating the selected entries with any changes made

- **Print Table Data**: This prints the table data to a printer
- **Refresh Records**: This refreshes the result set
- **Set to NULL**: This sets the selected entry to null
- **Set to default**: This sets the selected entry to its default value

As can be seen, the SQL window allows us to execute queries and statements against the database while displaying the results in the **Output** window. We can also manage databases directly from within the **Services** window.

If we expand a connection node in the **Services** window, the list of tables, views, and procedures for the selected connection is displayed.

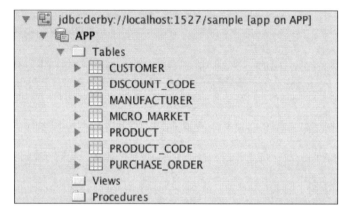

Right-clicking on any of these entries displays a context menu allowing us to interact with the selected entry. For example, right-clicking on the **Tables** node and selecting **Create Table...** displays a dialog where we can define the columns that make up a database table and then create the table directly without having to enter any SQL.

Right-clicking on a table and selecting the **View Data...** command acts as a shortcut to opening a SQL window and entering a `select * from` statement to view all the data within a table.

# Web Services

Invoking web services used to be a complicated procedure. You had to choose a client web services library to use and then usually write an Ant script that would parse a WSDL file and generate some client classes for you. Fortunately, NetBeans has made this whole process a lot easier. With NetBeans, we can now simply drag and drop a web service into a class, allowing us to easily invoke web service operations. Let's take a look at exactly what we mean by this.

Within the **Web Services** node of the **Services** window, NetBeans is preconfigured with many web service definitions from the following vendors:

- Amazon
- Delicious
- Flickr
- Google
- StrikeIton
- WeatherBug
- Zillow
- Zvents

Each of these categories contains one or more different web services that we can invoke from within our applications. For example, if we expand the **Amazon** node, we can see that there are web services for Amazon—**Associates Service**, **EC2 Service**, **S3 Buckets Service**, and **S3 Service**:

Expanding any service completely will result in individual web services being discovered. In the preceding screenshot, we can see that the **itemSearch** web service is located within the **Amazon | Associates Service | [xml]** category. Individual web services are denoted with a red ball icon (⬤), whereas their enclosing categories are marked with a hand holding the red ball icon (🤚).

To add code to your application to invoke the web service, simply drag the web service (**itemService** in the preceding screenshot) from the **Services** window into a Java source code file at the location you wish to invoke the web service. Upon dropping the web service, NetBeans will display a dialog, asking for any parameters for the web service to be defined; these, of course, will be web service-specific. The following screenshot gives an example of the web service parameters required for the Amazon Associates **itemSearch** web service:

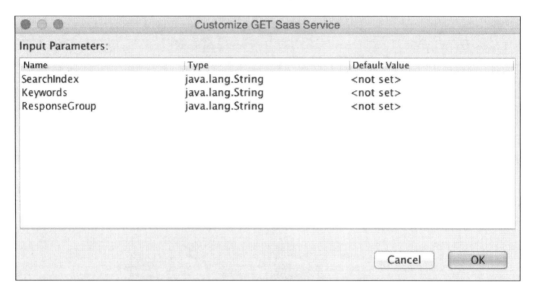

Upon entering any required values, NetBeans will generate the required code to invoke the web service creating the appropriate classes within your application; typically, these classes are within the `org.netbeans.saas` package and subpackages.

Some web services require authentication to invoke their web service API methods; Amazon and Google, for example, require an API key. When running your application using these web services, NetBeans will display an error message stating that the API key needs to be defined along with the information on what file the key needs to be defined within, for example, `java.io.IOException: Please specify your api key in the amazonassociatesserviceauthenticator.properties file.`

Invoking web services from NetBeans has been made immeasurably easier using the drag and drop technique described earlier, but how do we know what parameters a web service takes and whether they are optional and so on? Fortunately, NetBeans allows us to easily view the documentation for a web service by clicking on the top-level service (for example, **Associates Service**) and selecting the **View API Documentation** option. Selecting this option causes NetBeans to open your default system browser and display the relevant documentation for the selected web service. We can also view the WADL for an existing web service by right-clicking on the service and selecting the **View WADL** option.

For the WSDL-based web services (for example, the StrikeIron web services), we can do the same operations as described earlier, but we can also test the web services directly from within the **Services** window without having to drag and drop them into our applications. To test a web service, right-click on the web service itself and select the **Test Method** menu option. NetBeans will display a dialog, allowing all of the parameters for the web service method to be entered. Clicking on the **Submit** button in the dialog will invoke the web service and display the results toward the bottom of the dialog.

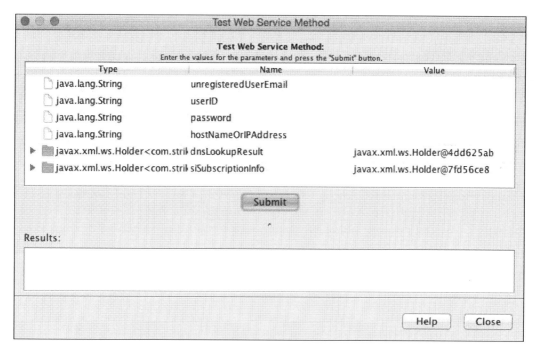

So far, we've seen how we can invoke and test a set of web service operations, all from within NetBeans, but what if we want to invoke a different web service, for example, one hosted elsewhere or even one we've written ourselves? Fortunately, NetBeans allows us to add any number of web services to the **Services** window that we can categorize into groups and then invoke by dragging and dropping into our Java source code.

Right-clicking on the **Web Service** node (or any of its descendant groups) and selecting the **Add Web Service** menu option displays a dialog where we can specify the WSDL or WADL file for the web service. This can either be a local file or can be a remote URL. We can also specify a default package for the web service to be stored in so that the default of org.netbeans.saas is not used.

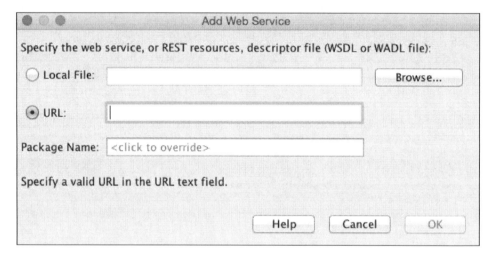

Finally, we can arrange the hierarchy of the web services in the **Services** window simply by dragging and dropping web services into other groups that we have made. Groups can be created at any point within the **Web Services** hierarchy by right-clicking and selecting the **Create Group** menu option at the required place.

# Application Servers

The **Servers** node in the **Services** window allows us to manage application servers such as GlassFish and Tomcat. The default enterprise distribution of NetBeans installs Tomcat and GlassFish and automatically registers them under the **Servers** node.

Right-clicking on the **Servers** node allows additional application servers to be registered within NetBeans. The following application server types can be registered:

- Apache Tomcat
- Apache TomEE
- GlassFish Server
- JBoss Application Server
- Oracle WebLogic Server
- WildFly Application Server

The procedure for registering an application server depends somewhat on the application server itself, but the general procedure is to specify the location and configuration of an application server, possibly registering the administrative credentials that can be used for managing the server. The GlassFish Server registration process is unique in that it allows you to download a copy of the GlassFish Server while registering the application server. That is to say the GlassFish application server does not need to already exist when adding an application server into NetBeans. This is unique to GlassFish; all the other application servers require an installed application server.

> The Payara Server (http://payara.co) can be registered as a GlassFish application server as the Payara Server is a drop-in replacement for the GlassFish application server.

Once an application server has been registered, it can be selected as the default server for running Java EE applications; this is typically performed when the application is created. When creating a new Java web application or EE application, NetBeans requires a server to be specified, as shown in the following screenshot:

If the required application server has not been registered within NetBeans, it can be added by pressing the **Add…** button.

Different application servers provide different functionality from within the **Services** window. Common functionality between all the servers, however, is to start and stop the server in either a run or debug configuration. For the GlassFish server, we can also easily view the admin console for the running server and view the server's logs and access the server's update center. All of this can be achieved by right-clicking on the **GlassFish Server** instance in the **Services** window:

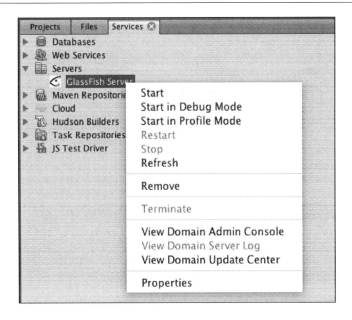

Similarly, once a server has been started, different application servers provide different functionality from within the **Services** window. With GlassFish, for example, we can see the applications that are deployed to the server along with any resources that are also deployed (such as JDBC resources and JDBC connection pools). We can also see any **JMS**, **JavaMail**, and **Web Services** that are deployed to the server, as shown in the following screenshot:

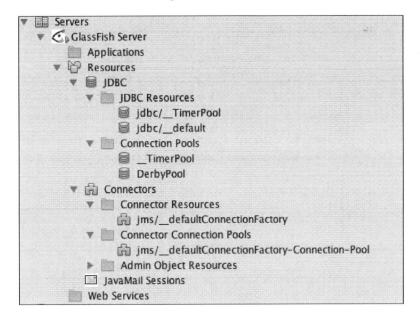

# Maven Repositories

Maven is one of the most popular build systems for Java programmers. With Maven, software libraries are published and stored on a central repository, unsurprisingly called **Maven central**. This repository is hosted on an `apache.org` domain since Maven is an Apache product. When a library is pulled from a Maven repository, it is stored locally for caching purposes; the next time the library is required, it is obtained from a local cache rather than from the central repository. You can imagine that as time goes on, both the central and, to a lesser extent, the local repositories grow at an enormous rate.

With the Maven repositories being so large, knowing the details about a package that we wish to use becomes increasingly complex. Fortunately, the **Maven Repositories** section of the **Services** window allows us to search and browse the packages that are installed on both the Maven central and our own local Maven repositories. Expanding the **Repositories** node shows a list of all the different Maven groups and artifacts within each group.

Say, for example, we wish to add JUnit support to our application, but want to know about the different version of JUnit and their dependencies. We can browse through the Maven central repository until we find the `junit` Maven artifact within the `junit` Maven group.

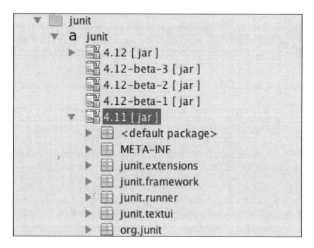

Extending the artifact, we can see a list of all the different versions of the artifact that are available (for example, `junit 4.12`, `junit 4.12-beta-3`, and so on). Expanding any artifact node lists all the classes and resources that are used within the particular version of the library.

Along with simply browsing for artifacts, we can search for them by right-clicking on the **Maven Repositories** node and selecting the **Find...** menu option. The **Find In Repositories** dialog is then displayed:

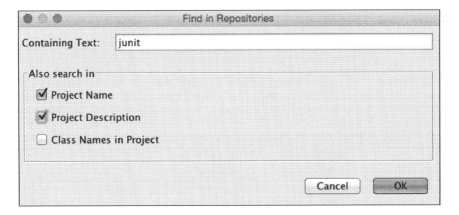

From here, we can specify criteria to find artifacts containing certain text. After selecting **OK** and performing a search, a list of suitable artifacts is displayed as the last node within the list of **Maven Repositories**.

Once we've found an artifact, either via searching or browsing the full repository, right-clicking on an artifact provides us with the following options:

- **View Details**: This opens the details window where all the details of the package such as its name, size, description, dependent projects, and others is displayed

- **Add as Dependency...**: This displays a dialog listing all of the currently open Maven projects, allowing us to add the selected artifact as a dependency of a selected project

- **Find Usages**: This finds usages of the specified artifact in both open projects and on the selected repository

- **View Javadoc**: This views the Javadoc for the selected artifact

- **Open**: This browses the packages and resources within the specified artifact

- **Download**: This downloads the artifact locally

- **Download Sources**: This downloads the source for the selected version of the selected artifact

- **Download Javadoc**: This downloads the Javadoc for the selected version of the selected artifact

- **Copy**: This copies the required Maven dependency so that the artifact can easily be used within a pom.xml file

Sometimes, organizations deploy their packages to repositories other than the Maven central. This is particularly common within organizations that do not wish to make their code public. Fortunately, NetBeans allows us to register third-party Maven repositories so that we can browse the packages installed on them and perform the same operations as we can on the Maven central and local repositories.

To add a Maven repository into the **Services** window, simply right-click on the **Maven Repositories** root node and select the **Add Repository...** menu option. Entering the repository's ID, name, and URL adds it to the list of registered repositories. Adding repositories to the **Services** window does not affect the way that your applications are built, it simply allows you to browse and find artifacts within the remote and local Maven repositories.

# Cloud services

The **Cloud** services node in the **Services** window allows us to view and manage different cloud services, all from within NetBeans. The default installation of NetBeans provides support for viewing Amazon Beanstalk clouds; however, plugins are available for other cloud vendors such as Jelastic, OpenShift, and Oracle Cloud. These additional plugins can be installed by selecting the **Plugins** menu option from the **Tools** menu.

To add a cloud service into the **Services** window, simply right-click on the **Cloud** node and select the **Add Cloud...** menu option. Select the required cloud provider from the **Add Cloud Provider** dialog, as shown in the following screenshot, and complete the wizard to register the provider. Different cloud providers require different information to be entered during the registration process, but typically, authentication and endpoint information are required.

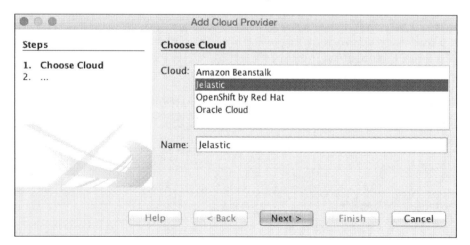

Once a cloud provider has been registered, we can view the applications deployed to the cloud provider, recycle them, and also view the logs for them. With the OpenShift provider, we can even create new applications to be deployed to the OpenShift cloud. The following screenshot depicts the Jelastic provider, showing how we have access to any deployed applications along with access to the server and log files created by the application:

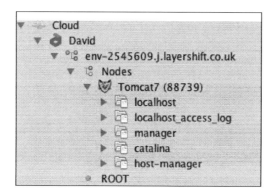

# Hudson Builders

Hudson is a continuous integration system that builds and runs tests on software at set intervals. Within Hudson, we can configure builds to be run at certain intervals, such as after code check-in or at timescales such as every hour. Each Hudson job can be configured to run when required and can check out or clone source code repositories to perform builds. Hudson then maintains a list of builds so that the quality of software can be monitored.

 For more information on Hudson, refer to http://hudson-ci.org.

Within NetBeans, we can register one or more Hudson servers so that we can monitor the status of builds directly from within the IDE. To add a new Hudson server into NetBeans, right-click on the **Hudson Builders** node in the **Services** window and select the **Add Hudson Instance...** menu option.

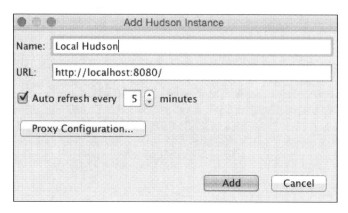

In the **Add Hudson Instance** dialog, we can enter name for the Hudson instance together with URL. If we need to route via a proxy server to gain access to the Hudson instance, we can configure this via the **Proxy Configuration...** button.

If we're running on a fresh instance of Hudson with no jobs defined, we can add a new job directly into Hudson from NetBeans by right-clicking on the Hudson instance and selecting the **New Build...** menu option. Upon selecting this menu item, NetBeans will display the **New Continuous Build** dialog, asking for details of **Build Server**, **Build Name**, and **Project to Build**. The **Project to Build** dropdown lists all the currently open projects within NetBeans. If you do not have the project open already, it can be opened by selecting the **Browse...** button:

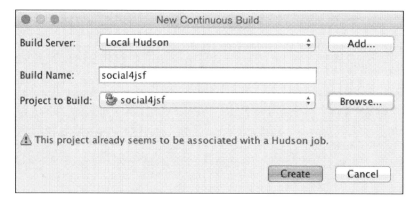

After creating a new continuous build, NetBeans will open the appropriate Hudson job in the default system browser so that the job can be completely defined within Hudson. Check out the Hudson documentation at `http://www.hudson-ci.org` for details on how to create build jobs in Hudson.

If there are already build jobs configured within Hudson, these will automatically be displayed within NetBeans, so there is no need to recreate the existing build jobs.

For each build job in Hudson, an entry will be displayed underneath the Hudson instance in the **Services** window.

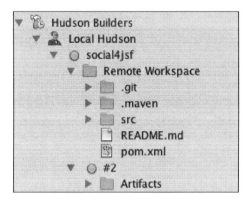

Each project is color coded with a ball icon to show whether the build has failed or not, with failed builds being displayed in red. For each project, the remote workspace can be viewed (this is the build workspace that Hudson used for the build) together with a list of all the previous builds that have been performed for the project.

For each build, we can right-click and perform these options:

- **Show Changes**: This shows the changes made to the source for this build
- **Show Console**: This shows the build console for this build
- **Show Test Failures**: This shows which tests failed for this build
- **Open in Browser**: This opens the Hudson build job in the system's default browser

# Task Repositories

NetBeans provides access to bug tracking systems such as Bugzilla, Jira, and Mantis through the **Task Repositories** node in the **Services** window. Bugzilla and Jira support are supplied prebundled with NetBeans, however, Mantis support requires adding via installing the appropriate plugin from the **Tools** and then **Plugins** menu options.

Configuring the different task repositories is a similar process for each of the different systems; however, we'll take a look at configuring Mantis here.

 For more information on Mantis, visit `http://mantisbt.org`.

To integrate a new task repository within NetBeans, simply right-click on the **Task Repositories** node in the **Services** window and select the **Create Task Repository...** menu option. On the **Create Task Repository** screen, enter the name we'll use to recognize the repository, along with the URL for Mantis and a username and password, as shown in the following screenshot:

Once the task repository has been registered, it is displayed in the **Services** window. In the case of Mantis, right-clicking on the task repository provides four options:

- **Find Tasks...**: This displays the **Find Tasks** window, allowing issues within the task repository to be searched for

- **Report Task...**: This displays the **Report a New Task** window, allowing new issues to be created within the task repository

- **Edit**: This edits the Mantis connection information
- **Remove**: This deletes the Mantis integration

With these options, we can, therefore, create new issues and search for the existing issues, all from within NetBeans itself. What about when we check in code to a source control system such as Subversion or Git? Can we mark issues as completed automatically?

Yes, we can! Fortunately, the task repository integration within NetBeans is available when code is committed to a source code repository. When the option is selected to commit code, a task repository and a task within it can be selected. The task can be updated with new information or can be marked as fixed. All of this is available from within the **Commit** dialog within NetBeans.

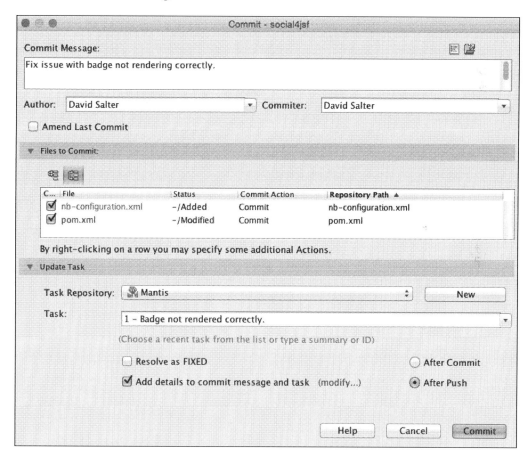

# Summary

In this chapter, we looked at many different types of services that developers typically use and saw how NetBeans can help developers take advantage of them.

In the next chapter, we'll look at database persistence and see how to interact with different databases from within NetBeans. We'll see how NetBeans can make the whole process a lot easier.

# Database Persistence

5

In the previous chapter, we looked at managing different services from within NetBeans. One of the services we looked at was managing different database connections and databases themselves. We saw how to perform SQL statements against a database and return result sets from queries.

In this chapter, we're going to look at how NetBeans helps us to perform database operations from within applications. We're going to look at the following topics:

- Creating persistence units
- Creating blank entity classes and entity classes from databases
- Creating JPA controllers
- Creating database schemas and database scripts from entity classes

## Java EE Persistence

From Java EE 5 onward, the **Java Persistence API (JPA)** allows us to persist and retrieve objects from databases. JPA provides an object/relational mapping tool that maps between Java objects and SQL statements. With JPA, therefore, it is not necessary to execute a number of `PreparedStatement` against the database `Connection` objects to get a `ResultSet` back from the database, like was necessary with JDBC. Additionally, as JPA abstracts developers away from SQL statements, we no longer have to worry about different "flavors" of SQL. For example, with JPA, we are generally removed from the problem of "how do we create auto-incrementing fields with Oracle/SQL Server/MySQL".

In this chapter, we're not going to explain all the different concepts of JPA; we will assume that you have some familiarity with it. The aim of this chapter is not to introduce or teach JPA, but to show how NetBeans aids developers who are handling relational data. We will concentrate on how NetBeans enhances our productivity when interacting with databases.

To learn more about JPA, refer to the Java Persistence API tutorial at `https://docs.oracle.com/javaee/6/ tutorial/doc/bnbpz.html`.

# JPA entities

JPA has the concept of entities that can be saved and retrieved to a database. To make things simpler, Java EE 5 added the concept of annotations so that Java classes could be annotated to add runtime information to classes. JPA provides a set of annotations that can be applied to Java classes, allowing developers to easily persist and retrieve objects from relational databases.

A simple Java class can be used to represent a JPA entity; however, there are several defining features that an entity class must possess. In Java EE 7, for a class to represent an entity, it must:

- Be annotated with the `@Entity` annotation located within the `javax. persistence` package

- Not be declared `final` or contain instance variables that are declared `final`

- Have a minimum of one `public` or `protected` no argument constructor

- Implement the `Serializable` interface if it is to be exposed outside of a remote session bean

- Ensure instance variables that are persisted are not public and can only be accessed via the accessor or business methods

# Creating blank entity classes

Now that we've seen the basic rules that allow a Java class to represent a JPA entity, how do we create an entity class? We can either create a Java class manually and ensure all the preceding rules are met, for example, adding the `@Entity` annotation as required or we can use the NetBeans wizards to automatically create classes for us.

To create a blank entity class, select the **File** and then **New File...** menu options from the NetBeans main menu. On the **New File** dialog, select the **Persistence** category and then **Entity Class** from the list of **File Types**:

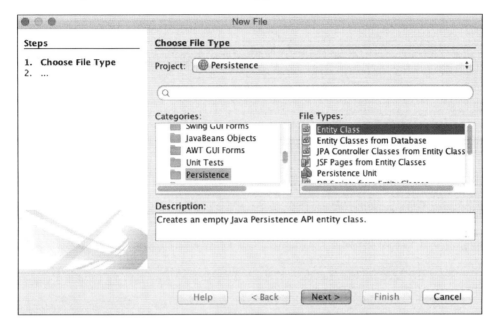

Within the **Persistence** category, we can see that there is also an option to create **Entity Classes from Database**. We'll see how this works shortly.

Upon selecting the **Next >** button, we're presented with the standard options to create classes, namely a **Class Name**, **Package**, and **Location** to create the class (**Source Packages** or **Test Packages**).

What's different on this dialog from the standard **New Java Class** dialog is that we can specify a primary key type. This defaults to **Long**, but can be changed as appropriate to different types. Choosing **Long** is probably the best bet for applications though unless you have a specific reason to use a different type. We can also specify whether a persistence unit will be created upon completion of the wizard. If we choose to not create a persistence unit, NetBeans will not allow the wizard to continue if there is no existing persistence unit in the project.

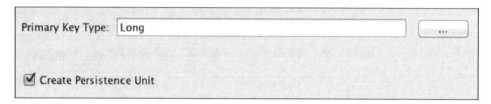

Continuing through the wizard, clicking on the **Next >** button takes us to the **Provider and Database** configuration screen where we can define settings that are stored in the persistence unit for the application.

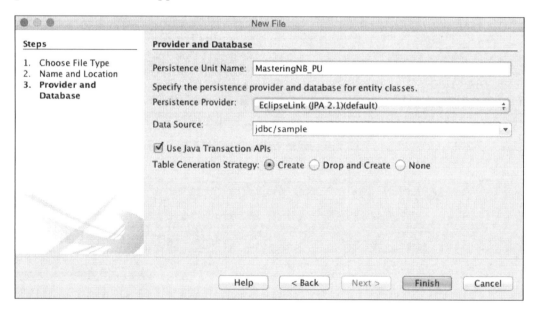

This screen allows several key concepts within the persistence unit to be defined:

- **Persistence Unit Name**: This is the name of the persistence unit. JPA uses this to distinguish between multiple persistence units defined in a project.

- **Persistence Provider**: JPA is a specification; however, there are multiple products that implement the specification. Within NetBeans, the default is EclipseLink, although Hibernate can also be chosen. If you wish to use a different persistence provider such as Apache OpenJPA, a new provider can be created by selecting the **New Persistence Library...** drop-down option and specifying the relevant .Jar files for the provider.

- **Data Source**: This drop-down list displays all the data sources defined within NetBeans. To create a new data source, select the **New Data Source...** option and then specify a JNDI name and a database connection in the resulting dialog. If you are unsure how to create data sources, refer back to *Chapter 4, Managing Services*.

- **Use Java Transaction APIs**: This option allows us to decide whether we want transactions to be managed for us or to have fine-grained programmatic control over transactions. Unless you have a specific reason not to use the Java Transactions API, this option should be kept selected.

> If you are creating an entity class in a standard Java application, the option to use the Java Transaction API will not be present. This option depends upon additional features provided by the application servers and is, therefore, generally only available for web applications.

- **Table Generation Strategy**: Here, we can specify how JPA creates and drops tables within the database. There are three options to select from:
    - **Create**: Database tables are created when the JPA application first runs.
    - **Drop and Create**: Database tables are dropped and then recreated when the JPA application first runs.
    - **None**: JPA does not create or drop tables. Tables must be created outside the application before it runs.

Upon completing the wizard, a blank entity class and a persistence unit are created (assuming the option to create a persistence unit was selected).

The basic form of the entity class is:

```java
@Entity
public class Customer implements Serializable {
    private static final long serialVersionUID = 1L;
    @Id
    @GeneratedValue(strategy = GenerationType.AUTO)
    private Long id;

    public Long getId() {
        return id;
    }

    public void setId(Long id) {
        this.id = id;
    }
}
```

The default persistence unit (`persistence.xml`) is defined as:

```xml
<?xml version="1.0" encoding="UTF-8"?>
<persistence version="2.1" xmlns="http://xmlns.jcp.org/xml/ns/
persistence" xmlns:xsi="http://www.w3.org/2001/XMLSchema-instance"
xsi:schemaLocation="http://xmlns.jcp.org/xml/ns/persistence http://
xmlns.jcp.org/xml/ns/persistence/persistence_2_1.xsd">
  <persistence-unit name="MasteringNB_PU" transaction-type="JTA">
    <jta-data-source>jdbc/sample</jta-data-source>
    <exclude-unlisted-classes>false</exclude-unlisted-classes>
    <properties>
      <property name="javax.persistence.schema-generation.database.
action" value="drop-and-create"/>
    </properties>
  </persistence-unit>
</persistence>
```

# Editing the persistence.xml file

Once we've created a `persistence.xml` file, we can edit it either as raw XML in a text editor window within NetBeans or use the NetBeans **Design** view from within the editor window.

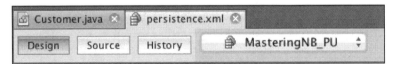

Selecting the **Design**, **Source**, and **History** options toggles the different views of the
`persistence.xml` file. When the **Design** view is selected, a pop-up menu is available
to the right of the **History** button (as shown in the preceding image). Selecting entries
from this dropdown selects different entries within the **Design** view. For example, if
we have multiple `persistence.xml` files, we can select the one to edit from here, we
can select the **General** details, or the specific **Properties** details for a `persistence.`
`xml` file to edit.

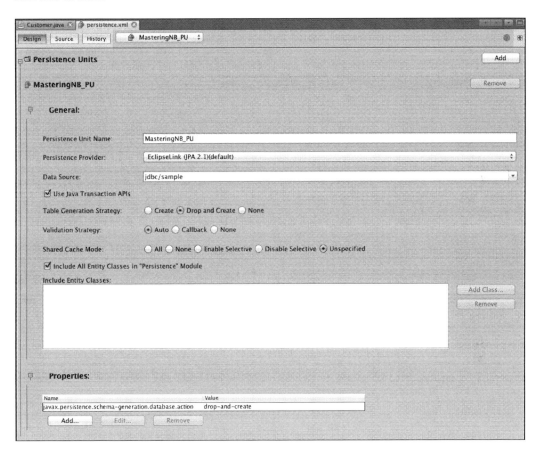

The first few options within the **Design** view of the persistence unit editor are the
same as when creating a persistence unit (**Persistence Unit Name**, **Persistence
Provider**, **Data Source**, **Use Transaction APIs**, and **Table Generation Strategy**).
Following on from these options, we have additional JPA configuration:

- **Validation Strategy**: This feature allows us to specify the validation mode
  for the provider of the persistence unit and is available when using JPA 2.0
  and above. Entries here map to the `<validation-mode />` entry within the
  `persistence.xml` file.

- **Shared Cache Mode**: Here, we can specify the caching mode that is provided by the persistence provider when using JPA 2.0 and above. Entries here map to the `<shared-cache-mode />` element within the `persistence.xml` file and correspond to the `javax.persistance.SharedCacheMode` enumeration values of ALL, NONE, ENABLE_SELECTIVE, and DISABLE_SELECTIVE. The **Unspecified** option is the equivalent of the `persistence.xml` file, not containing a `<shared-cache-mode />` element.

- **Include All Entity Classes in "Persistence" Module**: When this option is selected, all the classes annotated with `@Entity` will be included within the persistence unit. If this option is not selected, individual classes can be selected and removed from the persistence unit by selecting the **Add Class...** and **Remove** buttons, respectively, to the right of the **Include Entity Classes** list.

Finally, the **Properties** section allows us to define any custom properties required by the selected JPA provider.

 When editing a `persistence.xml` file, the **Navigator** window shows a hierarchical tree structure corresponding to the entries in the file. Selecting any of the entries in the hierarchy in the **Navigator** window highlights the corresponding entry in the source code editor window.

# Creating entity classes from databases

In the previous section, we took a code first approach and learned how to create empty entity classes within NetBeans. When applications using these entities are executed, we saw how the table generation strategy for the persistence unit can be used to create the schema for the database.

In this section, we're going to take a data first approach and see how NetBeans can help us to create entities when we already have a database schema.

In this section, we're going to create entities from existing database tables. To describe this feature, we're going to use the Java DB sample database that is provided as standard with GlassFish 4. Using the **Services** window, we can see that there are several tables in this database. Let's take a look at how these can be modeled as entities.

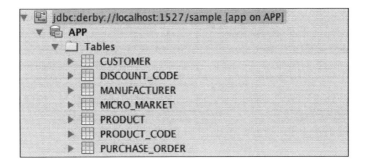

To create entities from a database, we must first ensure that we have a connection to the database we wish to model. If you are having difficulty creating a database connection, please refer to *Chapter 4, Managing Services*, where we detailed how to use the **Services** window to make connections to databases.

Once we have a connection to the appropriate database, we can start to map out the database entities by selecting the **File** and then **New File...** menu options.

In the **New File** dialog, select **Persistence** from the list of **Categories** and **Entity Classes from Database** from the list of **File Types** and continue with the wizard by pressing the **Next >** button.

The **New Entity Classes from Database** dialog is displayed, as shown in the following screenshot:

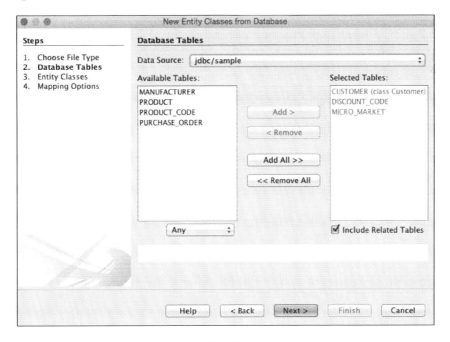

At the top of the dialog, the **Data Source** dropdown lists all of the database connections that we have defined within NetBeans in the **Services** window. From this list, we select the database that we wish to create entities from.

On the left-hand side of the dialog is a list of **Available Tables** that are present within the selected database. To map any of these tables into entities, we simply highlight the table and click on the **Add >** button. The list of selected tables on the right-hand side of the dialog shows which tables will be mapped to entities. Individual tables can be added or removed here, or we can add or remove all of the tables by pressing the **Add All >>** or **<< Remove All** buttons, respectively.

 If a table is already mapped (as in the `Customer` table in the preceding screenshot), the entity class name is displayed in brackets next to the table name.

Using the dropdown underneath the list of **Available Tables**, we can select to list:

- **Any**: All the available tables are listed and are available for mapping
- **New Only**: Only the new tables are available for mapping
- **Update Only**: Only the tables that have already been mapped to entity classes are available for mapping

If the **Include Related Tables** checkbox is checked when adding tables to the **Selected Tables** list, any tables that have foreign key relationships to the selected table are automatically added into the **Selected Tables** list. These tables names are displayed in gray to indicate that they have been automatically added. Hovering the mouse over these table names displays a tooltip, showing the table they have a foreign key to.

Selecting the **Next >** button in the wizard causes the **Entity Classes** page of the wizard to be displayed where we can map tables to the specific classes.

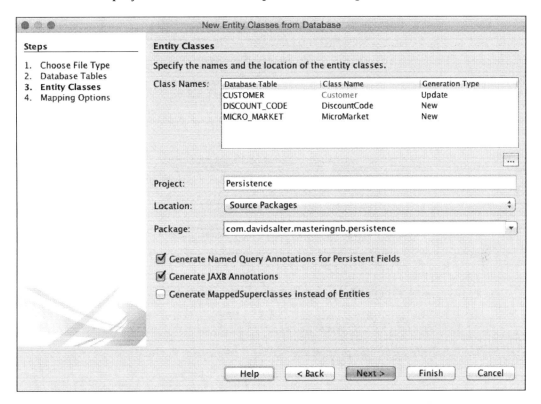

At the top of the dialog, a list of database tables that are to be mapped to entities is displayed together with **Class Name** of the entity and **Generation Type**. Class names default to the same name as the table, but are in camel case and have underscores removed. So, for example, the DISCOUNT_CODE table is mapped to an entity named DiscountCode. Double-clicking on the relevant Class Name field allows this to be changed if you require a different Java class name.

 The class name for existing entities cannot be changed using this wizard as they are fixed to the name of an existing Java class.

For tables that are not mapped to existing entities, the **Generation Type** is set to **New**. This means that a new class will be created for each table. For tables that are already mapped to entity classes (for example, `Customer` in the preceding screenshot), the **Generation Type** defaults to **Update**. This means that the existing Java class will be taken and updated to match the database schema. If you wish to completely overwrite any existing classes, set the **Generation Type** to **Recreate**.

To change the **Generation Type** to either **Update** or **Recreate** for all the existing classes listed in the dialog, select the **...** button below the table. You will then be prompted to select **Set All to Update** or **Set All to Recreate**.

Next, we have the standard fields when creating a Java class, namely **Project**, **Location**, and **Package**.

Finally, on the **Entity Classes** page, there are several checkboxes that describe the generated entity class:

- **Generate Named Query Annotations for Persistent Fields**: The generated entity class will have `@NamedQueries` defined for each of the fields in the class if this option is selected.

- **Generate JAXB Annotations**: The generated entity class will be annotated with `@XmlRootElement` so that it can be used from a **Java Architecture for XML Binding (JAXB)** web service.

- **Generate MappedSuperclasses instead of Entities**: This option causes NetBeans to generate a mapped superclass (annotated with `@MappedSuperclass`) instead of an `@Entity` class for each mapped table. If this option is selected, the option to generate named query annotations for persistence fields is not available.

- **Create Persistence Unit**: This option allows NetBeans to create a persistence unit for the specified data source. It is only available if an existing persistence unit does not exist in the project.

Selecting the **Next >** button takes us to the final page of the **New Entity Classes from Database** wizard:

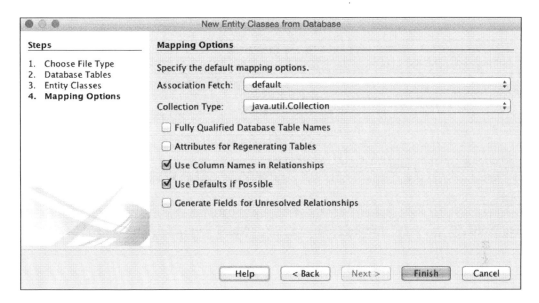

From the **Mapping Options** page, we can fine-tune how tables are mapped to entity classes with these options:

- **Association Fetch**: This option specifies how table relationships are fetched from the database as either eager or lazy fetching. For lazy fetching, the `fetch=FetchType.LAZY` fetch type is added into relationships. For eager fetching, the `fetch=FetchType.EAGER` fetch type is added into relationships. The default setting adds no fetch type into a relationship.

- **Collection Type**: This specifies the Java collection type that is used for the `@OneToMany` and `@ManyToMany` relationships. The different collection types available are `java.util.Collection`, `java,util.List`, and `java.util.Set`. Typically, a `java.util.Set` is used when repeated values are not allowed in the collection.

- **Fully Qualified Database Table Names**: This option specifies that the catalog and schema names are added into the `@Table` name when they exist.

- **Use Column Names in Relationships**: When this option is selected, the relationship field names (for one to many, many to one, and one to one relationships) are named after the database column names.

- **Use Defaults if Possible**: This option specifies that default values for annotations are to be used wherever possible, thereby reducing the amount of code used within annotations.

- **Generate Fields for Unresolved Relationships**: This option specifies that "default" fields be created within the entity for any table columns that are not referenced by the database schema for the selected tables.

Once the **Finish** button is selected, the appropriate entity classes are created in the project. If the database schema changes, running the wizard again will allow the entity definitions to be updated.

# Creating JPA controllers for entities

In the previous section, we saw how to create entities based upon an existing database schema. Once we've modeled database tables as entities though, we need to be able to perform CRUD operations—Create, Read, Update, and Delete operations on those entities.

Typically, when using JPA, we implement a repository or **Data Access Object** (**DAO**) pattern to enable us to perform CRUD operations on entities.

> For more information on the DAO pattern, refer to
> http://en.wikipedia.org/wiki/Data_access_object.

When you've written a data access object for a few classes, you realize that each DAO is pretty much the same as the other DAO; it's only accessing a different database table. Fortunately, NetBeans allows us to create DAOs for entity classes in a quick and efficient manner.

To create JPA controller classes (this is simply just another name for a JPA-based data access object), select **File** and then **New File...** from the NetBeans main menu. In the **New File** dialog, select **Persistence** from the list of **Categories** and **JPA Controller Classes from Entity Classes** from the list of **File Types**. Select **Next >** to continue.

At this stage in the wizard, NetBeans will search through your application looking for all the entity classes. These classes will then be displayed within the **Entity Classes** page of the wizard, as shown in the following screenshot:

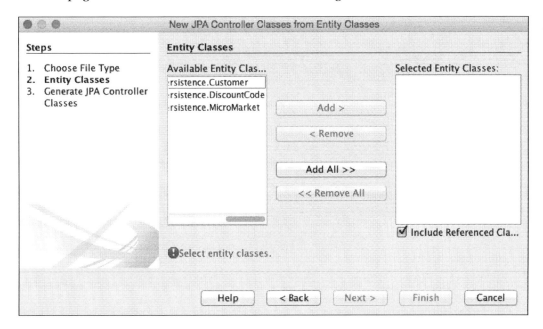

This dialog is very similar to the **New Entity Classes From Database** dialog. On the left-hand side of the dialog, NetBeans displays a list of all the entity classes that it has found within the project. To create a JPA controller class for a specific entity, simply select the entity and click on the **Add >** button to move it to the list of **Selected Entity Classes**. Conversely, selecting a class from the list of **Selected Entity Classes** and pressing the **< Remove** button will remove it from the list. As a shortcut, all the entity classes can be added or removed by pressing the **Add All >>** or **<< Remove All** buttons, respectively.

If the **Include Referenced Classes** checkbox is checked when a class is added, NetBeans will automatically add any classes that are joined to the originally selected entity class.

Pressing the **Next >** button moves the wizard onto the final stage where the **Project**, **Location**, and **Package** for the selected JPA controller classes can be specified. Upon selecting the **Finish** button, NetBeans will create the JPA controller classes in the specified package.

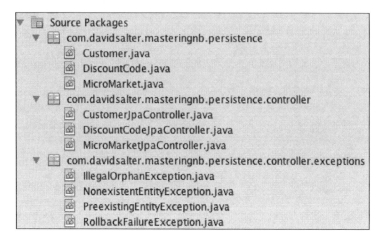

Once created, a JPA controller class contains methods to perform the CRUD operations for the given entity. For example, the Customer class we defined earlier has a corresponding CustomerJpaController class with the following methods:

```
public void create (Customer customer) throws ….
public void edit(Customer customer) throws …
public void destroy(Integer id) throws …
public List<Customer> findCustomerEntities(int maxResults, int
firstResult);
public List<Customer> findCustomerEntities(Boolean all, int
maxResults, int firstResult);
public Customer findCustomer(Integer id);
public int getCustomerCount();
```

It's also important to notice that several custom exceptions are defined when creating a JPA controller that is thrown at certain points within the CRUD life cycle. These exception classes are stored in the exceptions package, underneath the package containing the controller classes.

# Creating database scripts from entity classes

So far in this chapter, we've seen how to create entities and JPA controllers. However, to complete the round trip, NetBeans also provides facilities to create database schemas from the entities within our applications. This can be useful when we want to hand our schema creation scripts to DBAs so that they can check them over and possibly enhance them.

To create a database script from existing entities, we again invoke the **New File...** wizard. Within the wizard, we select **Persistence** from the list of **Categories** and **DB Scripts from Entity Classes** from the list of **File Types**.

When creating database schema scripts from a list of entities, there is very little configuration to be specified.

We need to specify **Script File Name**, **Project**, **Location**, and **Package**. Upon completing the wizard, NetBeans will create the schema script in the correct dialect for the specified data source and save it within the specified package.

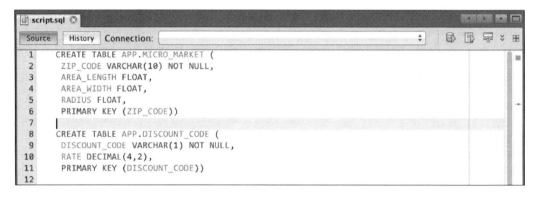

In addition to creating a script that represents the database schema, we can also create a database schema. Again, we use the **New File...** wizard to achieve this, selecting **Persistence** from the list of **Categories** and **Database Schema** from the list of **File Types**.

Creating a schema is a similar process to creating a database script except that we are creating a NetBeans schema file rather than a `.sql` file.

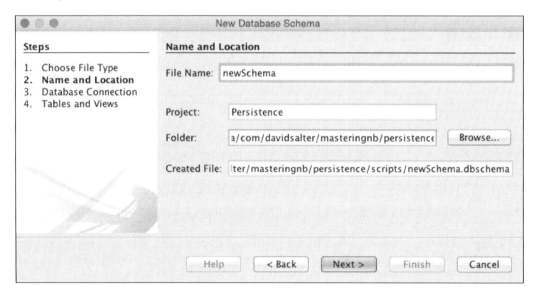

To complete the creation of the schema file, we must select a database connection (creating a schema does not depend upon the entity classes within the project) and then choose the tables and views to be included within the schema.

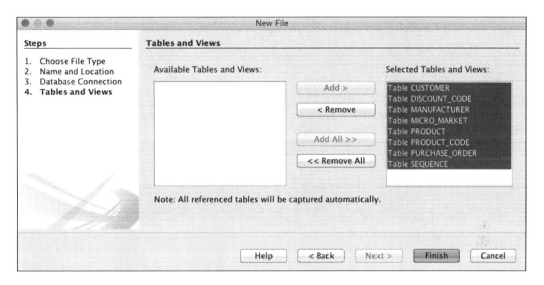

Once the schema file has been created, it is displayed within the standard package structure of the project within the **Projects** and **Files** windows.

The display of the schema file is very similar to that displayed when browsing the database schemas from the **Services** window. Within a schema file, however, we have the option to **Recapture Schema From Database** when we right-click on the schema node. When this option is selected, NetBeans requeries the database and generates a new schema file. Since the schema file is stored internally as XML data, we can then view the history of the file and see what changes were made to the schema between different revisions of the file. Therefore, this can be a very useful file to store within source control so that we can see how a database schema changes over time.

# Summary

In this chapter, we learned how NetBeans can make developing with persistence and JPA, in particular, a lot easier. We saw how we can create blank entity classes and entity classes from existing database schemas. We also looked at this from the opposite angle and saw how to create database schemas from the entity classes within our projects. We'll look at persistence again later in the book when we will learn to use it with session beans and web services.

In the next chapter, we'll take a look at desktop development and see the different tools that NetBeans provides to enable us to build desktop applications efficiently.

# 6
# Desktop Development

Java Standard Edition provides a native, lightweight toolkit for developing desktop applications. This framework, Swing, is one of the more common Java frameworks for developing desktop applications. Combined with the GUI editing tools, NetBeans provides excellent features for the Swing developer.

In this chapter, we're going to look at how we can use NetBeans to create Swing applications and how we can edit the bindings and interactions between components within those applications.

In addition to Swing, the Java platform also provides the JavaFX framework for GUI development. JavaFX isn't as well-known or commonly used as Swing, but we'll provide a brief overview of what JavaFX is and will compare it with Swing.

We're going to look at the following topics in this chapter:

- What is Swing and what support does NetBeans offer
- How to create Swing frames
- How to design Swing forms
- How to edit properties, events, and custom code for components
- How to bind components together using beans bindings
- A comparison between Swing and JavaFX

# Java Swing applications

Swing is Java's lightweight widget toolkit for creating desktop applications. When Java was first released, the **Abstract Window Toolkit (AWT)** was the standard. This was a platform-independent API where each component that was drawn by AWT depended upon the corresponding native component. AWT was the standard GUI toolkit for Java until J2SE 1.2 was released. With this release of Java, Swing was promoted as the GUI toolkit of choice. Swing provides many advantages over AWT, most particularly that it does not depend upon native GUI components like its predecessor AWT did. In fact, all the standard Swing components are all written in pure Java and do not depend upon native controls. Swing is, therefore, considered a lightweight GUI toolkit in comparison to AWT.

Swing support has been available within NetBeans since version 3. Swing support was completely rewritten in NetBeans 5 with the addition of project **Matisse**. This project was the new GUI builder that was added to NetBeans 5, and although it no longer holds the name Matisse, you may still see some members of the community referring to NetBeans Swing GUI builder as Matisse.

In this chapter, we're going to assume that you have some knowledge of Swing development.

# Creating Swing frames

In Swing, frames are top-level windows that typically have a title and a border. To get started with Swing development, therefore, it seems sensible that we should create an application with a frame (in Swing, frames are modeled via the `JFrame` class). In NetBeans, however, there is no wizard to create a `JFrame` or even, a GUI application. So, how do we get started with GUI development in NetBeans?

Since a GUI application is basically a standard Java application that displays a **graphical user interface (GUI)**, we create Swing applications as standard Java applications. To create a GUI application, therefore, we open the standard **New Project...** wizard and select **Java** from the list of **Categories** and then **Java Application** form the list of **Projects**.

Once we've created a Java application, we can add a top-level `JFrame` into it using the **New File...** wizard.

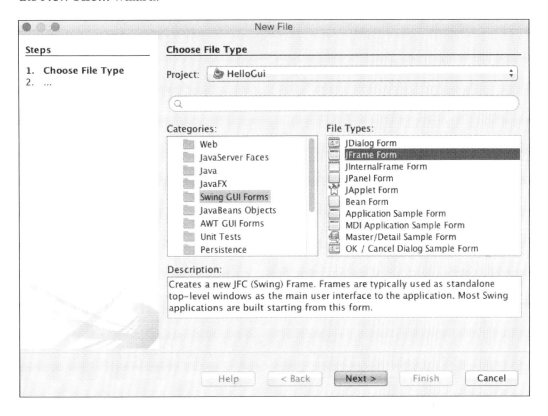

In this wizard, selecting **Swing GUI Forms** from the list of **Categories** provides us with several different file types that can be created:

- **JDialog Form**: This creates a new dialog within an application. Dialogs are typically modal (user input is only allowed in the selected dialog) or modeless (user input is allowed in all the windows of the application).

- **JFrame Form**: This creates a new form that is based on `JFrame` and is usually used as the top-level form within an application.

- **JInternalFrame Form**: This creates a new form that is based on `JInternalFrame`. Typically, these forms are used to implement **multiple document interface** (**MDI**) applications. These applications are typically identified as having multiple resizable windows that are all displayed within the bounds of the application window.

- **JPanel Form**: This creates a `JPanel` that can be used within Swing containers such as `JPanel`s and `JDialog`s.

- **JApplet Form**: This creates a Swing applet that can be run from within a browser window rather than from within a desktop application. Typically, applets have fallen out of favor and have been replaced by other technologies such as HTML and JavaScript components. We won't be discussing applets further in this book.

- **Bean Form**: This creates a new form based upon an existing Swing component, for example, a JButton or JPanel.

- **Application Sample Form**: This creates a form that is based on JFrame with standard **File**, **Edit**, and **Help** menus created within the form. This can be a very useful starting point for the main window in an application. The sample form also has a main() method declared in it that can act as the entry point for the application. This main() method simply creates an instance of the sample form and displays it on the screen.

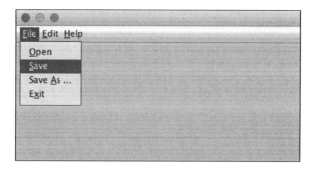

- **MDI Application Sample Form**: This creates a sample form that is based on JFrame with the intent of adding the forms that are based on JInternalFrame within it to create an MDI application. As with the **Application Sample Form**, the **File**, **Edit**, and **Help** menus are automatically added to the form along with a main() method to instantiate and display the form.

- **Master / Detail Sample Form**: This creates a sample master/detail form based upon a selected database table. During the creation of the form, NetBeans asks for a database connection and a table from that connection. A form is then generated, displaying a list of entries from the database table with the options to add, update, and delete entries from within a selected row in the table. Using this form can be a very effective way of creating data input applications.

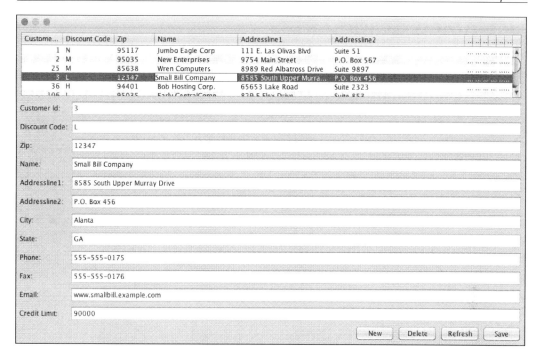

- **OK / Cancel Dialog Sample Form**: This creates a new class responsible for opening and displaying a sample dialog containing both **OK** and **Cancel** buttons. The class can be instantiated to either display the dialog in a modal or modeless fashion.

# Designing Swing forms

Upon opening a form for editing within NetBeans, the **Design** editing surface is displayed in the main editing window, as shown in the following screenshot:

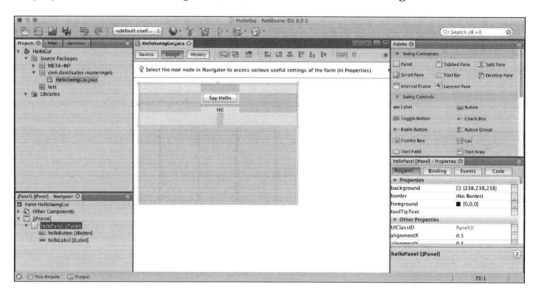

Within the main editing window are these three different views:

- **Source**: This displays the Java source code for the selected frame/dialog being edited.

- **Design**: This displays the design surface where components can be dragged and dropped onto the form to build up the user interface.

- **History**: This displays the local history of the class being edited. This can be very useful for comparing different edits of a class and reverting to the previous versions if required.

Of particular interest to GUI form developers is the **Design** view. This is where we build up the layout of components and most of your time will be spent when designing and developing forms.

To help us design forms, the **Palette** window contains all of the different GUI components that we can use within our applications. The **Palette** window is broken down into several categories:

- **Swing Containers**: This category contains Swing containers. These are the components that can hold other components such as `JPanel`, `JScrollPane`, and `JToolBar`.

- **Swing Controls**: All of the visual components that are used to build up forms are contained within this category. This includes controls such as `JLabel`, `JButton`, and `JTable`.

- **Swing Menus**: This category contains menu bars, menu items, and pop-up menus.

- **Swing Windows**: This contains the standard Swing windows, namely **Dialog, Frame, Color Chooser, File Chooser**, and **Option Pane**.

- **Swing Fillers**: When laying out forms, it can be useful to add fillers between the components such as horizontal or vertical fixed gaps. This category contains these types of components.

- **AWT**: This category contains the original Java AWT components. It's most likely that you will not use any components from this section as these components have all been replaced by more lightweight Swing components.

- **Beans**: Any Java Beans from the application classpath can be selected within this category.

- **Java Persistence**: Java Persistence components such as an `Entity Manager` or `Query` are available within this category.

To add a component onto a form, drag the component from the **Palette** window into the required location on the form. The **Navigator** window can be very useful to view a hierarchical representation of which components are on a form. Selecting a component within the **Navigator** window automatically selects it within the editor window so that its properties can easily be edited.

Once a component has been placed on a form, its location can be defined either by the layout of its parent container or its alignment to other components. This is where the NetBeans GUI editor really excels.

If the component that is being edited allows its layout to be defined (for example, a JPanel), this can be achieved via the **Set Layout** context menu option. To specify the layout of a component, right-click on the component and select the **Set Layout** menu option. The following screenshot gives an example of the context menu displayed when you right-click on a JPanel component:

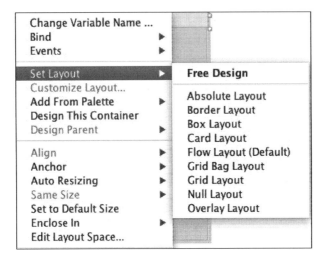

From this menu, we can select a components layout as **Free Design** or one of the standard Swing layout managers (**Absolute Layout, Border Layout, Box Layout, Card Layout, Flow Layout (Default), GridBag Layout, Grid Layout, Null**, and **Overlay Layout**).

 For more information on layout managers, visit http://docs.oracle.com/javase/tutorial/uiswing/layout/visual.html.

The **Free Design** layout allows us the most flexibility by providing us with the ability to autoresize components and anchor components to other components.

# Anchoring and autoresizing components

Typically, when a form is resized, we expect the components within the form to be resized and moved accordingly. For example, if we make a form wider and taller, we don't want all of our components to stay at the top-left of the form surrounded by lots of whitespace. For a good user experience, we want the controls to expand, contract, and move when we resize forms. Let's first take a look at anchoring the components.

When we say we have anchored a component, what exactly do we mean? We mean that the component remains at a fixed location relative to another component or boundary on either the left, right, top, or bottom of the component.

When we anchor a component, we are basically saying that when we resize the form, we want the component to stay aligned with another component. So, for example, if we anchor a button to the right and bottom of a JFrame, when we expand and contract the frame, the button will stay at the bottom-right. To indicate that an item is anchored to another object, NetBeans displays a dotted horizontal or vertical line, ending at the boundary that the component is anchored to. If a component is not anchored on a particular edge, a zigzagged line is displayed indicating that the location of the component may expand in the specified direction. In the following screenshot, the button is anchored to the bottom-right of the frame. There is, therefore, a dotted line between the button and the right and bottom edges of the JFrame. There is a zigzagged line between the left and top edges of the JFrame:

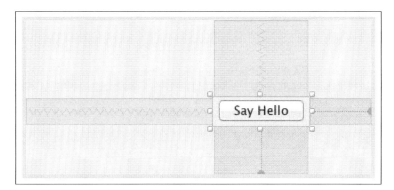

When a component is anchored to another component, it therefore moves when the form is resized, but the component itself does not resize. If we want a component to resize when a form is resized, we must specify that the component can autoresize.

Components can be set to autoresize by right-clicking on them and selecting the **Auto Resizing** menu option. From there, you can select to either autoresize horizontally or vertically.

When a component is set to autoresize, it is displayed within the NetBeans design window with a straight dotted line on both sides of the component. If the component is set to autoresize horizontally, there will be a straight dotted line to the left and right of the component. Conversely, if the component is set to autoresize vertically, there will be a straight dotted line to the top and bottom of the component. The following screenshot gives an example of a button that is set to autoresize both vertically and horizontally:

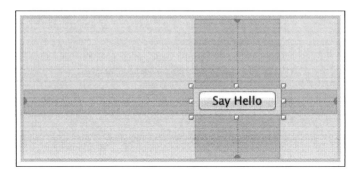

To complete the anchoring and resizing of components on forms, we need to be able to specify the layout space around the components. This can be achieved in the first instance by simply dragging the component to the desired location on the design window. Sometimes, however, it's useful to have a finer grained control and to be able to specify the layout space in pixels. This can be achieved by double-clicking on the spacing on any of the four sides (top, right, bottom, and left) around the component.

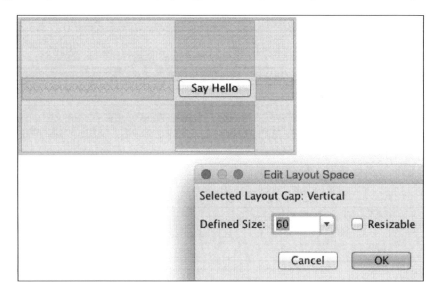

Upon double-clicking on the layout space, the layout space being edited is displayed in green, as shown in the preceding screenshot. On the **Edit Layout Space** dialog, we can specify the exact size in pixels of the layout, with the dialog indicating whether we are editing a **Vertical** or **Horizontal** layout gap. From this dialog, we can also specify whether the gap is resizable or not.

Right-clicking on a layout gap and selecting the **Edit Layout Space...** menu option performs the same operation as double-clicking on it.

To help us lay out controls within a form, NetBeans provides a toolbar along the top of the design view, containing tools to align and preview forms.

| | |
|---|---|
| | **Selection Mode**: This allows the components to be selected and edited within the form. |
| | **Connection Mode**: This allows connections to be made between two components so that, for example, a click event on one component can trigger an event on another component. |
| | **Preview Design**: This displays the form in a pop-up window, showing the expected layout at runtime. |
| | **Align Left In Column**: When more than one component is selected, this option allows them all to be aligned to the left in a column. |
| | **Align Right In Column**: When more than one component is selected, this option allows them all to be aligned to the right in a column. |
| | **Center Horizontally**: When more than one component is selected, this option allows them all to be centered horizontally in a column. |
| | **Align Top In Row**: When more than one component is selected, this option allows them all to be aligned at the top. |
| | **Align Bottom In Row**: When more than one component is selected, this option allows them all to be aligned at the bottom. |
| | **Center Vertically**: When more than one component is selected, this option allows them to be centered vertically. |
| | **Change Horizontal Resizability**: When selected, this option specifies that a component will resize horizontally rather than being anchored to the left and right of other components. |
| | **Change Vertical Resizability**: When selected, this option specifies that a component will resize vertically rather than being anchored to the top and bottom of other components. |

# Defining properties and events

So far, we've looked at how to create forms (for example, various `JFrame` and `JDialog`), by laying out components and specifying their layout relationship to other components.

To complete a user interface, we need to define the properties and events for each component. Fortunately, with NetBeans, this is relatively straightforward using the **Properties** window:

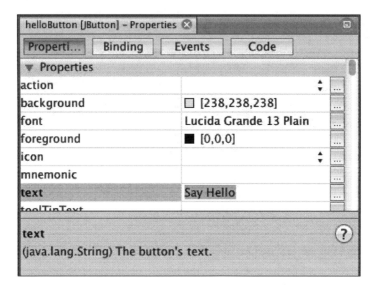

The **Properties** window is broken down into four categories:

- **Properties**: All of the properties for a selected component can be edited within this section.

- **Binding**: This allows events from components to trigger actions on other components. For example, if we were writing an application to display pages of a book, scrolling through the book using a scroll bar could automatically update a label stating the page that was currently being viewed.

- **Events**: This section allows us to determine what actions are performed on a component when certain events (for example, click, mouse moved, key pressed) are triggered.

- **Code**: This allows us to define the code aspects of a component, for example, the variable name or any pre/post initialization code.

Let's take each of these categories in turn and take a deeper look at each.

# Editing properties

The **Properties** category allows all the properties for the specified component to be edited. The properties that exist differ depending upon the component selected, but in general, they are categorized into **Properties** (the most common properties, such as foreground color and text), the **Layout** properties (such as horizontal or vertical resizable), the **Accessibility** properties (such as accessible name and description) and the **Other** properties (everything else such as maximum and minimum size or cursor).

For each property, the value can be changed either as text or via custom editors.

The custom editors for each property are accessed via the ⟨⋯⟩ button to the right of the property definition.

If we take the **foreground** property as an example, we can simply click on the color (**[0,0,0]** in the following example) and enter any color we want. So, for example, we could enter a color as `[255, 255, 255]` to change the components foreground color to white.

Again, for the **foreground** property, clicking on the custom editor button displays a custom editor, allowing the color to be selected, as shown in the following screenshot. For all the color-related properties, a graphical set of color choosers are displayed, providing many ways of selecting colors (for example, via **RGB**, **CMYK**, or **System Palette**):

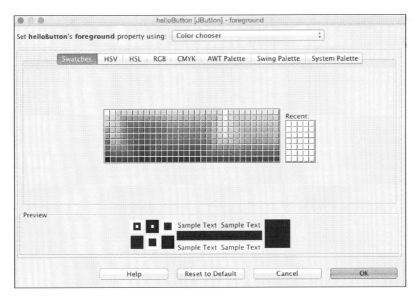

Each different property generally has a custom editor page that is displayed when clicking on the custom edit button. On the dropdown at the top of every custom editor, however, are the options to select a value from existing component and to use custom code.

When selecting a value from an existing component, we have the option to select a component and then choose either a property or method call on the component that will return the required value:

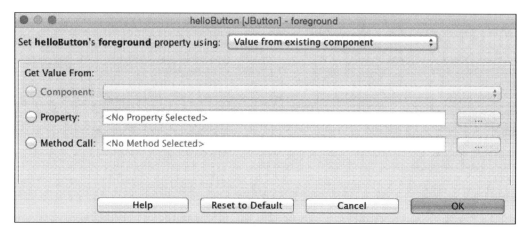

When selecting to set a property via custom code, we are shown the code fragment that NetBeans will create (`helloButton.setForeground(...)` in the following screenshot) for setting the property. To complete the custom code, we need to enter valid Java code within the edit box that returns the type expected by the Swing API. This type is displayed underneath the edit box as a reminder of the required type.

NetBeans doesn't validate the custom code that you type into a custom code editor, so you won't know until runtime that what you've entered is valid. This is very powerful as you can enter custom code that relies upon the existing members of a class or create completely new objects to return the required value. A consequence of this is that it's easy to write invalid code into a custom code editor. Be mindful of this and try to keep your custom code as clean and simple as possible to help reduce errors.

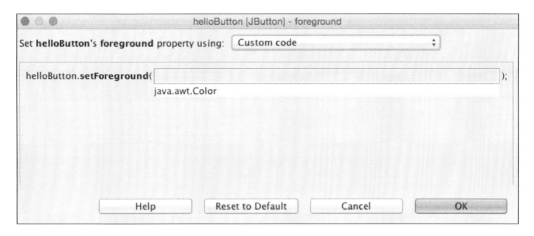

# Editing bindings

In the **Binding** category, we can "bind" components together. By this, we mean that we can automatically wire up two components so that when an event occurs in one component, an action is triggered in another.

 When binding components within NetBeans, the JSR-295 framework is used behind the scenes to perform the actual bindings. This framework is not a part of standard Java framework, and as such, any applications build that use bindings will have to be deployed with the JSR-295 library jar.

As can be seen in the preceding screenshot, the **Binding** category allows us to choose a property on the source control that when changed will fire a property changed binding.

To give a better understanding of how binding works, let's take a look at implementing a simple binding between a JEdit control and a JLabel control. To do this, perform the following steps:

1. Create a standard Java application within NetBeans and add a JFrame form to the application called HelloSwingGui.

2. Within the form, add a JTextField called nameEdit and a JLabel called helloLabel and layout the form so that it looks similar to the following:

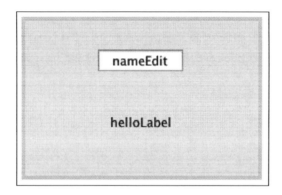

All we've created here is a simple form with an edit box and a label. When we change the text in the edit box, we are going to use bindings to automatically update the text in the label. Let's now define the bindings between the edit box and the label:

1. Right-click on the helloLabel component and select **Bind**. NetBeans now provides a list of all the properties that can be bound. From the list, select text. This is the display text of the label component. The **Bind** properties window will now be displayed:

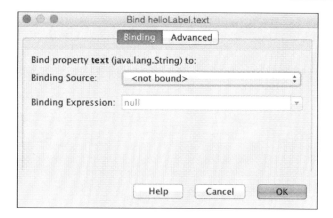

2. Within the **Bind helloLabel.text** dialog, NetBeans allows us to specify the binding source and binding expression. Binding source is where we want to get our source data from and binding expression is what we want to do with that data.

3. From the **Binding Source** dropdown, select **nameEdit**. This signifies that we are to be using data from the `nameEdit` control.

4. From the **Binding Expression** dropdown, select **text java.lang.String**. This signifies that we want to use the input text on the edit box in our binding:

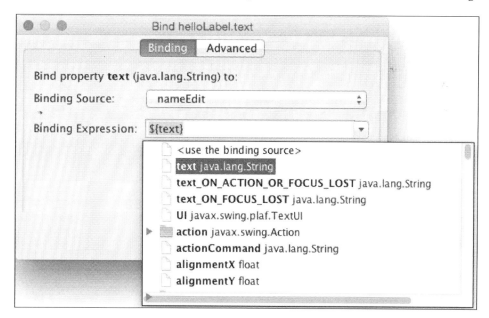

5. Click on the **OK** button to complete configuring the bindings.

Let's quickly reap what we've achieved here. We've created an edit box and a label and configured bindings on the label. We configured the bindings on the label so that the text of the edit box is the source of our data and whatever that data is, we're going to set it into the text property of the label. When we run the application, what we expect to see now is that whatever we type into the edit box will be echoed into the label.

If we run the application and enter some text into the edit box, we can see that this does indeed happen.

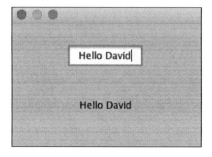

This simple example shows the power of binding components without the need for writing event change listeners.

Typically, when wiring up two components using standard Swing events, we need to write code to get the text from one control and set it into another. When we've written the code, we need to run our application to see the effects on the screen. When we use bindings, however, NetBeans is clever enough to use those bindings when previewing a form. So, instead of running our application, we can simply press the **Preview Design** button and potentially save a lot of time during the development.

# Advanced binding properties

When specifying the bindings for a control, you may have noticed that there was a tab to specify the advanced properties.

On this screen, we can configure extra properties, such as what to do when the source value is null or how to convert the source value into the correct class. The following properties can be set:

- **Name**: Here, you can name the binding.

- **Update Mode**: This specifies how the target and source properties are updated. The update mode can take one of these three values:

    ° **Always sync (read/write)**: Whenever a source is made to the target or source property, the other property is updated. Both properties are kept in sync. This is the default option.

- ○ **Only read from source (read only)**: The target property is updated when the source property is initially set and whenever changes are made to the source property. Changing the target property never causes the source property to be updated.

  - ○ **Read from source once (read once)**: The target property is updated only when the source property is initially set. Subsequent changes to the source property do not update the target property. Changing the target property never causes the source property to be updated.

- **Converter**: If both your source property and destination property are not of the same type (or types that can be automatically converted), NetBeans allows you to define a converter class to convert between the source and target formats. We'll describe converter classes later.

- **Validator**: When you require changes to a source property to be validated before they are written to the target property, you can specify a validator class. We'll describe validator classes later.

- **Null Source Value**: This contains the binding value to use when the source value is null.

- **Unreadable Source Value**: This contains the binding value to use when the source value is unreadable, for example, when the binding expression cannot be resolved.

When specifying the advanced properties for either a JTextField or a JSlider, additional properties are available.

For a JTextField, the **Update Source When** property is available. This allows us to specify that the target property can be updated while typing, when focus leaves, or when *Enter* is pressed or focus is lost.

For a JSlider, the **Ignore Adjusting** property is available. When this is selected, the target property is only updated after the user has finished dragging the slider. No changes are made to the target property while the user is dragging the slider.

## Converters

When binding components, the source and target properties are not always of the same type. To convert between different types, NetBeans allows a converter class to be supplied.

As standard, the following conversions do not require a converter class and can be converted both forward and backward automatically by the binding framework:

- BigDecimal to String
- BigInteger to String
- Boolean to String
- Byte to String
- Char to String
- Double to String
- Float to String
- Int to String
- Long to String
- Short to String
- Int to Boolean

Converter classes must be derived from the org.jdesktop.beansbinding. Converter base class and must provide methods to perform a forward conversion from the source to target property type and also a backward conversion from a target to the source property type:

```
public class SampleConverter extends
            org.jdesktop.beansbinding.Converter {

    @Override
    public Object convertForward(Object source) {
        // Convert from source property to target property
    }

    @Override
    public Object convertReverse(Object target) {
        // Convert from target property to source property
    }

}
```

## Validators

A validator class allows you to perform validation on a source property before it is written to a target property. To create a validator, a class must extend the `org.jdesktop.beansbinding.Validator` class and must override the `validate` method. This method must return null if the source has validated successfully or a `org.jdesktop.beansbinding.Result` object if the validation has failed. In the case of failed validation, an error code and description may be added to the `Result` class:

```
public class SampleValidator extends
            org.jdesktop.beansbinding.Validator {

    @Override
    public Result validate(Object value) {
        // Perform validation and return null or a Result
    }

}
```

# Editing events

The **Events** category allows us to define what happens when events occur within our application, such as when a key is pressed in an edit box, or when the mouse is moved over a certain component.

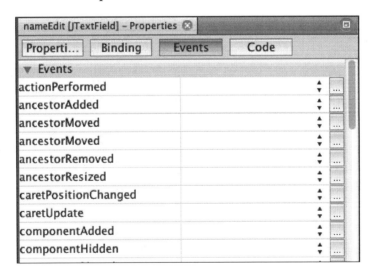

The list of events for each component is categorized in alphabetical order. Upon clicking on the edit box to the right of an event, a popup is displayed, suggesting a name for the event handler. This name consists of the name of the control being edited together with the name of the event. For example, when creating a new event handler for the key pressed event of the `nameEdit` control, NetBeans would suggest an event handler name of `nameEditKeyPressed`, as shown in the following screenshot:

Upon selecting the name for the event handler, NetBeans automatically opens up the **Source** window for the code, placing the caret ready for entering the event handler code.

```
private void nameEditKeyPressed(java.awt.event.KeyEvent evt) {
    // TODO add your handling code here:
}
```

When editing GUI code, the standard Java source editor is slightly different from editing standard Java classes as there are grayed out areas of text that cannot be edited. This is shown in the preceding screenshot. This is required by NetBeans as a large amount of GUI code is automatically generated by NetBeans depending upon the layout and bindings of a form. If a developer were to edit this code outside of the GUI editor, the chances of NetBeans being able to provide graphical editing of the file again would be slim. NetBeans, therefore, takes precautions to stop the code it needs to allow forms to be edited from being modified outside of the graphical editor.

The obvious consequence of this is that it's not possible from the source code editor to delete the event handler code or to rename the event handler methods. If you try to do this, you'll see that NetBeans won't let you type within the grayed out areas of the code. So, how do we delete or rename event handler code?

Fortunately, NetBeans makes this a simple process. From the **Events** category in the **Properties** window, we can simply press the button, ⟨...⟩, to the right of an event name.

Selecting this option displays a dialog, listing all the handlers for the specified method. From within this dialog, we can add new event handlers, remove the existing ones, or simply rename the existing ones.

# Editing code

The final option in the **Properties** window is the **Code** category. From here, we can fine-tune how components are created.

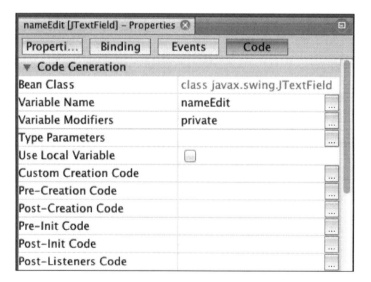

The important areas within the **Code** category are the code categories where we can write custom Java code for different aspects of the components life cycle:

- **Custom Creation Code**: This allows us to write custom code for instantiating the component
- **Pre-Creation Code**: This lets us write the code that is executed before the component is created
- **Post-Creation Code**: This lets us write the code that is executed after the component has been created
- **Pre-Init Code**: This lets us write the code that is executed after the component has been instantiated, but before it's properties are set
- **Post-Init Code**: This lets us write the code that is executed after the component's properties are set
- **Post-Listeners Code**: This lets us write the code that is executed after all the components properties have been set and event listeners have been registered
- **Pre-Adding Code**: This lets us write the code that is executed before the component is added into its parent container
- **Post-Adding Code**: This lets us write the code that is executed after the component has been added into its parent container
- **After-All-Set Code**: This lets us write the code that is executed after the component has been completely configured
- **Pre-Declaration Code**: This lets us write the code that is executed before the component is declared
- **Post-Declaration Code**: This lets us write the code that is executed after the component has been declared

# Creating connections

So far, we've seen how NetBeans can enable us to easily create bindings between the components and how we can register and respond to events for individual components. NetBeans, however, has one final tool that allows us to make connections between the components. This is very similar to bindings, however, it allows us to write the standard Swing code to listen for the events and then perform actions. Using the **Connection Mode** tool does nothing that we can't write in the standard code, but it makes it a lot easier to wire the components together.

To see how this tool works, let's modify the application we wrote earlier to add a clear button that clears the value in the input edit box. When complete, the application should look similar to the following:

To add a **Clear** button, perform the following steps:

1. Add a JButton to the form we created earlier so that the form looks similar to the preceding screenshot. Set the text property of the button to read **Clear**.

2. Click the **Connection Mode** button (⌗) at the top of the **Design** window. Upon clicking this button, NetBeans will display a message, asking for the component that will generate the event to be selected:

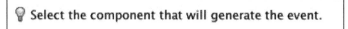

3. Click on the **Clear** button. Upon selecting the component, NetBeans will display a message, asking for the component that will receive the event to be selected:

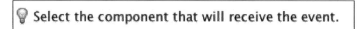

4. Click on the `nameEdit` edit box as this is the target component. This is the component that we want to update when an event occurs on the source component. Upon selecting a component to receive the event, NetBeans will display the **Connection Wizard** window:

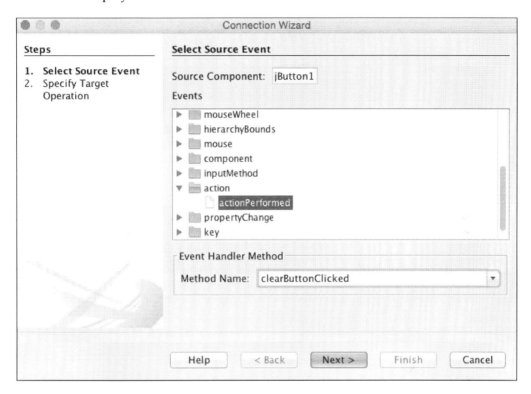

Within the **Connection Wizard** window, all the events that can be triggered on the source component are displayed. To connect the components, we need to select a source event and then specify a target operation. For our sample application, the source event will be the `actionPerformed` event of the button.

1. Select the **actionPerformed** event from the list of **Events** and change the event handler method name to be `clearButtonClicked`.

2. Click on the **Next >** button.

Now that we've specified the source event handler, we need to specify what happens to the target controller. NetBeans displays the **Specify Target Operation** page to allow us define this.

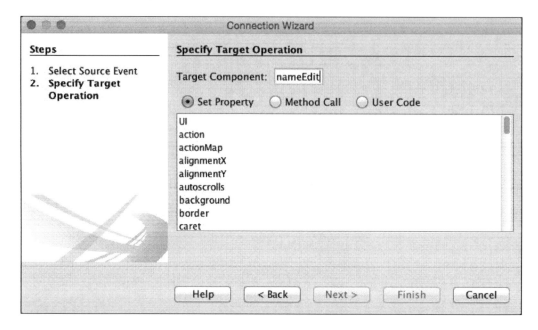

Within this page, we can specify that we want to update a property, call a method, or define some custom user code.

> Note that as before, any user code entered here is not validated, so ensure that you check your code carefully before continuing. It's better to add your code to a method and invoke it from user code as it will be easier to manage, test, and debug this way.

For our sample application, we're simply going to empty the contents of the edit box on the screen.

1.  Ensure that the **Set Property** radio button is selected and select the text property from the list of properties.
2.  Click on the **Next >** button.

NetBeans will now display the final page of the **Connection Wizard**.

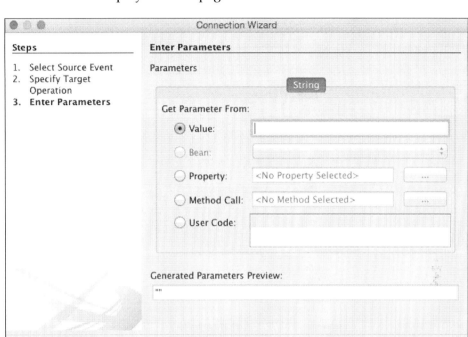

Within this page, we can specify how any properties are set on the target component. We can set the property via **Value**, **Bean**, **Property**, **Method Call**, or **User Code**. These options are similar to how we've specified binding values previously.

For our sample application, we simply want to set the text of the `nameEdit` to an empty string.

1. Ensure the **Value** radio button is checked and the corresponding edit box contains no value.
2. Click on the **Finish** button to complete the wizard.

At this point, NetBeans closes the wizard and opens the source code editor to allow any other modifications to be made. We can run our application at this stage and see how it performs. You'll notice that within the application, we can now click on the **Clear** button and the contents of the edit box will be cleared out.

This is a very simple example, but it shows the power of the **Connection Mode** tool. With this tool, we're able to wire up two components, and change the state of the target component based upon some event occurring on the source component. All of this can be achieved without writing a line of code.

# JavaFX applications

JavaFX is the Java Platform's newest lightweight toolkit for developing rich client applications and is described by Oracle as "the next step in the evolution of Java as a rich client platform". JavaFX is intended to be the long-term replacement for Swing. It was first announced in 2007 with version 1.0 being released shortly afterwards. With the release of Java 7 Update 6, JavaFX was supplied as standard with the Java JDK, whereas previously, it was a separate download. Since the release of Java 8, JavaFX has used the same numbering system as that of Java itself; hence, the latest version of JavaFX is version 8.

JavaFX allows developers to separate their user interface from their Java code in a simple manner using FXML markup (essentially XML files) for defining user interfaces that can then be styled using CSS.

To get an idea of the differences between Swing and JavaFX, consider the following two code snippets to create a button.

In JavaFX, user interfaces are typically defined in FXML markup language (although they can be defined within Java code if required). To create a button with the text `Click Me!` having an `onAction` handler associated with it, we would typically declare the following:

```
<Button text="Click Me!" onAction="#handleButtonAction" fx:id="button"
/>
```

To define a similar button within a Swing application, we would write the following code:

```
JButton jButton = new javax.swing.JButton();
jButton.setText("Click Me!");
jButton.addActionListener(new java.awt.event.ActionListener() {
    public void actionPerformed(java.awt.event.ActionEvent evt) {
        handleButtonAction(evt);
    }
});
```

Looking at these two code fragments, it's easy to see how the separation of user interface markup into a separate file gives JavaFX a lot of power when designing applications.

# JavaFX Scene Builder

Out of the box, NetBeans provides only basic text-based editing for FXML files—it doesn't provide enhanced GUI development tools like it does for Swing. This is fine for making quick changes to an FXML file or creating small files, but for comprehensive user interfaces, we require a better FXML editing tool.

This is where Scene Builder comes in. It provides a similar set of design tools to those that we've discussed earlier in this chapter, except for JavaFX applications instead of Swing applications.

In early 2015, Oracle announced that it would no longer be providing binary packages for Scene Builder. The final release of Scene Builder binaries from Oracle is version 2.0 and can be downloaded `http://www.oracle.com/technetwork/java/javase/downloads/javafxscenebuilder-info-2157684.html`.

For details of Oracle's announcement not to provide Scene Builder binaries, visit `http://www.oracle.com/technetwork/java/javase/downloads/sb2download-2177776.html`.

So, after discussing JavaFX, is this the end of Scene Builder? Fortunately, this is not the case as a company called Gluon is building Scene Builder binaries and distributing them to the JavaFX community. For more information on Gluon Scene Builder, visit `http://gluonhq.com/gluon-supports-scene-builder/`.

# Summary

In this chapter, we started by looking at how to create Swing applications within NetBeans. We then continued and looked at creating Swing frames and saw how these could easily be created from ready built templates. We also learned to design forms by adding and arranging components onto a design surface. We then saw how to control the properties, bindings, events, and custom code for all the components we put on a form.

Finally, we took a brief look at JavaFX and saw how this differs from Swing. We saw that Scene Builder can be used to provide similar GUI editing facilities to NetBeans and got to know that a company called Gluon, instead of Oracle, now provides binaries for Scene Builder.

In the next chapter, we'll move on to the next level of the application stack and see how we can effectively create a business layer for our applications.

# 7
# Creating the Business Layer

Java EE is one of the foremost Java technologies for developing enterprise applications. In this chapter, we'll see how to become a productive EJB developer. We're going to look at the following topics in this chapter:

- Creating enterprise projects
- Creating enterprise applications with multiple modules
- Creating EJBs
- Creating session beans for entity classes
- Performing bean validation
- CDI injection points/notifications within the editor window
- Adding CDI support to a project
- Creating qualifiers, stereotypes, interceptor bindings, and scope types

## Creating enterprise projects

In *Chapter 2*, *Editing Files and Projects*, we learned about the **Projects** window within NetBeans and saw how it is used for Java projects. In this section, we're going to look at the "business" type of projects that NetBeans supports. Within a Java EE environment, business projects typically correspond to EJB projects.

When we invoke the **New Project** wizard within NetBeans, there are several additional NetBeans project types that are available within the EE distribution of NetBeans:

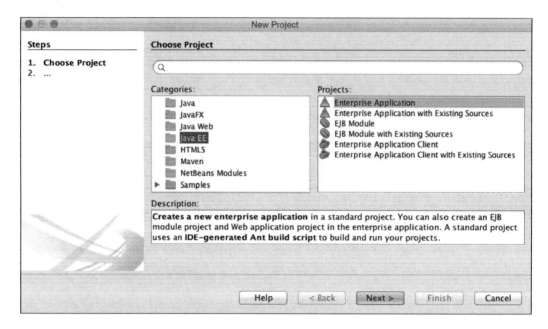

- **Enterprise Application**: This creates a new enterprise application (packaged as an .Ear archive) and provides the option of creating web and EJB modules for inclusion within the .Ear archive (we will discuss web modules in the next chapter).

- **Enterprise Application with Existing Sources**: This creates a new enterprise application based upon existing sources. For this option to complete successfully, the existing source must be stored within the format specified by the J2EE BluePrints Project Conventions for enterprise applications.

- **EJB Module**: This creates a new EJB project and provides the option of adding the EJB module into an existing .Ear archive.

- **EJB Module with Existing Sources**: This creates a new EJB project based upon the existing sources. As with the EJB module, the option of adding the module to an existing .Ear archive is available.

- **Enterprise Application Client**: This creates a new enterprise application client project.

- **Enterprise Application Client with Existing Sources**: This creates a new enterprise application client project based upon the existing sources.

In addition to these new project types in the EE distribution of NetBeans, there are several new Maven project types that support enterprise applications. We'll discuss those shortly.

First, however, let's take a look at these new project types and see how we can create a multi-module project within NetBeans.

# Creating a NetBeans multi-module project

From the previous section, you'll remember that NetBeans allows us to create an enterprise application, but what exactly is an enterprise application?

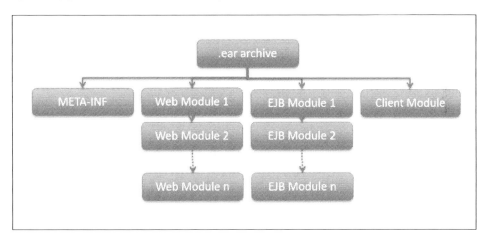

Simply put, an enterprise application is an archive containing any required deployment descriptors, a collection of zero or more web archives, a collection of zero or more EJB archives, and an optional client module. Enterprise archives can hold more content than this (for example, libraries of .jar files or resource adapters), but for the purpose of this discussion, we'll be considering web, EJB, and client modules.

We'll be looking at web modules in the next chapter, so we'll just concentrate on EJB and client modules in this chapter.

For simple applications, we can deploy all of our code (web and EJB) into a single .War file, which may be sufficient for most purposes. When, however, we wish to deploy multiple web applications connected to multiple EJB projects, the enterprise application project type make a lot more sense.

Let's now walk through the steps required to create an enterprise application that contains an EJB and a client module. The client module could be a Swing or Java FX application, however, for this demonstration, we'll be using a simple command-line application. The basic modules within our application will be as follows:

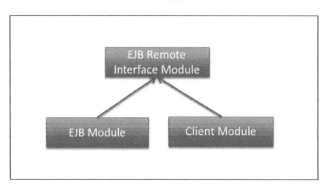

We're developing an application with an EJB and a client module, so why do we need a third module? As we're implementing our business logic as a remote EJB, we will need to reference the EJB in our client module. It's not a good practice for a client module to depend explicitly on an EJB module, so we typically create a module that contains only the EJB remote interfaces. The EJB and client module projects then both refer to the module that contains the remote interfaces. That way, we have a clean separation of code, and the client module does not have an explicit knowledge of the EJB module. All of these modules will be packaged together into an enterprise application, although it should be noted that recent versions of GlassFish do not require this to be the case. From GlassFish v3.1 onwards, EJB and client modules can be deployed separately to the server.

The first stage is to create an empty enterprise application within NetBeans by performing the following steps:

1.  Select the **File** and then **New Project...** menu options.

2.  Select **Java EE** from the list of **Categories** and **Enterprise Application** from the list of **Projects**.

3.  Click on **Next >** and then enter the project name as `GreeterEnterprise`. Click on **Next >** to continue to the **Server and Settings** page.

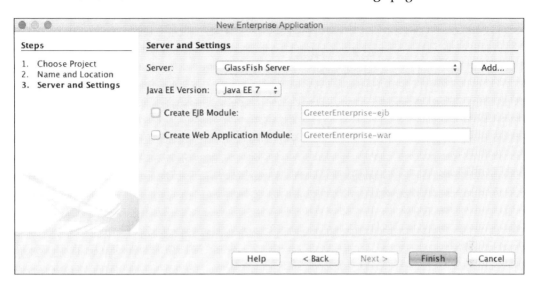

On the **Server and Settings** page, we can specify whether we want to create a new EJB or web application module. As we need to create an EJB module with remote interfaces in a separate `.Jar` file, we will need to create these projects separately. Follow these steps:

1.  Ensure that **Create EJB Module** and **Create Web Application Module** are unchecked. (Note that we could have left the **Create EJB Module** option checked here to automatically create the modules when the project is created. In this instance, we've chosen to show how to create an EJB module outside of this new project wizard.)

2.  Click on **Finish** to create the enterprise application.

The enterprise project will be created within NetBeans. If we expand all of the nodes within the **Projects** window, we can see that there are no files in the enterprise application, except a solitary, empty MANIFEST.MF file (this isn't surprising since we elected not to create any modules in the application).

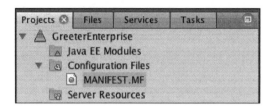

Now that we've created an enterprise application to host our code, let's create an EJB module by performing the following steps:

1.  Select the **File** and then **New Project...** menu options.

2.  Select **Java EE** from the list of **Categories** and **EJB Module** from the list of **Projects**.

3.  Click on **Next >** and then enter the project name as GreeterEJB. Click on **Next >** to display the **Server and Settings** page.

The **Server and Settings** page is similar to that displayed when creating the enterprise application, except that this time, there's an additional input where we can specify the enterprise application to add the EJB module to. For our example application, we need to ensure that the enterprise application we've just created is specified.

1.  Ensure that **GreeterEnterprise** is selected in the **Add to Enterprise Application** drop-down box and that a valid instance of GlassFish is selected for the **Server** drop-down box.
2.  Click on **Finish** to create the EJB module and add it to the enterprise application.

To enable us to store the remote interfaces for any EJBs we may write, we need to create an empty **Java Class Library** project.

Use the **New Project** wizard to create a **Java Class Library** project named `GreeterEJBRemote`.

The final project we need to create is for the **Enterprise Application Client**. This project needs to be added to the enterprise application project in the same way as the EJB module.

Use the **New Project** wizard to create an EJB module project named `Greeter`. Ensure that **GreeterEnterprise** is selected in the **Add to Enterprise Application** drop-down box and that a valid instance of GlassFish is selected on the **Server and Settings** page.

Once completed, the projects should be displayed within the **Projects** window, as shown in the following screenshot. We've created four projects (**Greeter**, **GreeterEJB**, **GreeterEJBRemote**, and **GreeterEnterprise**). From these projects, we can see that **GreeterEJB.jar** and **Greeter.jar** are defined as Java EE modules in the **GreeterEnterprise** application.

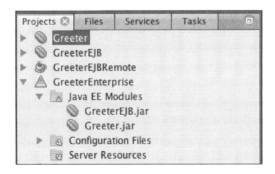

# A Maven multi-module project

Creating a NetBeans multi-module project is an efficient way of creating enterprise applications. Sometimes, however, we wish to build and run our applications outside of NetBeans. In these situations, building a Maven multi-module project is probably a better strategy as it provides all of the benefits of a Maven project such as the ability to easily add dependencies or the ability to build and deploy the project from a continuous integration system.

[  For more information about Apache Maven, visit https://maven.apache.org. ]

Within NetBeans, there are many different types of Maven project that can be created. From an EJB perspective, the following types of Maven projects can be created using the **New Project** wizard:

- **EJB Module**: This creates a standard EJB Maven project, allowing the user to specify the version of Java EE and the server to deploy to.

- **Enterprise Application**: This creates a Maven enterprise application project optionally, comprising of an EJB and web modules. The generated Maven project is assembled into a .Ear archive. As with the EJB project, the version of Java EE and server to deploy to can be specified.

- **Enterprise Application Client**: This creates a standard enterprise application client project, allowing the user to specify the version of Java EE and the server to deploy to.

- **POM Project**: This creates a Maven POM project that can act as the parent application, consisting of multiple Maven subprojects. No source code is generated for this project type as it is a placeholder for subprojects.

- **Project from Archetype**: This creates a Maven project based upon a user-selected Maven archetype. This type of project can be used to generate any type of application (for example, EJB, web, or JavaFX) and is not specific to EJB projects.

- **Project from Existing POM**: This allows an existing Maven project to be opened. This type of project simply defers to the **Open Project** dialog, allowing a Maven pom.xml project file to be opened.

The most powerful of these project types are **POM Project** and **Project from Archetype** as these allow us to build many different combinations of multi-module projects. Let's take a look now at how we can create a multi-module Maven project using these project types. To keep things simple, we'll create an application that uses POJOs only rather than EJBs so that we can concentrate on how NetBeans interacts with Maven projects. The techniques we will use are equally applicable for EJB projects though (or for that matter, web, JavaFX projects, and so on).

# Creating a Maven multi-module project

The first stage in creating a Maven multi-module is to create a parent POM project. As discussed earlier, this is simply a placeholder for all the other modules, effectively collecting all the child projects within one umbrella. Follow these steps to create a parent POM project:

1.  Invoke the **New Project** wizard and select **Maven** from the list of **Categories** and **POM Project** from the list of **Project Types**. Click on **Next**.

2.  Enter the name and location details as follows:

    ○   **Project Name**: MavenGreeter
    ○   **GroupId**: com.davidsalter.masteringnb
    ○   **Version**: 1.0-SNAPSHOT
    ○   **Package**: com.davidsalter.masteringnb.mavengreeter

3.  Click on **Finish** to create the project.

At this stage, the project will be created within NetBeans. In the **Projects** window, we can see that there is only one file, pom.xml, created in the project.

Indeed, if we look at this generated `pom.xml` file, we can see that we've declared a project but not much else:

```xml
<?xml version="1.0" encoding="UTF-8"?>
<project xmlns="http://maven.apache.org/POM/4.0.0" xmlns:xsi="http://
www.w3.org/2001/XMLSchema-instance" xsi:schemaLocation="http://maven.
apache.org/POM/4.0.0 http://maven.apache.org/xsd/maven-4.0.0.xsd">
    <modelVersion>4.0.0</modelVersion>
    <groupId>com.davidsalter.masteringnb</groupId>
    <artifactId>MavenGreeter</artifactId>
    <version>1.0-SNAPSHOT</version>
    <packaging>pom</packaging>
    <properties>
        <project.build.sourceEncoding>UTF-8</project.build.
sourceEncoding>
    </properties>
</project>
```

Adding a new module into this parent module is a simple procedure using NetBeans. To show the power and simplicity of a multi-module Maven project, we'll add two new modules. The first will be an application, while the second will hold some business logic to greet clients.

1. Right-click on the **Modules** node within the **MavenGreeter** project in the **Projects** window and select **Create New Module**.

2. The **New Project** wizard will now open defaulting to the **Maven** category. From the list of projects, select **Java Application** and click on **Next**.

3. As we're declaring a child module of our parent project, a lot of default details are already specified for us. On the **Name and Location** page, we should only need to enter the project name as `MavenGreeterClient`.

4. Click on **Finish** to create the project.

We've just added a new Java project called `MavenGreeterClient` and added it as a subproject of the `MavenGreeter` project. We now need to add another project that can be used to hold business logic. Repeat steps 1 through 4, this time specifying the project name as `MavenGreeterBusiness`.

Within the **Projects** window, we should now see that we have three projects created with our client and business projects listed as modules for the main parent POM project.

If we look at the pom.xml file for the MavenGreeter project, we can also see that our child projects have been added as modules:

```xml
<?xml version="1.0" encoding="UTF-8"?>
<project xmlns="http://maven.apache.org/POM/4.0.0" xmlns:xsi="http://
www.w3.org/2001/XMLSchema-instance" xsi:schemaLocation="http://maven.
apache.org/POM/4.0.0 http://maven.apache.org/xsd/maven-4.0.0.xsd">
    <modelVersion>4.0.0</modelVersion>
    <groupId>com.davidsalter.masteringnb</groupId>
    <artifactId>MavenGreeter</artifactId>
    <version>1.0-SNAPSHOT</version>
    <packaging>pom</packaging>
    <modules>
        <module>MavenGreeterClient</module>
        <module>MavenGreeterBusiness</module>
    </modules>
    <properties>
        <project.build.sourceEncoding>UTF-8</project.build.
sourceEncoding>
    </properties>
</project>
```

Since we have just created our projects, we need to set up the dependencies between them. For our sample application, the `MavenGreeterClient` project is going to have a dependency on the `MavenGreeterBusiness` project.

In order to specify the project dependencies with Maven, we first need to build the projects so that they are installed into our local Maven repository. After building the projects, we can open up the `pom.xml` file for the `MavenGreeterClient` project and add a dependency on the `MavenGreeterBusiness` project.

Maven dependencies can be added manually by typing into the `pom.xml` file, however, with NetBeans, we can right-click on the body of the `pom.xml` file and choose the **Insert Code...** option.

Whenever inserting code this way, NetBeans provides context-sensitive insertion options. For the case of a Maven `pom.xml` file, the following options are provided:

- **Dependency**: This adds a Maven dependency. The user is presented with a search dialog, allowing them to find the required dependency to add.

- **Dependency Exclusion**: This allows the user to exclude dependencies from the project.

- **Plugin**: This allows a Maven plugin to be added into the project. On the resulting dialog, the user can query for the name of a plugin and then select which goals the plugin will be configured for.

- **Profile**: This adds a new Maven profile into the `pom.xml` file. The name of the profile can be defined along with the options of how the profile can be activated.

- **License**: This displays a list of licenses known to NetBeans (for example, MIT, BSD, GPL). Selecting a license adds the relevant code to the `pom.xml` file.

For now, we want to add a dependency within the `MavenGreeterClient` project.

1. Ensure the `pom.xml` file for the `MavenGreeterClient` project is open for editing and then right-click within the editor and select **Insert Code...** and then **Dependency...**.

2. The **Add Dependency** screen will now be displayed. Within here, enter MavenGreeterBusiness in the **Query** edit box:

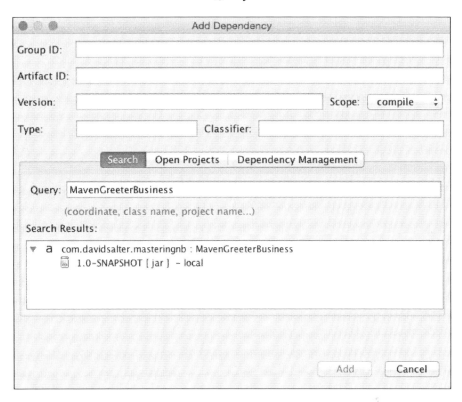

Within the **Search Results** list, all matches to the query entered will be displayed. In this case, the MavenGreeterBusiness module is displayed.

3. Select version **1.0-SNAPSHOT** from the **Search Results** list and click on **Add** to add the dependency.

 When adding dependencies, the **Open Projects** tab displays a list of currently open Maven projects. Instead of searching for a project previously, we could have simply selected the project from here and added it as a dependency.

Looking at the `pom.xml` file for the `MavenGreeterClient` project, we can now see that the required dependency has indeed been specified:

```xml
<?xml version="1.0" encoding="UTF-8"?>
<project xmlns="http://maven.apache.org/POM/4.0.0" xmlns:xsi="http://
www.w3.org/2001/XMLSchema-instance" xsi:schemaLocation="http://maven.
apache.org/POM/4.0.0 http://maven.apache.org/xsd/maven-4.0.0.xsd">
    <modelVersion>4.0.0</modelVersion>
    <parent>
        <groupId>com.davidsalter.masteringnb</groupId>
        <artifactId>MavenGreeter</artifactId>
        <version>1.0-SNAPSHOT</version>
    </parent>
    <artifactId>MavenGreeterClient</artifactId>
    <packaging>jar</packaging>
    <dependencies>
        <dependency>
            <groupId>${project.groupId}</groupId>
            <artifactId>MavenGreeterBusiness</artifactId>
            <version>${project.version}</version>
        </dependency>
    </dependencies>
    <properties>
        <maven.compiler.source>1.7</maven.compiler.source>
        <maven.compiler.target>1.7</maven.compiler.target>
    </properties>
</project>
```

Now that we've defined all the dependencies required, we can finally add some sample code to the projects to see how they work.

Add the `com.davidsalter.masteringnb.mavengreeterbusiness.Greeter` class to the `MavenGreeterBusiness` project:

```java
package com.davidsalter.masteringnb.mavengreeterbusiness;

public class Greeter {

    public Greeter() {
    }

    public String greet(String name) {
        return "Hi " + name;
    }
}
```

Add the `com.davidsalter.massteringnb.mavengreeterclient.Main` class to the `MavenGreeterClient` project:

```
package com.davidsalter.masteringnb.mavengreeterclient;

import com.davidsalter.masteringnb.mavengreeterbusiness.Greeter;

public class Main {
    public static void main(String args[]) {
        Greeter greeter = new Greeter();

        System.out.println(greeter.greet("David"));
    }
}
```

Finally, we can run the client application. Right-click on **MavenGreeterClient** and select **Run**.

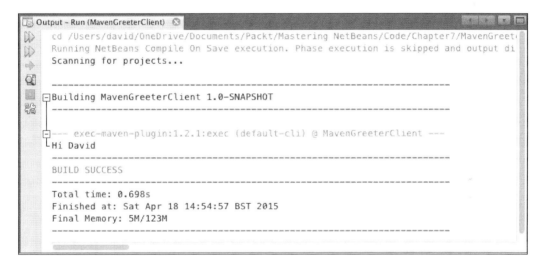

# Creating EJBs

Within a Java EE application, business logic is usually implemented within EJBs or behind an EJB façade.

NetBeans provides support for creating the different types of EJBs using the standard **New File** wizard. Using this wizard, we can create:

- **Session Bean**: This creates either a stateless, stateful, or singleton session bean optionally with a local or remote interface.

- **Timer Session Bean**: This creates either a stateless or singleton session bean annotates with `@Schedule` optionally with a local or remote interface.

- **Message Driven Bean**: This creates a message-driven bean which is capable of receiving messages from JMS queues or topics.

- **Service Locator**: This creates a J2EE service locator class. This pattern is typically not used as much with Java EE applications.

- **Caching Service Locator**: This creates a J2EE service locator class which caches lookups. As with the **Service Locator** pattern, this pattern is typically not used as much with Java EE applications.

- **Session Beans For Entity Classes**: This creates an EJB session bean façade for one or more entity classes.

- **Standard Deployment Descriptor**: This creates an empty `ejb-jar.xml` file.

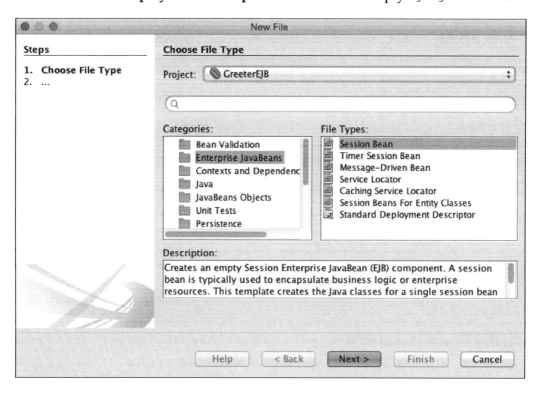

Earlier in this chapter, we created an enterprise application called `GreeterEnterprise`. Let's see how we can easily add an EJB with a remote interface and then invoke that from an enterprise client. For this example, we'll create a stateless session bean and invoke a business method from an application client.

To create a stateless session bean, we use the **New File...** wizard within NetBeans:

1.  Invoke the **New File** wizard on the `GreeterEJB` project and select **Enterprise JavaBeans** from the list of **Categories** and **Session Bean** from the list of **File Types** and then click on **Next >**.

2.  On the **Name and Location** page, enter the following information:

    ○  **EJB Name**: `WelcomeBean`
    ○  **Source Package**: `com.davidsalter.masteringnb.greeter`
    ○  **Session Type**: `Stateless`
    ○  **Create Interface**: Ensure **Remote in project** is checked, selecting to create the interface in the `GreeterEJBRemote` project:

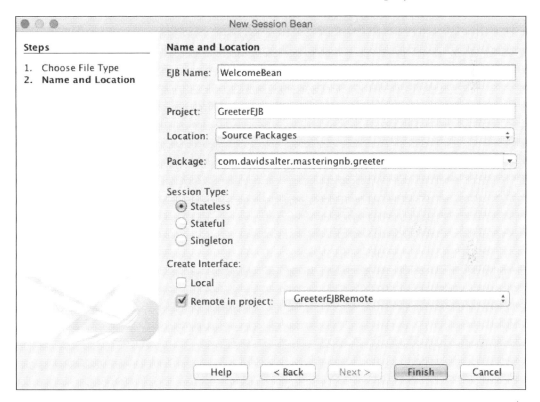

3.  Click on the **Finish** button to create the EJB.

NetBeans will now create the EJB in the `GreeterEJB` project and open the `WelcomeBean.java` file for editing.

The WelcomeBeanRemote interface is automatically created in the GreeterEJBRemote project.

The WelcomeBean class has been created as an implementation of a stateless session bean. So far, we haven't added any business methods into the class, so the implementation of the class is as follows:

```
package com.davidsalter.masteringnb.greeter;

import javax.ejb.Stateless;

@Stateless
public class WelcomeBean implements WelcomeBeanRemote {

    // Add business logic below. (Right-click in editor and choose
    // "Insert Code > Add Business Method")
}
```

Similarly, the WelcomeBeanRemote interface has no methods in it at present and is implemented as follows:

```
package com.davidsalter.masteringnb.greeter;

import javax.ejb.Remote;

@Remote
public interface WelcomeBeanRemote {

}
```

Now that we've created an EJB, we can of course fill in the missing parts and add a business method into the implementation class and then add the corresponding method signature into the appropriate interface. This of course is error-prone as there's a chance we will enter the method signature differently between the implementation and the interface. We may even forget to add the method signature to the interface all together. Additionally, if we're implementing both a local and a remote interface, we will need to type the method signature three times: once in the implementation class and once each in the local and remote interfaces.

Fortunately, NetBeans makes this whole process a lot easier as we can use NetBeans to add our business method. NetBeans will then automatically add the method signature to the corresponding interface files automatically.

To add a business method into an EJB, we need to invoke the **Insert Code…** option within the editor window of an EJB. This wizard has many options for a Java class, but within an EJB, we have the additional options of **Add Business Method…** and **Call Enterprise Bean…**. Let's take a look at both these methods now by adding a business method and then invoking it.

If you remember, our `GreeterEnterprise` project has both an EJB and a client application module. First, we'll add a method into the EJB and then invoke it from the client application by performing these steps:

1.  Ensure the `WelcomeBean.java` file from the `GreeterEJB` project is open for editing. Right-click in the body of the class and select the **Insert Code…** option. From the pop-up window, select **Add Business Method…**.

2.  On the **Add Business Method…** dialog, enter the following information:
    - **Name**: greet
    - **Return Type**: String
    - **Parameter Name**: name
    - **Parameter Type**: java.lang.String
    - **Use in Interface**: Ensure **Remote** is checked

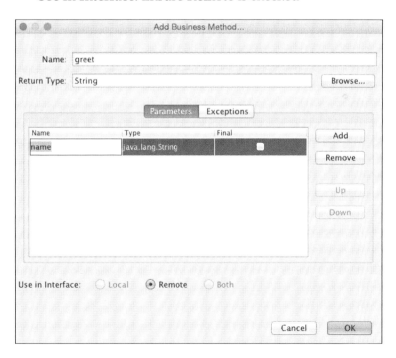

3.  Click on **OK** to add the business method.

On the **Add Business Method...** dialog, NetBeans allows us to first specify the name and return type of the business method to add. We can add and remove parameters by pressing the **Add** or **Remove** buttons, respectively. For each parameter we add, we can specify the parameter's name, type, and whether the parameter is declared as `final` or not. We can then reorder the parameters using the **Up** and **Down** buttons.

When we created the EJB within NetBeans, we specified whether the EJB was to implement a local, remote, or both interfaces. This choice is echoed on the **Add Business Method...** dialog so that we can optionally choose which interfaces our business method must implement.

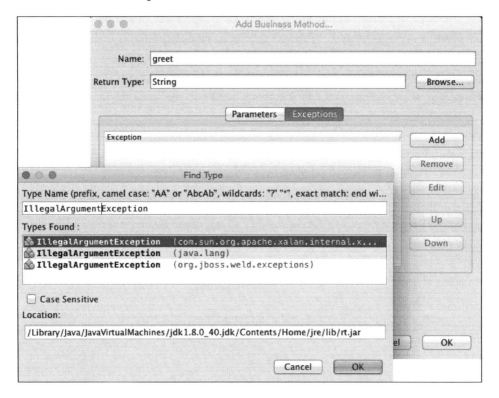

If we require our business method to throw any exceptions, these can be declared within the **Exceptions** tab of the dialog. Within this tab, we can search for exceptions and then add them to the list of exceptions that are thrown from the method. As with parameters to the method, we can add, remove, and reorder the exceptions that are thrown.

When searching for an exception on the **Find Type** dialog shown previously, we can enter camel case shorthand or use wildcards to find the names of exceptions we wish to throw. For example, to find the `IllegalArgumentException` shown earlier, we could search for either `IllegalArgumentException`, or `IAE`, or `*ArgumentEx*`, or any number of combinations of these.

Upon completing the **Add Business Method...** wizard, NetBeans will create a blank implementation of the business method:

```
public String greet(String name) {
    return null;
}
```

To continue with our example, let's implement the simplest possible version of this method as:

```
public String greet(String name) {
    return "Hello " + name;
}
```

We can also open the `WelcomeBeanRemote` interface and verify that NetBeans has added the correct method signature:

```
@Remote
public interface WelcomeBeanRemote {

    String greet(String name);

}
```

Now that we've implemented our EJB, let's write some code to invoke it from a standalone Java client application.

Invoking an EJB is a straightforward process when the EJB implements a local interface as we can simply inject the EJB into our code using the @EJB annotation. We'll see use of this in the next chapter when we will look at invoking EJBs from within a web application.

When an EJB implements a remote interface, we need to look up for a reference to the EJB before we can use it. This typically involves creating an `InitialContext` class and performing a `lookup()` on it, passing in the JNDI name for the EJB. As we'd expect, however, NetBeans makes this process simple using the **Insert Code…** wizard. To see how this wizard works, let's create a Java application and invoke our EJB by following these steps:

1. Add a new `Main` class with a `main(String args[])` method into the `Greeter` project. This can be added using the **New File…** wizard and selecting to create a new Java `Main` class from the **Java Category**. Ensure the class is called `Main` and is in the `com.davidsalter.masteringnb.greeter` package.

2. Right-click on the body of the `main(String[] args)` method and select **Insert Code…** and then **Call Enterprise Bean…**.

The **Call Enterprise Bean** dialog will now be displayed. This dialog displays all of the EJBs that can be found within the currently open NetBeans projects. From this dialog, we can browse through the projects that support EJBs and select the EJB we wish to invoke. Toward the bottom of the dialog, the interfaces for the selected bean are displayed. Selecting one of these interfaces determines how the code is generated for invoking the EJB.

For a remote interface, a `lookup()` method will be performed on an `InitialContext` to get a reference to the bean. For a local interface, the EJB will be injected into the client code using the `@EJB` annotation.

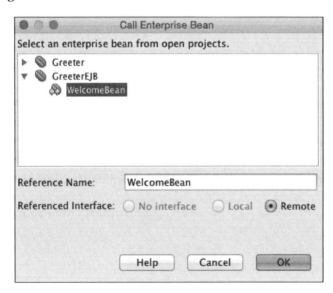

Select the **WelcomeBean** within the **GreeterEJB** node and press the **OK** button to add the code to the Main class.

Upon closing the dialog, NetBeans will insert the code into the Main class to lookup the EJB, however, the code to invoke the EJB will not be written; this has to be manually added. At this stage, the Main class looks similar to the following:

```
package com.davidsalter.masteringnb.greeter;

import java.util.logging.Level;
import java.util.logging.Logger;
import javax.naming.Context;
import javax.naming.InitialContext;
import javax.naming.NamingException;

public class NewMain {
    WelcomeBeanRemote welcomeBean = lookupWelcomeBeanRemote();

public static void main(String[] args) {
        // TODO code application logic here
    }

    private WelcomeBeanRemote lookupWelcomeBeanRemote() {
        try {
            Context c = new InitialContext();
            return (WelcomeBeanRemote) c.lookup("java:global/
GreeterEnterprise/GreeterEJB/WelcomeBean!com.davidsalter.masteringnb.
greeter.WelcomeBeanRemote");
        } catch (NamingException ne) {
            Logger.getLogger(getClass().getName()).log(Level.SEVERE,
"exception caught", ne);
            throw new RuntimeException(ne);
        }
    }
}
```

By looking at this code, we can gain an understanding of what NetBeans has done to allow us to invoke a method on the EJB. NetBeans has created a local variable welcomeBean of the type WelcomeBeanRemote. This bean is then assigned the result of the lookupWelcomeBeanRemote() method. Within this method, an InitialContext is created and the lookup() method is called passing in a JNDI name of java:global/GreeterEnterprise/GreeterEJB/WelcomeBean!com. davidsalter.masteringnb.greeter.WelcomeBeanRemote.

This JNDI name is used by GlassFish. If you are using a different application server, check your documentation to find the exact format of the JNDI name of a remote EJB.

To finally invoke a method on our EJB, we must call the business method on the welcomeBean. This can be achieved by changing the Main class as follows:

```
package com.davidsalter.masteringnb.greeter;

import java.util.logging.Level;
import java.util.logging.Logger;
import javax.naming.Context;
import javax.naming.InitialContext;
import javax.naming.NamingException;

public class Main {

    com.davidsalter.masteringnb.greeter.WelcomeBeanRemote welcomeBean
= lookupWelcomeBeanRemote();

    public static void main(String[] args) {
        Main main = new Main();
        main.welcome();
    }

    private void welcome() {
        System.out.println(welcomeBean.greet("David"));
    }

    private com.davidsalter.masteringnb.greeter.WelcomeBeanRemote
lookupWelcomeBeanRemote() {
        try {
            Context c = new InitialContext();
            return (com.davidsalter.masteringnb.greeter.
WelcomeBeanRemote) c.lookup("java:global/GreeterEnterprise/GreeterEJB/
WelcomeBean!com.davidsalter.masteringnb.greeter.WelcomeBeanRemote");
        } catch (NamingException ne) {
            Logger.getLogger(getClass().getName()).log(Level.SEVERE,
"exception caught", ne);
            throw new RuntimeException(ne);
        }
    }

}
```

To test out the application, ensure that GlassFish is started and deploy the `GreeterEnterprise` application by right-clicking on the project and selecting **Deploy**. A notification will be displayed in the **GlassFish Server Output** window when the application is deployed.

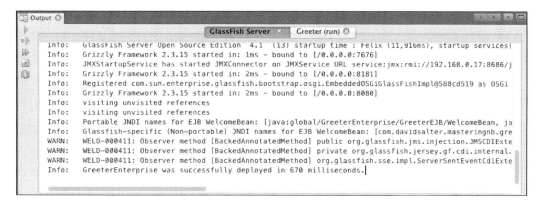

Run the `Greeter` application by right-clicking on the **Greeter** project and selecting **Run**.

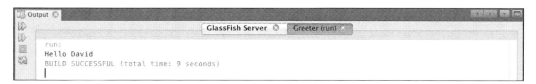

In this example, we've seen how to create a stateless session bean and invoke it via a remote instance. Creating a stateful or a singleton session bean follows the exact same procedure, except that we specify the session type as appropriate within the **New Session Bean** wizard.

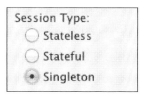

# Creating a session bean façade for entity classes

In the previous section, we saw how we can use NetBeans to help us create business methods within EJBs and easily invoke EJB from client applications.

In all but the most simple application, however, we usually have a database component and a graph of database objects modeled with the @Entity annotation within our application.

Since one of the benefits of EJBs is that they offer transactional support, EJBs make a good candidate for a session façade for entity classes. A session façade is a design pattern that abstracts the implementation of methods away from callers in order to decouple business objects from callers. In this instance, NetBeans can create a session façade that abstracts away all of the database functionality from clients, making the clients unaware of how business objects are persisted. This is only one use of a session façade though, and as a developer, we can add more methods into the façade to provide the exact services that our clients need.

 For more information on the session façade pattern, visit http://www.oracle.com/technetwork/ java/sessionfacade-141285.html.

A typical database session façade provides **CRUD (Create, Retrieve, Update, and Delete)** functionality to its clients. Let's take a look at how NetBeans can help us to create a façade.

Let's assume we have a class, Customer, representing a customer in a relational database. A simplified representation of a customer may look similar to the following in Java code:

```
@Entity
public class Customer {

    @Id
    private long id;
    private String name;
    private BigDecimal creditAmount;
    private String emailAddress;

    public Customer() {
    }

    // Getters and setters omitted for brevity.
}
```

To create a session façade for this entity, we can use the **New File...** wizard and select the **Session Beans For Entity Classes** file type:

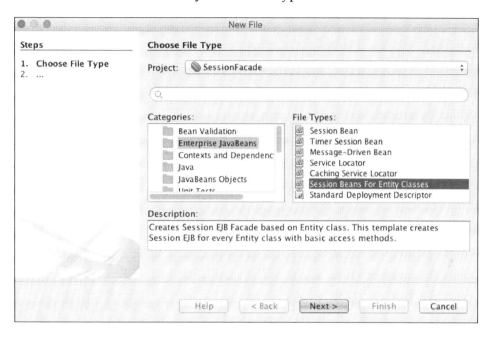

The first stage in creating a session façade is to select the `@Entity` classes that we wish to create a façade for.

NetBeans searches through our codebase and displays a list of all the classes that have the @Entity annotation. To continue, we must simply select the classes that we wish to implement a façade for. If some classes reference other classes (for example, we have @ManyToMany or @OneToMany relationships), we can easily add those by checking the **Include Referenced Classes** option.

The next stage is to specify the package for our session façade and whether we wish to use local or remote interfaces for the generated EJB(s). Typically, we only implement local interfaces for session facades that access database logic. This is because we do not want a remote EJB interface to have a dependency on JPA objects (this is simply because a database is typically a server-side object and our clients have no knowledge of our databases).

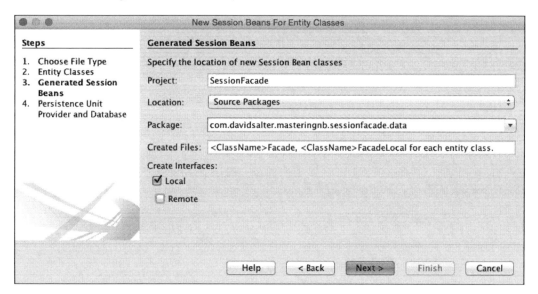

This stage of the wizard also gives us some information on the name of the created façade files. In the preceding example, we will have the following files created for each entity:

- `<ClassName>`Façade, for example, `CustomerFacade.java`
- `<ClassName>`FacadeLocal, for example, `CustomerFacadeLocal.java`

Finally, if we have not specified a database provider and data source for our project, the **Provider and Database** page will be displayed. If we're running through this wizard for the second or more time on a particular project, this final page will not be displayed as NetBeans will assume that we've already configured our database connection details.

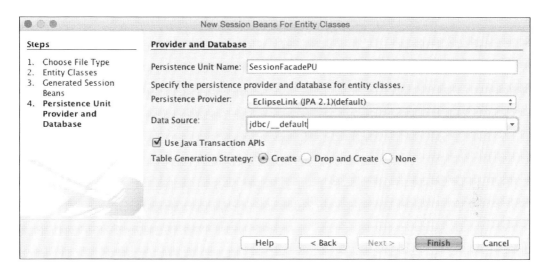

Within this final page of the wizard, we specify the persistence unit name, persistence provider, data source, and table generation strategy. All of this information is used to create a persistence unit. For more information on persistence units and their support in NetBeans, refer to *Chapter 5, Database Persistence*.

For this example, the `persistence.xml` file created will look similar to the following:

```
<?xml version="1.0" encoding="UTF-8"?>
<persistence version="2.1" xmlns="http://xmlns.jcp.org/xml/ns/
persistence" xmlns:xsi="http://www.w3.org/2001/XMLSchema-instance"
xsi:schemaLocation="http://xmlns.jcp.org/xml/ns/persistence http://
xmlns.jcp.org/xml/ns/persistence/persistence_2_1.xsd">
  <persistence-unit name="SessionFacadePU" transaction-type="JTA">
    <jta-data-source>jdbc/__default</jta-data-source>
    <exclude-unlisted-classes>false</exclude-unlisted-classes>
    <properties>
      <property name="javax.persistence.schema-generation.database.
action" value="create"/>
    </properties>
  </persistence-unit>
</persistence>
```

As shown on the **Generate Session Beans** page of the wizard, NetBeans creates a façade consisting of several files when the wizard is complete.

A session bean interface, `CustomerFacadeLocal`, is generated, providing the signatures for all of the CRUD methods we will expect:

```
@Local
public interface CustomerFacadeLocal {
    void create(Customer customer);
    void edit(Customer customer);
    void remove(Customer customer);
    Customer find(Object id);
    List<Customer> findAll();
    List<Customer> findRange(int[] range);
    int count();
}
```

This class is implemented by the `CustomerFacade` class:

```
@Stateless
public class CustomerFacade extends AbstractFacade<Customer>
implements CustomerFacadeLocal {
    @PersistenceContext(unitName = "SessionFacadePU")
    private EntityManager em;

    @Override
    protected EntityManager getEntityManager() {
        return em;
    }

    public CustomerFacade() {
        super(Customer.class);
    }
}
```

Finally, an `AbstractFacade` class is created if it does not already exist. This class uses JPA to implement the CRUD methods for each façade we choose to create:

```
public abstract class AbstractFacade<T> {
    private Class<T> entityClass;

    public AbstractFacade(Class<T> entityClass) {
```

```java
        this.entityClass = entityClass;
    }

    protected abstract EntityManager getEntityManager();

    public void create(T entity) {
        getEntityManager().persist(entity);
    }

    public void edit(T entity) {
        getEntityManager().merge(entity);
    }

    public void remove(T entity) {
        getEntityManager().remove(getEntityManager().merge(entity));
    }

    public T find(Object id) {
        return getEntityManager().find(entityClass, id);
    }

    public List<T> findAll() {
        javax.persistence.criteria.CriteriaQuery cq =
getEntityManager().getCriteriaBuilder().createQuery();
        cq.select(cq.from(entityClass));
        return getEntityManager().createQuery(cq).getResultList();
    }

    public List<T> findRange(int[] range) {
        javax.persistence.criteria.CriteriaQuery cq =
getEntityManager().getCriteriaBuilder().createQuery();
        cq.select(cq.from(entityClass));
        javax.persistence.Query q = getEntityManager().
createQuery(cq);
        q.setMaxResults(range[1] - range[0] + 1);
        q.setFirstResult(range[0]);
        return q.getResultList();
    }

    public int count() {
        javax.persistence.criteria.CriteriaQuery cq =
getEntityManager().getCriteriaBuilder().createQuery();
```

```
        javax.persistence.criteria.Root<T> rt = cq.from(entityClass);
        cq.select(getEntityManager().getCriteriaBuilder().count(rt));
        javax.persistence.Query q = getEntityManager().
createQuery(cq);
        return ((Long) q.getSingleResult()).intValue();
    }
}
```

# The Java Bean Validation framework

The Java Bean Validation framework 1.0 (JSR 303) was introduced into Java EE 6 to allow validation constraints to be added onto Java beans. The latest release of the Bean Validation framework, version 1.1 (JSR 349), further enhances the validation model, allowing additional features such as method level validation and full support for CDI.

Bean Validation works by adding a constraint onto a field, method, or class in the form of an annotation. The framework provides many constraints as well as an API, allowing new constraints to be developed. Some of the more common annotations are:

- `@NotNull`: The value of the property must not be null
- `@Pattern`: The value of the property conforms to the specified regular expression
- `@Max` / `@Min`: The value of the property must be an integer with the specified maximum/minimum value
- `@Future` / `@Past`: The value of the property must be a data in the future/past

Of course, there are many more validation constraint annotations than these. For full details, refer to the Bean Validation site at `http://www.beanvalidation.org`.

## Creating a Bean Validation constraint

A lot of the time when you want to perform validation on Java Beans, the standard validation constraints will suffice. For example, we typically want to check that a value is not null or it has a maximum length or follows a particular pattern. In these cases, we can use the standard constraints.

Sometimes, however, we wish to perform some other validation that just doesn't quite fit into the standard constraints. Creating a new constraint can look daunting, but with the help of NetBeans, creating new constraints is a straightforward matter.

Consider the following Java bean:

```
public class Customer {

    @Id
    private long id;

    @NotNull
    private String name;
    private BigDecimal creditAmount;

    private String emailAddress;

    public Customer() {
    }

    // Getters and setters omitted for brevity.
}
```

Within this class, we can see that there is a @NotNull constraint added to the name property, ensuring that a name value is specified.

If we wanted to add a constraint onto the emailAddress property, to ensure that the emailAddress is valid, we can do this using the **New File** wizard from within NetBeans. To create a new constraint, we launch the New File wizard, select **Bean Validation Category** and then choose **Validation Constraint** from the list of **File Types**.

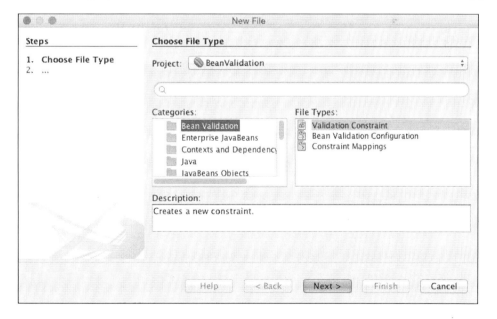

After clicking on the **Next >** button, the **Name and Location** page of the wizard is displayed. This is where we specify the details about the constraint that we wish to add.

Here, **Class Name** is the name of the interface that represents the constraint validation. In the following screenshot, **Class Name** of `SimpleEmail` will correspond to an annotation of `@SimpleEmail`.

Next, we must specify the usual project, location, and package fields that are present on most of the NetBeans **New File** wizards.

Finally, we can select the **Generate Validator Class** option. By selecting this option, NetBeans will create a constraint with a `@Constraint` annotation on it. This simply means that we have a separate class that can be used to validate a constraint. To create a validator class, we must specify **Validator Class Name** and **Java Type to Validate**. The validator class name is the name of the class that NetBeans will generate to validate the constraint, whereas the Java type to validate specifies what type of object this class will validate.

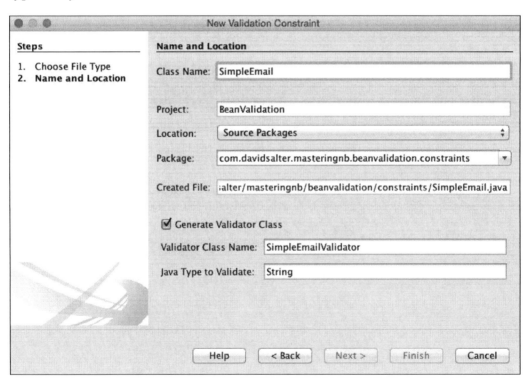

Upon completing the wizard, NetBeans will create both the constraint and constraint validator class. For the preceding example, these will be the `SimpleEmail.java` and `SimpleEmailValidator.java` classes.

The `SimpleEmail.java` class specifies the constraint that we wish to implement. It's basic structure is as follows:

```
@Documented
@Constraint(validatedBy = SimpleEmailValidator.class)
@Target({ElementType.METHOD, ElementType.FIELD, ElementType.
ANNOTATION_TYPE})
@Retention(RetentionPolicy.RUNTIME)
public @interface SimpleEmail {

    String message() default "{com.davidsalter.masteringnb.
beanvalidation.constaints.SimpleEmail}";

    Class<?>[] groups() default {};

    Class<? extends Payload>[] payload() default {};
}
```

The annotation is created using the `@interface` keyword, which is annotated by several annotations:

- `@Documented`: This specifies that the annotation will be included in the JavaDoc
- `@Constraint`: This specifies which class will be used to validate the constraint
- `@Target`: This specifies whether the annotation will apply to methods, fields, or annotations
- `@Retention`: This specifies that the annotation will be available at runtime

The constraint validator class, `SimpleEmailValidator.java`, is initially created with a blank implementation:

```
public class SimpleEmailValidator implements ConstraintValidator<Simpl
eEmail, String> {

    @Override
    public void initialize(NewConstraint constraintAnnotation) {
        throw new UnsupportedOperationException("Not supported yet.");
    }

    @Override
```

```
        public boolean isValid(String value, ConstraintValidatorContext
    context) {
            throw new UnsupportedOperationException("Not supported yet.");
        }
    }
```

The validator class contains two methods. The `initialize()` method can be used to obtain any optional information required from the validator annotation, while the `isValid()` method returns `true` or `false` depending upon whether the constraint is successful or not.

To complete the `@SimpleEmail` constraint, we need to specify that the annotation is only available to fields and not to methods or other annotations. To achieve this, we need to amend the `@Target` annotation accordingly:

```
@Documented
@Constraint(validatedBy = SimpleEmailValidator.class)
@Target({ElementType.FIELD})
@Retention(RetentionPolicy.RUNTIME)
public @interface SimpleEmail {

    String message() default "{com.davidsalter.masteringnb.
beanvalidation.constaints.SimpleEmail}";

    Class<?>[] groups() default {};

    Class<? extends Payload>[] payload() default {};
}
```

To complete the implementation, we need to implement the `isValid()` method of the `EmailValidator.java` class. For this example, checking that the e-mail address contains an @ symbol will suffice:

 This example has been chosen to showcase creating a constraint rather than how to validate an e-mail correctly. A full approach to validating e-mail addresses can be found in the third-party libraries such as in the Apache Commons EmailValidator at http://commons.apache. org/proper/commons-validator/apidocs/org/apache/ commons/validator/routines/EmailValidator.html.

```
public class SimpleEmailValidator implements ConstraintValidator<Simpl
eEmail, String> {

    @Override
    public void initialize(SimpleEmail constraintAnnotation) {
```

```
    }

    @Override
    public boolean isValid(String value,
                           ConstraintValidatorContext context) {
        if (value == null) {
            return true;
        }

        if (value.contains("@")) {
            return true;
        } else {
            return false;
        }
    }
}
```

The final stage of creating a custom constraint is to specify any messages that may be returned to the client as a result of failed validation. Looking at the `SimpleEmail.java` class, we can see the message property defining the name of a message within a message bundle file:

```
String message() default "{com.davidsalter.masteringnb.
beanvalidation.constaints.SimpleEmail}";
```

For constraint validation, the message bundle file must be called `ValidationMessages.properties`. To define an appropriate message for the `SimpleEmail` validator, the contents of this file will look similar to this:

```
com.davidsalter.masteringnb.beanvalidation.constaints.SimpleEmail=This
does not appear to be a valid email address
```

Having created a custom validator and defined any output messages, we can now annotate our original class to ensure that it is defined correctly:

```
public class Customer {

    @Id
    private long id;

    @NotNull
    private String name;
    private BigDecimal creditAmount;

    @SimpleEmail
```

```
    private String emailAddress;

    public Customer() {
    }
    // Getters and setter omitted for brevity


}
```

# Contexts and Dependency Injection

One of the hot new features in Enterprise Java over recent years has been the **Contexts and Dependency Injection (CDI)** framework.

CDI allows us to interact with the context of objects by enabling binding to the different lifecycle methods of stateful components using annotations such as `@PostContruct` and `@PreDestroy`. It also provides a dependency injection framework, allowing components to be injected into other components using the `@Inject` annotation. We can choose different implementations of components to inject at deploy time, allowing a looser coupling of components leading to better and more structured architectures.

 For more information about CDI, refer to the Java EE 6 tutorial at `http://docs.oracle.com/javaee/6/tutorial/doc/giwhb.html`.

CDI is a huge subject that can be described in entire books such as *JBoss Weld CDI for Java Platform, Ken Finnigan, Packt Publishing*. In this section, we're assuming that you are familiar with CDI.

## Adding CDI support

When using CDI, a special file, beans.xml, must be present in order for the runtime to detect and initialize the CDI framework. Within an EJB JAR project, this file is stored within the `META-INF` folder, whereas in a `.War` archive, the file is stored within the `WEB-INF` folder.

NetBeans provides support for creating a beans.xml file using the standard **New File** wizard.

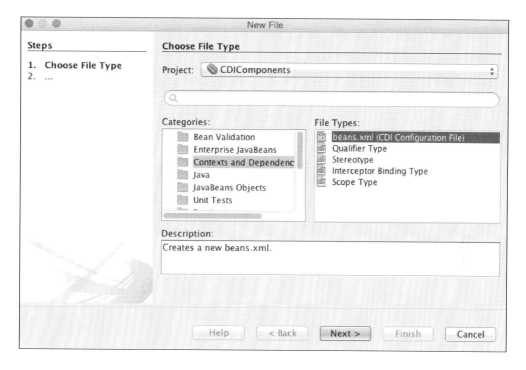

Using this wizard, we can also create other CDI components, namely:

- **Qualifier Type**: This defines a new `@Qualifier`. Qualifier types allow different implementations of a component to be injected into other components, for example, a JDBC or JPA factory can be defined using different qualifier types.

- **Stereotype**: This defines a new `@Stereotype`. Stereotypes are annotations that define a set of other CDI annotations such as scope and interceptor bindings and alternative implementations for beans. A good use of a stereotype would be to define a mock object, replacing an existing bean with a mock implementation.

- **Interceptor Binding Type**: This creates a new `@InterceptorBinding`. Interceptor bindings work with interceptors to allow methods to be invoked around the execution of target class methods. This implements a cross-cutting concern, and typically applies to tasks such as security or logging where the activity being added is not related to the target methods logic, hence the phrase cross-cutting is used.

- **Scope Type**: This defines a new `@Scope`.

# CDI injection points editor support

When looking at the code that supports CDI, it can sometimes be a bit confusing working out where components come from, and navigating between them.

NetBeans overcomes this issue by providing icons in the left gutter of the source code editor, showing that a component is being injected into another component.

```
46      @Inject
47      @MongoConnection
        MongoSettings mongoSettings;
49
```

In the preceding screenshot, for example, we can see that an object of type `MongoSettings` called `mongoSettings` is being injected. NetBeans displays a blue I in the gutter on the left-hand side of the editor window to indicate that this is an injection point. Clicking on this icon opens the source code for the Java object that is being injected.

The preceding screenshot also shows an example of the use of a custom qualifier to denote a `MongoConnection`.

# Summary

In this chapter, we looked at how to create multi-module EJB projects using both standard NetBeans projects and Maven. We saw how these projects can contain multiple modules and how the Maven multi-module project type is especially powerful as it allows an almost unlimited project hierarchy to be created. We also noted that for simpler projects, a simple `.War` file deployment may be sufficient instead of a multi-module EJB project.

We looked at the different types of EJBs that can be created within NetBeans and created an example project to deploy an EJB and then invoke it from a remote client. We also saw how we can use NetBeans to easily generate a session bean façade for the existing `@Entity` classes within our applications.

Finally, we looked at some of the more advanced and newer features of Java EE. We saw how NetBeans can help us perform bean validation and create new bean validation constraints, and how it can be helpful when using CDI within our applications.

In the next chapter, we'll move over to the web tier and see what features NetBeans has to help us develop web applications.

# 8
# Creating the Web Tier

One of the most common uses for Java EE is to create web applications that can be deployed to servlet containers such as Apache Tomcat, or to full-blown application containers such as WildFly or GlassFish. In this chapter, we're going to look at some of the tools that NetBeans provides to help developers build modern web applications.

We're going to look at the following topics in this chapter:

- Creating/configuring web projects
- Configuring application servers
- Web project run options
- Creating Spring Web MVC projects
- Adding components to web applications
- CSS preprocessors
- JavaScript support

## Creating web projects

NetBeans provides first class support for developers wishing to write web applications whether they are simple HTML websites or complex Java web applications using HTML, JavaScript, and backend Java code, or anywhere in between.

As with enterprise projects we saw in the previous chapter, NetBeans provides the ability to create projects using either NetBeans project templates (based upon Apache Ant) or as Maven applications.

To create and run a web application, we need to have an application server we can deploy and run the application on. The Java EE distribution of NetBeans comes bundled with GlassFish Server Open Source Edition Version 4.1 and Apache Tomcat 8.0.15. GlassFish allows developers to deploy full Java EE stack applications, including EJB and JMS among other Java EE technologies. Tomcat is more focused on the web tier and is the de facto standard for Spring applications.

The application servers registered for web (and EJB) deployment are listed within the **Servers** node of the **Services** window:

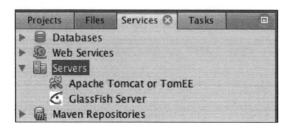

From within this window, we can start and stop application servers and view the applications that are deployed to them. Different application servers provide additional functionality, for example, with GlassFish, we can also view the admin console or update center for the application server.

If GlassFish and Tomcat are not the application servers of choice, we can easily add new application servers to be controlled from within NetBeans.

# Configuring application servers

The easiest way to add and configure an application server is directly from within the **Services** window by right-clicking on the **Servers** node and selecting **Add Server...**.

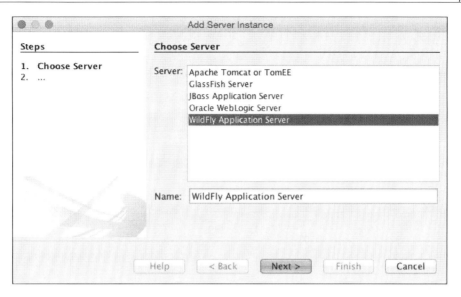

Selecting this option displays the **Add Server Instance** wizard, the first stage of which is to select the new server type. In this list, the most common Java application servers are displayed:

- **Apache Tomcat or TomEE**: This option allows us to configure a Tomcat application server (`http://tomcat.apache.org/`) or an Apache TomEE application server (`http://tomee.apache.org/`). NetBeans is supplied with Apache Tomcat 8.0.15, so newer instances of Tomcat can be configured via this option. Apache TomEE is a full Java EE Web Profile application server composed of Apache Tomcat and other Apache components (such as OpenEJB and MyFaces JSF). Since TomEE is based upon Tomcat, it can be configured and controlled from within NetBeans in the same way as Tomcat.

- **GlassFish Server**: This is the reference implementation of Java EE. Prior to version 4.1, Oracle provided a fully supported production-ready version of GlassFish that could be configured via this option within NetBeans. Since Oracle stated that they will not support a production-ready version of GlassFish, Payara (`http://www.payara.co`) has taken up the challenge and provides 24/7 support for GlassFish using Payara Server. This server is based upon GlassFish and is indeed a drop-in replacement for GlassFish. As such, Payara Server can be added and configured from within NetBeans using this option.

- **JBoss Application Server**: JBoss was one of the first Java EE application servers. Versions 4, 5, 6, and 7 of JBoss application server can be configured using this option.

- **Oracle WebLogic Server**: WebLogic is Oracle's fully supported application server and is described as "#1 Application Server Across Conventional and Cloud Environments".

- **WildFly Application Server**: WildFly (`http://wildfly.org/`) is the successor to JBoss Application Server and is RedHat's community-supported Java EE 7 application server.

Upon choosing an application server, the **Add Server Instance** wizard continues and requires details of the server instance to be configured. The first stage of this is to configure the location of the application server. The following screenshot shows an example of configuring WildFly 8.2.0 within NetBeans:

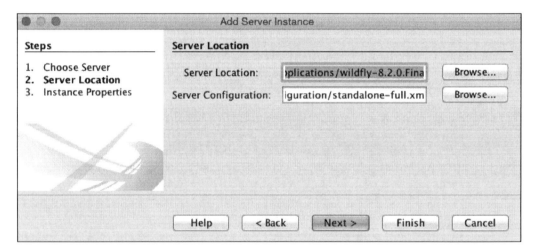

Upon specifying the application server location, NetBeans continues and allows any additional configuration data to be specified. In the case of WildFly, this is the **Domain**, **Host**, and **Port** of the application server instance.

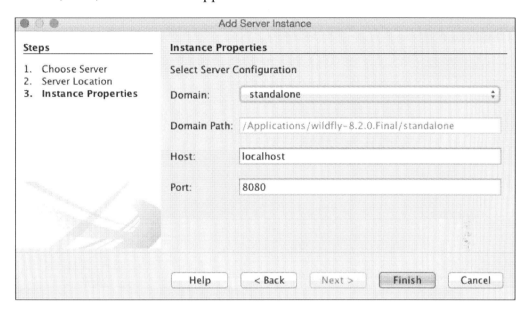

# Creating a web application

Having configured a new application server or selected one of the existing GlassFish or Tomcat instances, we can create a web application.

We can also define new application server instances while creating web projects. So, if you've forgotten to define a server or wish to use a different server, they can be configured in the **New Project** wizard.

In a similar fashion to how we created EJB projects in *Chapter 7*, *Creating the Business Layer*, NetBeans allows us to create both NetBeans-formatted web projects and Maven web projects. NetBeans projects are based upon Apache Ant and provide an excellent quick start when developing web projects. With a Maven project, however, we gain all of the advantages of Maven, including different archetypes, dependencies, and ease of build/deployment on other machines (including continuous integration).

Let's first take a look at the NetBeans standard project types for web applications.

# Creating a NetBeans web application

To create a NetBeans web application, we use the standard **New Project** wizard and select **Java Web** from this list of **Categories**:

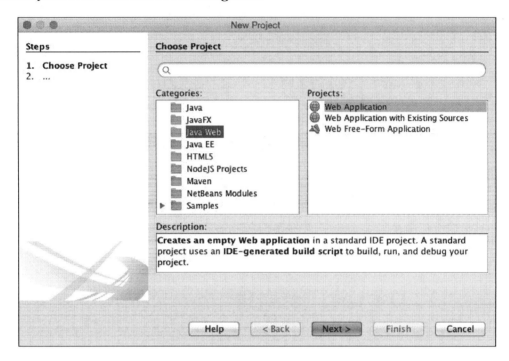

NetBeans then provides the following project types:

- **Web Application**: This creates a new empty web application using an IDE-generated Ant build script.

- **Web Application with Existing Sources**: This creates a new web application using an IDE-generated Ant build script. This option allows the user to specify the location of the existing sources for a web application and is useful when an application has been developed outside NetBeans.

- **Web Free-Form Application**: This imports an existing Ant-based web application into NetBeans. This option allows the user to specify the locations of the web content, Java source, and Java test sources. The project-specific Ant options (**Build, Clean, Test**, for example) can then be mapped to the appropriate NetBeans menu and keyboard shortcuts.

In addition to specifying project types and locations, NetBeans allows us to specify any additional project options such as additional frameworks that are to be used by the web application. Both the **Web Application** and **Web Application with Existing Sources** project types allow us to configure additional frameworks. Let's now create a standard web project and see what options we have to configure the project.

After launching the **New Project** wizard and selecting to create a web application, NetBeans displays the **Name and Location** page where we can specify the project name, location, and whether we want to use a dedicated folder for storing libraries used by the application.

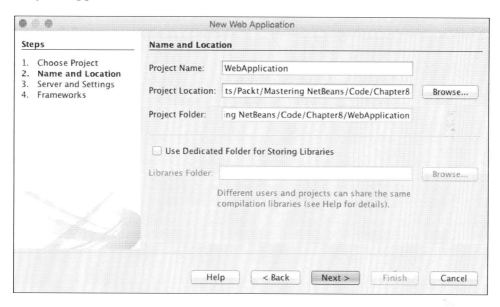

The **Use Dedicated Folder for Storing Libraries** option allows us to specify a folder outside the project's structure that can be used for storing any third-party JAR files that are to be used by this (or other) applications. This option is useful when the project you are working on is to be accessed by more than one developer as it makes it easy to share libraries between different instances of a project.

Upon defining a project's name and location, NetBeans allows us to configure the server that the application is to be deployed against along with the version of Java EE to use and whether we wish to add the web application to an existing enterprise application. If we choose to add the web application to an enterprise application, the generated .War file will be added into the enterprise application's .Ear file. If we choose not to add the web application to an enterprise application, NetBeans will generate a standalone .War file for deployment.

The Java EE version depends upon the application server that is selected. For example, GlassFish 4 and WildFly 8 will allow Java EE 7 Web profile to be selected for web applications.

Finally, we can specify the context path of the application we are creating. This is the address that the application will deployed to and accessible from within a browser.

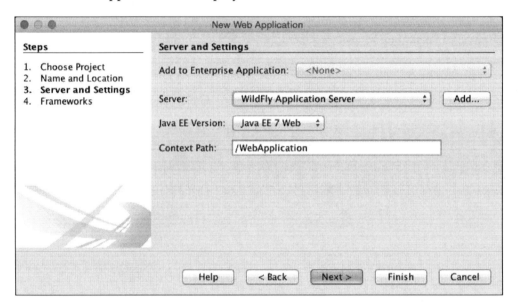

After specifying the settings for a web application, NetBeans prompts for any frameworks that may be used within the web application.

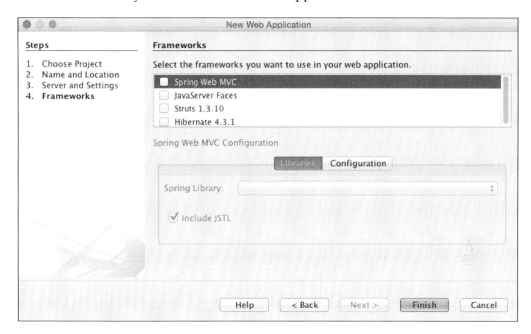

NetBeans allows the following frameworks to be specified:

- **Spring Web MVC**: This option allows a Spring Web MVC application to be created using either Spring 4.x or 3.x. The configuration tab provides the options to specify the name of Spring's dispatcher servlet and its mappings. The option to include the JSTL library within the web application is also provided.

> For more information on Spring Web MVC development, check out the Spring home page at `http://spring.io`. We will look at the alternative ways of creating Spring Web MVC applications later in this chapter.

- **Java Server Faces**: **Java Server Faces (JSF)** is the standard view technology for Java EE web applications. When selecting to use JSF within an application, NetBeans provides the option of specifying which version of JSF to use. We can opt to use **Server Library** (one that is supplied with our chosen application server), **Registered Libraries** (one that is registered within NetBeans, typically JSF 2.2 or JSF 1.2) or **Create New Library**. When creating a new library, we can select a set of .Jar files that makes up the library along with a name to give the new library.

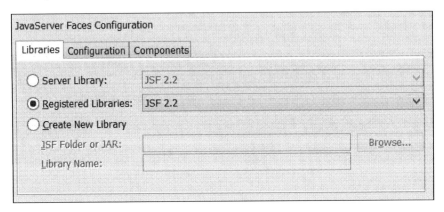

  - **Configuration**: This tab allows us to configure the JSF Servlet URL pattern to be used by JSF. This defaults to /faces/*, but can be changed to any other appropriate JSF mapping such as *.jsf or *.page.

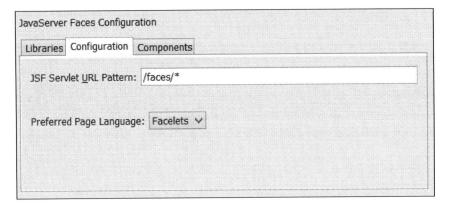

○ **Components**: Finally, we can specify which JSF component libraries we wish to use within the web application. We can choose from **PrimeFaces**, **ICEFaces**, and **RichFaces**. Clicking on the **More...** button to the right of each libraries' name allows us to create the relevant component library's within NetBeans. NetBeans comes bundled with the libraries for PrimeFaces 5, but for ICEFaces and RichFaces, the component libraries need to be downloaded prior to the configuration so that the relevant libraries can be created successfully.

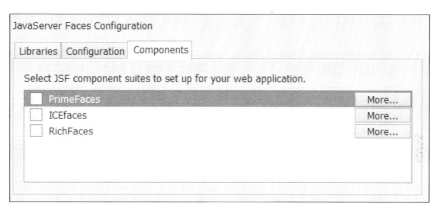

- **Struts 1.3.10**: Struts is one of the oldest web frameworks for Java web applications, however, NetBeans still provides support for it. When selecting Struts, we can configure the action URL pattern for the Struts action servlet. This defaults to the typical configuration of `*.do`, but can be configured to any other reasonable value. We can also configure the Struts application resource. For more information about Struts, refer to `https://struts.apache.org/`.

- **Hibernate 4.3.1**: The final framework we can add to our application is Hibernate. It is an open source Object Relational Mapping framework used to map Java classes to relational databases. When configuring Hibernate, we can select a database connection; NetBeans will then automatically select the appropriate database dialect for Hibernate to use. The **Database Connection** dropdown lists all the database connections that have been defined within NetBeans and also provides the facility to create new connections. Please refer to *Chapter 5, Database Persistence,* for details on how to configure database resources within NetBeans.

## Modifying a NetBeans web application

After creating a web application, the chances are very high that we want to add additional frameworks into the application. We can do this manually by adding additional libraries into a web application and then adding any necessary configuration files.

Fortunately, NetBeans allows us to easily add any of the preceding frameworks into a web application in the same way as when the application was created.

By accessing the project properties (right-click on the project in the **Projects** window and select **Properties**), we can change which frameworks are used in the project.

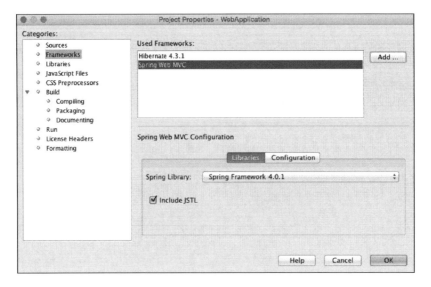

In the **Project Properties** dialog, selecting the **Frameworks** category displays a list of the frameworks that we have already added into an application and provides the option to add any of the recognized frameworks (JSF, Struts, Spring Web MVC, Hibernate) into the application if they are not already added.

# Creating a Maven web application

In the previous section, we've seen how we can create a NetBeans web project and add different frameworks into the application. The list of frameworks that we can add, however, is fairly limited, and we're restricted by the versions that NetBeans provides. To give us better control over the contents of web applications, we can create them as Maven projects.

To create a Maven web project, we have two options:

- Create a Maven web project
- Create a Maven project from Archetype and select one of the many different web project types

The first of these options creates a Maven web application project. This option is accessible within the **New Project** wizard by selecting **Maven** from the list of **Categories** and **Web Application** from the list of **Projects**.

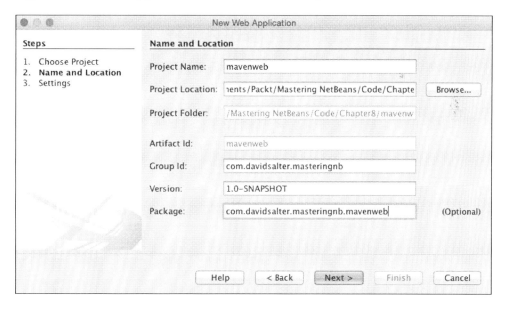

Upon selecting to create this type of web project, we are first asked for the following information:

- Project name
- Project location
- Maven group ID
- Version
- Default package

After entering this information, NetBeans asks for the server to deploy and run the application against together with the version of Java EE to build the project against. These are the same options as when creating a NetBeans web project.

When creating a Maven web project, we are not given the option of specifying the context root of the web application. The context root defaults to the name of the generated `.War` file, which is typically the project name concatenated to the project version. For example, if we deploy the application created in the preceding screenshot, the URL to access the application will be: `http://localhost:8080/mavenweb-1.0-SNAPSHOT/`

The simplest way that will work with all application servers is to change the name of the generated `.War` file to the name of the context root that is required. So, for example, to change the context root to be the same as the `artifactId`, add a `<finalName />` element into the `pom.xml` file:

```
<build>
    <finalName>${artifactId}</finalName>
    ...
</build>
```

Different application servers have different techniques for setting the context root for an application. For WildFly, for example, changing the context root requires adding a `WEB-INF\jboss-web.xml` file with the following contents:

```
<?xml version="1.0" encoding="UTF-8"?>
<jboss-web version="8.0"
        xmlns="http://www.jboss.com/xml/ns/javaee"
        xmlns:xsi="http://www.w3.org/2001/XMLSchema-instance"
        xsi:schemaLocation="http://www.jboss.com/xml/ns/javaee
        http://www.jboss.org/schema/jbossas/jboss-web_8_0.xsd">
    <context-root>/mweb</context-root>
</jboss-web>
```

Fortunately, NetBeans helps us here again as we can set the context root from within the project's Run options.

# The web project's Run options

Right-clicking on a project in the **Projects** window and selecting **Properties** displays the **Project Properties** page. Selecting **Run** from the list of **Categories** displays the project's **Run** options.

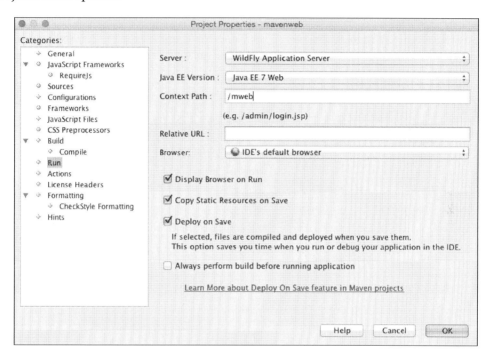

This page displays the options that are available to control how an application is deployed and executed.

The first two options allow the server and Java EE version to be configured for the application. When changing the Java EE version, a notification is displayed, indicating that there could be potential problems when changing the versions of Java EE:

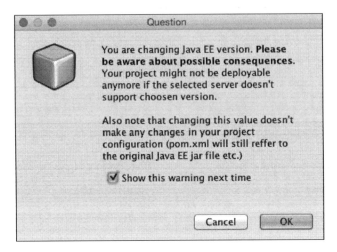

Consider, for example, if you have developed a Java EE 7 application and you change the supported Java EE version to Java EE 5. The Java EE 5 version supports far fewer features than Java EE 7, so your code base will likely be referencing features that do not exist. Care should also be taken when changing the application server as there may be some features that are implemented slightly differently in alternate application servers. NetBeans doesn't warn about changing the server, but the same consideration needs to be thought of when changing the version of Java EE.

Next, we have the context path of the application. You'll remember that, in the previous section, we stated that the default context path of a Maven web application consists of `artifactId` and the version number, but we can easily change it by modifying the name of the generated `.war` file. We also gave an example of how to change the context path in WildFly. Changing the context path setting modifies a web application accordingly for the specified application server. So, for example, if we modify the context path for an application we are deploying to WildFly, the appropriate entries will be changed in the `WEB-INF\jboss-web.xml` file.

The relative URL and browser to use when running the application are configured next. The relative URL specifies the address relative to the context path that will be opened within the browser. So, for example, to open the page, `http://localhost:8080/mweb/manage/console.jsf`, we would set **Context Path** to `/mweb` and **Relative URL** to `/manage/console.jsf`. By default, the operating system's default browser is opened (whether it is Firefox, Safari, Chrome, or something else). The browser can be changed to open inside NetBeans by selecting **Embedded WebKit browser**. With this option selected, a new tab is opened within NetBeans when the application is executed and the page is rendered directly inside the **IDE** tab. For testing mobile applications, a connected Android device or emulator can be selected. For advanced debugging, **Chrome with NetBeans Connector** can be selected.

Finally, within the **Run** options, we can specify what to do when we run and save an application. **Display Browser on Run** tells NetBeans to open up the defined browser when the application is executed. This defaults to on, but if we are developing a JAX-RS application, for example, we may wish to configure this to be off so that a browser window is not opened every time we deploy the application. **Copy Static Resources on Save** enables NetBeans to copy non-Java resource files to the build directory whenever files are saved. This option defaults to on when the **Deploy on Save** option is selected. **Deploy on Save** causes NetBeans to attempt to hot-deploy the application when any files are saved, irrespective of whether they are static (for example, `.html` or `.css`) or Java source code files. This option defaults to on and can help to save considerable time as NetBeans performs a hot deploy (the `.War` file is deployed without having to stop and start the application server). When turning off the **Deploy on Save** option, NetBeans provides a warning about the possible consequences. If this option is turned off, any modified files will not be deployed to the application server and you are manually responsible for deploying your application to the server. For large applications that can take a long period of time to deploy, it is sensible to turn off the automatic deployment on saving files.

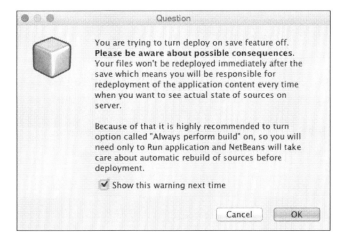

Finally, we can specify that NetBeans will always perform a build before running the application. With this option selected, NetBeans will perform a build of the application before running it. This defaults to off, but can be turned on if, for example, you have a suite of tests that you wish to run as a part of your build before running an application.

# Adding components to a web application

Once a web application project has been created in NetBeans, either as a standard NetBeans project or a Maven project, we can add additional components into the project. These components can be anything from frontend code such as HTML or CSS files, server-rendered code such as JSF pages, or general utility classes such as service locators that can help when developing applications.

Using the **New File** wizard and selecting the **Web** category, we can add the following types of files:

- **JSP**: This creates a new JSP page or JSP segment using either standard or XML-based JSP syntax.
- **JSF Page**: This creates a new JSF page using either Facelets or JSP as the view engine.
- **Servlet**: This provides the ability to create a new servlet. The servlet can be optionally registered within the `web.xml` file or can be registered using annotations.
- **Filter**: This provides the ability to create a new filter. The HTTP request mappings or servlet that apply to the filter can be specified. The filter declaration can optionally be registered within the `web.xml` file.
- **Web Application Listener**: This creates a web listener class, implementing one or more of the following interfaces:
    - Context Listener
    - Context Attribute Listener
    - HTTP Session Listener
    - HTTP Session Attribute Listener
    - Request Listener
    - Request Attribute Listener
- **WebSocket Endpoint**: This provides the ability to create a web socket endpoint at a specific URI.
- **HTML**: This creates an empty HTML page.

- **XHTML**: This creates an empty XHTML page.

- **Cascading Style Sheet**: This creates an empty CSS file.

- **JavaScript File**: This creates an empty Java Script file.

- **JSON**: This creates a JSON file (a default entry is added to show the format of the file).

- **Tag Handler**: This provides the ability to create a tag handler class used for creating JSP tags extending either `javax.servlet.jsp.target.SimpleTagSupport` or `javax.servlet.jsp.tagext.BodyTagSupport`.

- **Tag Library Descriptor**: This creates a tag library descriptor file.

- **Tag File**: It creates a JSP 2.0 tag file.

- **Service Locator**: This creates a class representing an instance of the J2EE Service Locator design pattern.

- **Caching Service Locator**: This creates a class, representing an instance of the J2EE Caching Service Locator design pattern.

- **JSF Pages from Entity Classes**: This creates a set of JSF pages (including page and JPA controllers) based upon a set of the `@Entity` classes.

- **Standard Deployment Descriptor (web.xml)**: This creates a standard `web.xml` file within the project's `WEB-INF` folder.

NetBeans also provides wizards within other categories that allow us to quickly add components into a web application. Some of the file types that can be created within one category are duplicated in different categories. The resultant files that are created are the same, but NetBeans simply puts them into multiple categories to make finding them easier. For example, we can create an HTML file from within either the **Web** or **HTML5** category.

From within the **HTML5** category of the **New File** wizard, we can create the following:

- **HTML File**: This creates an empty HTML page.

- **JavaScript File**: This creates an empty JavaScript file.

- **Cascading Style Sheet**: This creates an empty CSS file.

- **Sass File**: This creates and configures an empty Sass file. We will discuss Sass files and their support in NetBeans later in this chapter.

- **LESS File**: This creates and configures an empty Less file. We will discuss Less files and their support in NetBeans later in this chapter.

- **JSON File**: This creates a JSON file (a default entry is added to show the format of the file).

- **RESTful JavaScript Client**: This creates a JavaScript client with the ability to consume a RESTful web service. This can be a useful starting point for a web application that communicates with the server via web services. We will discuss web services further in the *Chapter 9, Creating and Consuming Web Services*.

- **Gruntfile.js**: This creates a JavaScript Grunt file. This file type is useful for JavaScript developers who wish to perform multiple tasks such as minifying JavaScript and CSS files, running JavaScript tests, and so on. Roughly translated, a grunt file provides similar facilities to an Ant file within the Java ecosystem.

Finally, NetBeans provides facilities for creating components used by different frameworks, namely JSF, Struts, and Spring (although the Spring support is more geared towards Spring 3 than Spring 4).

Within the **JavaServer Faces** category of the **New File** wizard, NetBeans allows us to create:

- **JSF Page**: This creates a new JSF page using either Facelets or JSP as the view engine.

- **JSF Managed Bean**: This creates a new JSF Managed Bean. The name and scope of the bean can be specified and optionally registered within the `faces-config.xml` file for the project.

- **JSF Faces Configuration**: This creates a new `faces-config.xml` file in the `WEB-INF` folder of the project.

- **JSF Composite Component**: This creates a JSF 2 composite component.

- **JSF Pages from Entity Classes**: This creates a set of JSF pages (including page and JPA controllers) based upon a set of the `@Entity` classes.

- **JSF Resource Library Contract**: This creates a JSF Resource Library Contract, optionally creating an initial template. The initial template specifies a header, footer, left and right sidebars, and main content, and can be created using either CSS or HTML tables for the layout.

- **JSF Faces Component**: This creates a new class annotated with `@FacesComponent`.

- **Facelets Template**: This creates a new template, specifying a header, footer, left and right sidebars, and main content. The template can be created using either CSS or HTML tables for the layout.

- **Faces Template Client**: It creates a new JSF Facelets template client based upon an existing template.

Within the **Struts** category of the **New File** wizard, NetBeans allows us to create:

- **Struts Action**: This creates a new Struts action class

- **Struts ActionForm Bean**: This creates a new Struts `ActionForm` bean

 Since 2013, the Apache Struts 1.x has reached its end of life and is no longer officially supported. For more information on Struts 2, refer to `http://struts.apache.org`.

Finally, the **Spring Framework** category of the **New File** wizard allows us to create:

- **Spring XML Configuration File**: This creates an empty Spring configuration file

- **Abstract Controller**: This creates a Spring Web MVC controller class that extends from `org.springframework.web.servlet.mvc.AbstractController`

- **Simple Form Controller**: This creates a Spring Web MVC controller class that extends from `org.springframework.web.servlet.mvc.SimpleFormController`

 Note that although NetBeans allows us to create `AbstractControllers` and `SimpleFormControllers`, these are not necessarily the best way to create controllers in modern versions of Spring. For example, `SimpleFormController` was deprecated in Spring 3.0. For more information on the latest version of the Spring Framework and how to build controllers in its web-based counterpart, Spring Web MVC, refer to `http://spring.io`.

# Creating Spring web applications

So far, we've covered creating web applications, with the primary focus on standard Java EE. NetBeans, however, also provides support for creating Spring applications. The NetBeans support for Spring applications, however, is not completely up to date with the latest version of Spring, so as well as highlighting the features available to a Spring developer, we'll also discuss a more up-to-date way of creating Spring applications in this section.

An empty Spring application in NetBeans can be created using the standard **New Project** wizard we've discussed earlier in this chapter. On the **Frameworks** page of the **New Web Application** wizard, NetBeans allows Spring to be configured.

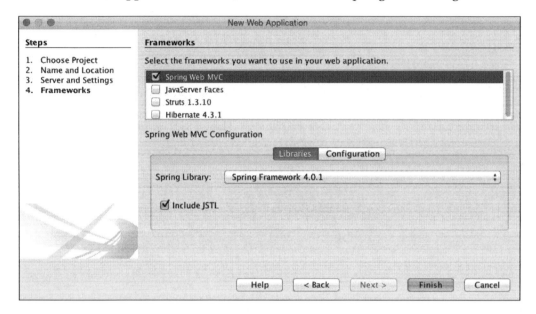

Upon selecting the **Spring Web MVC** framework, NetBeans allows the version of the Spring Library to be configured. NetBeans provides options for using Spring 4.0.1 and Spring 3.2.7, depending upon the version of the Spring Framework that you are targeting. These versions will get updated with new releases of NetBeans. For a more fine-grained control of the versions of NetBeans, and greater control over all of the versions of third-party libraries, a Maven project is recommended rather than a standard web application.

If you are using JSP syntax for a Spring Web MVC application, you'll probably want to check the **Include JSTL** checkbox to add JSTL support to the application. When selected this will add the JSTL libraries into the web application, adding both the `jstl-impl.jar` and `jstl-api.jar` libraries.

Finally, when creating a Spring Web MVC application, the **Configuration** tab allows the name of the dispatcher servlet to be defined along with its servlet mapping.

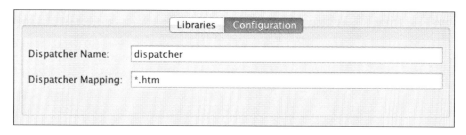

In the preceding screenshot, the dispatcher servlet is called `dispatcher` and has a mapping of `*.htm`. NetBeans creates the relevant sections within the application's `web.xml` file to support Spring:

```
<servlet>
    <servlet-name>dispatcher</servlet-name>
    <servlet-class>
        org.springframework.web.servlet.DispatcherServlet
    </servlet-class>
    <load-on-startup>2</load-on-startup>
</servlet>
<servlet-mapping>
    <servlet-name>dispatcher</servlet-name>
    <url-pattern>*.htm</url-pattern>
</servlet-mapping>
```

NetBeans creates that classic Spring structured application creating a sample view (`index.jsp`) within the `WEB-INF/jsp` folder of the application. An application context file for the dispatcher servlet is created at `WEB-INF/dispatcher-servlet.xml` (the name here depends upon the name of the dispatcher servlet, for example, if we'd defined the dispatcher servlet to be called `myapp`, the corresponding configuration file would have been named `WEB-INF/myapp-servlet.xml`). Finally, an application context XML file is created at `/WEB-INF/applicationContext.xml` where Spring beans can be defined.

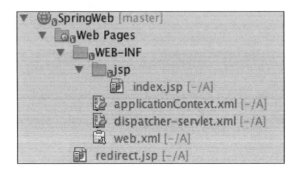

# Changing the version of Spring used

When creating a web application with Spring support, NetBeans provides the options of using Spring 4.0.1 or Spring 3.2.7. Given that the Spring Framework is constantly being upgraded with new features and new fixes (for example, Spring 4.2 has now been released), we would probably want to use the latest version of Spring within an application. How can we do this? If we're using Maven, we can simply change the versions of the libraries we wish to use within the `pom.xml` file. If we're developing a NetBeans web application, however, we need to update the library that defines all of the Spring `.Jars` and dependencies.

To access the libraries used within the application, we must access the project's **Properties**. This is achieved by right-clicking on the project within the **Projects** window and selecting **Properties**. On the **Properties** screen, selecting **Libraries** from the list of **Categories** displays all the libraries used within the application.

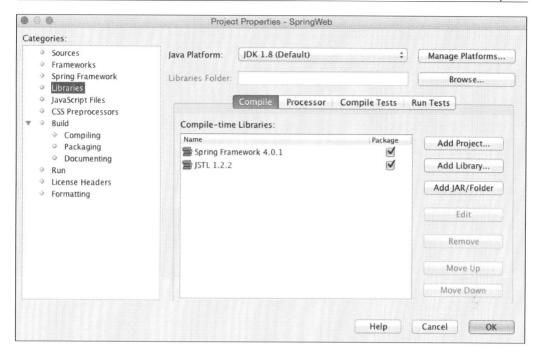

Within the **Project Properties** window, we can add new dependencies to a project (this is not specific to web projects, but can be done on any type of NetBeans project). We can add a project, a library, or a .Jar file/folder as a dependency. This works similar to the way Maven projects use dependencies so that we can have one project depending upon some other code, which is possibly written by a third party altogether.

For example, if we create a MyWebApp project and add a dependency to the MyEJBApp project, we could define a set of EJBs within the MyEJBApp project and access them from MyWebApp.

To change the version of a framework being used by an application, we have two choices:

- Create a new library for the new version of the framework and set that as a dependency instead of the original library being used

- Edit the existing library and change the set of .Jar files references within it to those of the new version of the library

The choice of options here depends on whether the changes to the library are significant and whether we'll possibly need to use the old version of the framework. In the case of Spring, we have two libraries defined within NetBeans. We have the Spring 4.0.1 and Spring 3.2.7 library. The creators of NetBeans decided that when writing a Spring application, we would want to target the application at either Spring 3 or Spring 4. In this case, we can simply add the Spring 3 or Spring 4 library to an application to add the required support. Since its quite likely that we may want to create different applications, targeting different versions of Spring, in this case, we would probably be better off updating one of the existing Spring libraries rather than creating a new one. For example, we could change the Spring 4.0.1 library to reference Spring 4.2.0 (the latest version). This way, we still have two Spring libraries, with one targeting Spring 3 and the other, Spring 4.

So, how do we update a library? Within the **Libraries** section of the project's properties, we must select the library to update and then click on the **Edit** button. This causes the **Customize Library** dialog to be displayed.

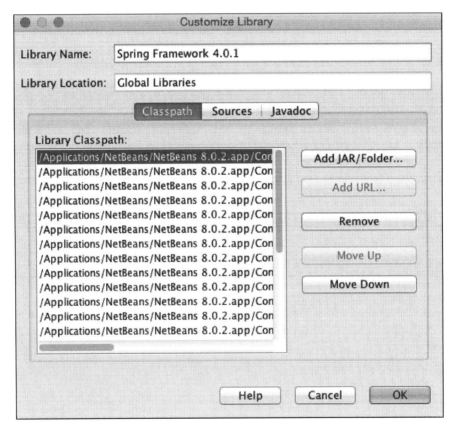

In this dialog, we can select .Jar files from the **Library Classpath** list and click on the **Remove** button to remove them from the library.

> The **Library Classpath** list allows multiple .Jar files to be selected at one time and then removed or moved up/down.

Once we've removed all of the old versions of a library, we can click on the **Add JAR/Folder...** button and browse for the updated version of the library's .Jar files.

If the order of the .Jar files in the library is important (for example, if we always want a particular .Jar file to be accessed before another), we can change the ordering by selecting an entry in the **Library Classpath** list and clicking on either the **Move Up** or **Move Down** buttons.

In addition to specifying the .Jar files within a library, we can also define the sources and JavaDoc used by the library. Defining the source code and documentation for a library helps when writing applications against it as we can debug into the source code and get the pop-up tips, showing how APIs work. It's recommended to enter this information for third-party libraries if at all possible. With the default Spring libraries used within NetBeans, however, this information is not specified as there are no source code or documentation files defined. When updating the Spring libraries (or any other libraries for that matter), it's recommended to update these sections.

Finally, if the version of the library has changed (for example we've upgraded from Spring 4.0.1 to Spring 4.2.0), we can change the library name appropriately.

# Spring application development shortcuts

After creating a Spring application, is there any other support that NetBeans provides to make development easier?

As discussed earlier, the **New File** wizard in NetBeans allows us to create both controllers (based upon AbstractController and SimpleFormController). These two options do a little more than creating new classes. Of more interest, however, is the ability to create new Spring XML configuration file(s).

When using XML configuration files for Spring, it's a best practice to store different facets in different configuration files. For example, all the database-related beans would be stored in one configuration file, while all the web-related beans would be stored in a different configuration file. Each configuration file within a Spring application can make use of different Spring namespaces. These allow us to define what we can specify within the XML file. Getting the namespaces correct within XML files is critical, and can be prone to errors when entered manually. Fortunately, the **New File** wizard provides the option to select which Spring namespaces are required when creating an XML configuration file.

On the final page of the **New File** wizard when creating Spring configuration files, we are presented with a list of Spring namespaces from which we can choose those that are required for the new file.

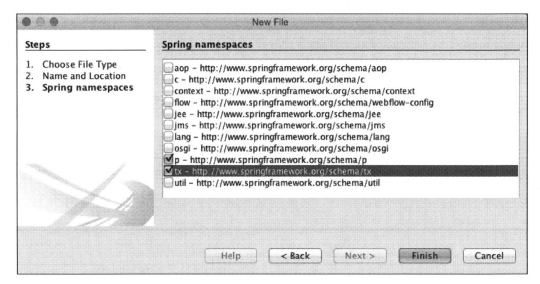

Upon completing the wizard, the XML configuration files are created with the specified namespaces defined:

```
<?xml version="1.0" encoding="UTF-8"?>
<beans xmlns="http://www.springframework.org/schema/beans"
  xmlns:xsi="http://www.w3.org/2001/XMLSchema-instance"
  xmlns:p="http://www.springframework.org/schema/p"
  xmlns:tx="http://www.springframework.org/schema/tx"

  xsi:schemaLocation="http://www.springframework.org/schema/beans
```

```
    http://www.springframework.org/schema/beans/spring-beans-4.0.xsd
    http://www.springframework.org/schema/tx
    http://www.springframework.org/schema/tx/spring-tx-4.0.xsd
"> 

</beans>
```

Once we've created a configuration file, we can use the *Ctrl + Insert* keyboard shortcut to create a reference to a new bean within a file.

 Right-clicking within a Spring configuration XML file doesn't display a pop-up menu to insert code like you would see in a Java source code file, so in this instance, the *Ctrl + Insert* keyboard shortcut is a good one to remember.

Upon selecting the **Declare Spring Bean** option, the **Declare Spring Bean** dialog is displayed in which you can enter the ID and class of the bean to be declared:

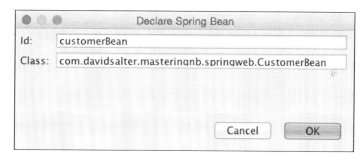

Selecting the **OK** button adds the bean definition to the configuration file:

```
<bean id="customerBean"
    class="com.davidsalter.masteringnb.springweb.CustomerBean"/>
```

# Modern Spring development

In the previous sections, we've seen how we can use NetBeans to create Spring Web MVC applications. We also saw how we can use Maven dependencies or edit the project's libraries to change the versions of Spring being used.

With the recent versions of Spring, the trend has been to move away from configuration stored within context XML files and to use annotations instead. The current version of NetBeans doesn't provide any wizards to allow us to rapidly create applications conforming to this pattern, but does, as you would expect, allow us to develop these types of applications.

So, how do we create a Spring application in a "modern" way? We could simply create a new Maven project and define all our dependencies. This would certainly work and would provide excellent control over exactly what libraries and what versions of libraries to use. An alternative, however, would be to use the Spring Initializr at `http://start.spring.io`.

Although not NetBeans-specific, the Spring Initializr provides rapid support for creating Spring applications as Maven projects that can then be loaded directly into NetBeans.

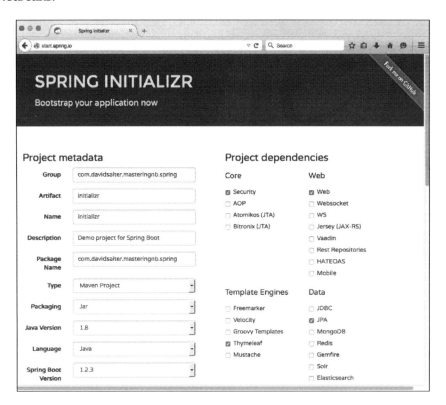

Spring Initializr provides different options, allowing the definition of a project to be specified along with details of which Spring aspects are required (for example, web, security, template engines). Upon completion, a zipped archive can be downloaded that includes a Maven project that can be opened directly within NetBeans. The downloaded application uses Spring Boot to provide access to the latest Spring technologies.

For more information on Spring Boot, refer to
`http://projects.spring.io/spring-boot/`.

# Enhancing Spring Boot support

Out of the box, NetBeans provides fantastic support for Maven applications, but very little support for Spring Boot applications.

Within Spring Boot, a lot of application configuration can be achieved by editing values in the `application.properties` file. For example, this file can specify the database connection details for an application, or the default port that the embedded Tomcat server uses.

NetBeans allows us to edit this file as a simple text file. This, however, doesn't provide any advanced editing such as autocomplete support as the base NetBeans product has no knowledge of Spring Boot. Fortunately, we can add support for editing Spring Boot configuration files by installing the **Spring Boot Configuration Support** plugin. To install this plugin, browse to the project's home page at `http://keevosh.github.io/nb-springboot-configuration-support/` and click on the **Download** link to download the latest plugin to your local system.

At present this plugin is not available via the NetBeans Update Center, so it has to be downloaded and installed manually.

Next, open up the NetBeans plugins by selecting **Tools** and then **Plugins** from the main NetBeans menu. Click on the **Downloaded** tab and then the **Add Plugins...** button to locate the downloaded file. The downloaded file will be called something like this: `nb-springboot-configuration-support-1.0.nbm`

Click on the **Install** button to complete the installation. At this point, NetBeans may ask to restart the system.

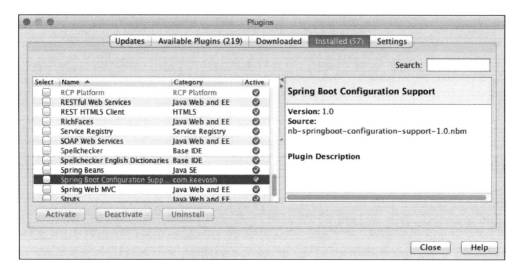

Once the **Spring Boot Configuration Support** plugin has been installed, pressing *Ctrl* + spacebar within an `application.properties` editor window will display autocompletion help, as shown in the following screenshot:

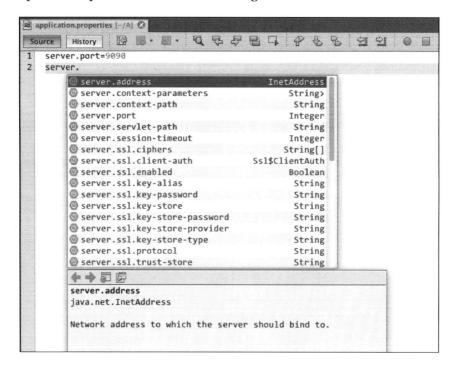

# CSS preprocessors

When developing web applications, we typically style applications using CSS. It gives us advantages when developing HTML in that the style of our applications is kept separate from the markup for a page, thus allowing us to easily change the styling of an application without modification to the page itself.

Unfortunately, CSS is a fairly simple rudimentary language and can, for example, lead us to the duplication of definitions. Consider the case where we wish to declare several classes with the same color font:

```
.main_text {
  color: #ff0000;
}

.sidebar_text {
  color: #ff0000;
}
```

In these two classes, we've had to duplicate the color value (#ff0000) twice. If we wanted to change this to, say, #0000ff, we'd need to change it in multiple places in the CSS file. An even bigger problem would be if we needed to change this color depending upon some other trigger. Using CSS, it would become terribly complex and error-prone to achieve these scenarios.

Fortunately, NetBeans allows us to use the CSS preprocessors—Less and SASS— which will allow us to overcome these problems. Both these CSS preprocessors enhance what we can do with CSS by adding features such as variables, mixins, and functions, allowing us to maintain CSS in a much simpler way. CSS preprocessors take an input file, perform some processing, and then generate a standard CSS file.

> For more information on Less, refer to http://lesscss.org, and for more information on SASS, visit http://sass-lang.com.

To give an example on why we may want to use a preprocessor instead of CSS, let's take a look at a simple scenario described earlier, but using Less instead of plain CSS. Using Less, we can define our `.main_text` and `.sidebar_text` classes as:

```
@CompanyStyleColor: #ff0000;
.main_text {
  color: @CompanyStyleColor;
}

.sidebar_text {
  color: @CompanyStyleColor;
}
```

This is a fairly simple example, but shows the power of the Less CSS preprocessor. The color used within the `.main_text` and `.sidebar_text` classes is defined in a `@CompanyStyleColor` variable. Changing the value of this variable (in one single place) would change all the references to it within the CSS file.

We said earlier that a CSS preprocessor takes an input file and then generates standard CSS. How is this configured within NetBeans?

# Configuring Less and SASS in NetBeans

In order to configure NetBeans so that it use Less and SASS, we first need to ensure that our chosen preprocessor is installed correctly. Less is typically installed as a NodeJS module, whereas SASS is installed via a Ruby gem. A thorough description of NodeJS and Ruby gems is outside the scope of this book, however, the installation process for both of these products is straightforward and described in detail on each of the project's sites.

 For Less installation details, refer to `http://lesscss.org/usage/index.html`, and for SASS installation details, visit `http://sass-lang.com/install`.

To configure NetBeans, we need to access the **Miscellaneous** options from the NetBeans **Preferences** main menu option. Within this screen, we must access the **CSS Preprocessors** tab, as shown in the following screenshot:

Within this tab, there are the options to configure both the Sass path and Less path. These must specify the full path to Sass and Less, respectively. The **Browse** and **Search** buttons can be used to help locate your installation of the appropriate preprocessor if you are unsure of its location. To the right of the dialog are two links—**Install Sass** and **Install LESS**. Clicking on these links opens up your default browser at the installation page for Sass and Less.

For each preprocessor, there are also two checkboxes—**Open Output on Error** and **Generate extra information (debug)**. When a Sass or Less file is saved within NetBeans, it is automatically compiled into the corresponding CSS. If any errors occur during the compilation stage, the NetBeans **Output** window will automatically be opened if the **Open Output on Error** checkbox is selected.

If the **Generate extra information (debug)** option is selected, then a CSS .map file will be created when the Sass or Less file is compiled. The .map file allows the Chrome Developer Tools to edit the source Sass or Less file instead of the generated CSS file when debugging through Chrome. We'll see an example of this shortly.

# Configuring Less and Sass on a project basis

Once we've configured NetBeans and told it where the executables are for the CSS preprocessors, we need to configure a project by defining which preprocessor to use and where the source and destination files are. This is achieved within the **Project Properties** dialog, which is accessible by right-clicking on a project in the **Projects** window and selecting the **Properties** option. Selecting the **CSS Preprocessors** category allows us to configure the project.

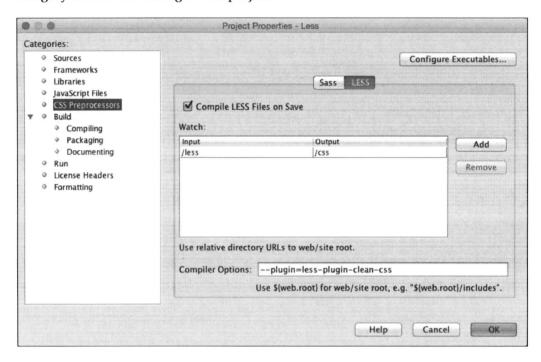

In this dialog, the first button that we see is the **Configure Executables...** button. Clicking on this button takes us to the **CSS Preprocessors** tab within the NetBeans **Options** dialog, as discussed earlier in this chapter. If NetBeans is already configured with the locations of the Sass and Less executables, this option can be ignored.

Next, NetBeans provides two tabs, **Sass** and **LESS**, where we can configure how NetBeans interacts with these file types. Each of these tabs offers the same functionality except for the different preprocessors, so let's take a look at the **LESS** tab. The first option, **Compile LESS Files on Save**, instructs NetBeans to compile any configured Less files when they are saved. This means that every time you save a Less file, the corresponding CSS file is generated along with the debug .map file if this is configured within the NetBeans options.

The **Watch** section allows us to configure which folders contain input LESS files and where to store the generated CSS file after compilation. The default options here are to store LESS files in a folder called /less and to store the generated CSS files in the /css folder. Additional folders can be configured using the **Add** and **Remove** buttons. These folders are relative to the web application's root folder.

Finally, any compiler options for Sass or Less can be configured within the **Compiler Options** edit box. In the preceding screenshot, the compiler options instruct NetBeans to use less-plugin-clean-css when compiling Less files. This plugin has the effect of minimizing the generated CSS.

Given the preceding configuration, if we create a Less file — \less\site.less, when the file is saved, a corresponding CSS and .map file will be created as \css\site.css and \css\site.css.map, as shown in the following screenshot:

We can use the Less file \less\site.less as an example:

```
@Red:    #f00;
@Green:  #0f0;

@Bold:  700;
@Light: 100;

@CompanyStyleFontColor:@Green;
@CompanyStyleFontWeight:@Light;

h1 {
    color: @CompanyStyleFontColor;
    font-weight: @CompanyStyleFontWeight;
}
```

Here's the HTML:

```
<!doctype html>
<head>
    <link rel="stylesheet" href="css/site.css">
</head>
<body>
    <h1>The Less preprocessor made me narrow and green!</h1>
</body>
</html>
```

We can see exactly how the Less file is compiled into a CSS file, which has the simple effect of changing the `<h1>` element's color and weight.

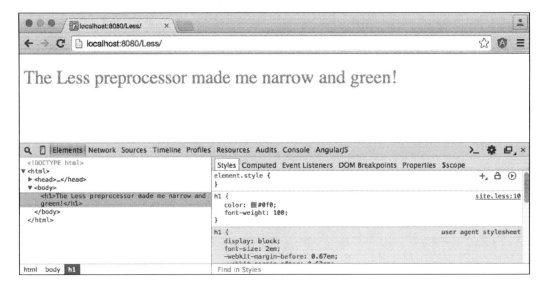

The important thing to spot here, however, is that because we told NetBeans to generate debug information, a `.map` file was created. This `.map` file allows the Chrome Developer Tools to enable editing of the source Less file rather than the generated CSS file. The following screenshot, for example, shows that the styles for the `<h1>` element are defined within the `site.less` file at line 10:

```
Styles | Computed  Event Listeners  »
element.style {                        +,  🔒  ⊙
}

h1 {                                    site.less:10
    color: ▩ #0f0;
    font-weight: 100;
}
```

 Remember, when editing web application styles using an external tool such as the Chrome Developer Tools or from within NetBeans itself, any changes made to the CSS file will be lost when the Less or Sass files are compiled. When using Less and Sass, only make changes to the source files and not the generated CSS files.

# Creating CSS rules

Within a CSS file, sometimes there is a need to define styles for the nested `<div/>` elements. Consider the following HTML:

```
<div class="header">
  <h1>Header</h1>
  <div class="content">
    <h1>Content Header</h1>
  </div>
</div>
```

If we wanted to define the styling for the `<h1/>` element within the Content Header, we could add a CSS rule:

```
.content h1 {
  // Some styling
}
```

Although this is a pretty simple example, it illustrates the cascading nature of CSS and how we can declare selectors built up from more than a single class name or ID.

Within NetBeans, we can invoke the **Css Rule** code generator (by right-clicking inside a CSS file or selecting the *Ctrl + Insert* keyboard shortcut) to help us create this type of CSS.

Upon selecting this option, the **Style Rule Editor** dialog is displayed:

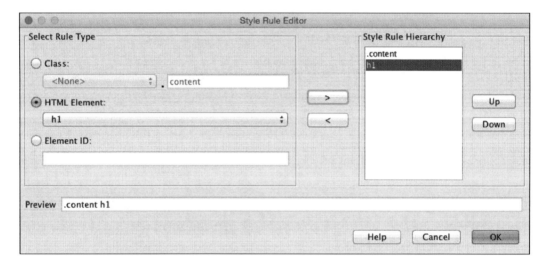

In this dialog, we can add either one or more of the following rules:

- **Class**: This adds a CSS class rule, for example, `.content`.

- **HTML Element**: This adds an HTML element rule, for example, `h1`.

- **Element ID**: This adds an HTML element ID rule, for example, `#submitButton`. Note that it is not necessary to add the # for an ID as NetBeans will automatically add this.

The rules that are created are displayed towards the right hand side of the dialog within the **Style Rule Hierarchy** list. From within this list, we can reorder the style rules by selecting a rule and clicking on either the **Up** or **Down** buttons. Selecting the **OK** button creates the specified style rule within the open CSS, Less, or Sass file.

# Adding JavaScript to a web application

So far in this chapter, we've seen how to create both standard Java EE web and Spring Web MVC applications and how to use CSS preprocessors. To complete our look at creating web applications, let's now turn to JavaScript and see what support does NetBeans offer.

The majority of modern web applications are now developed using some sort of JavaScript framework. This ranges from adding simple scripts to a page to enhance the user experience to developing complex **single-page applications** (**SPAs**) entirely in JavaScript.

On any web project, NetBeans provides support to add different JavaScript frameworks into the application. From within the **Project Properties** page, the **JavaScript Files** category lists a huge number of JavaScript frameworks and libraries that can easily be added to your applications.

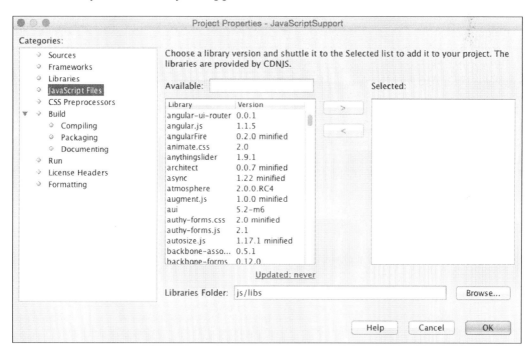

The first list displays all of the JavaScript libraries that are available. To add a library into your application, simply select it and click on the > button to move it into the selected list. By default, all the selected libraries will be copied into the js/libs folder of your web application.

The first time the **JavaScript Files** property page is displayed, the **Updated: never** label is displayed underneath the list of available libraries. Although not obvious, this link can be clicked to refresh the list of available libraries. It's recommended to update this list of libraries periodically to ensure the latest versions of the libraries are available for use. Updating the libraries can take a few minutes though, so be prepared to wait as you can't add and remove libraries into your application while the update is proceeding.

This technique provides an excellent way of quickly adding JavaScript into an application.

# Checking JavaScript files

Given the nature of JavaScript as a dynamic language, it's easy to make errors in JavaScript code that don't get caught when your Java web applications are compiled and built. For anyone working with JavaScript within a web application, NetBeans provides support for the popular JSLint tool. This tool examines JavaScript code and reports code violations, and is an essential tool when developing with JavaScript in a NetBeans web application.

To install JSLint support, access the **NetBeans Plugins** page from the main menu and ensure that the **JSLint** plugin is installed. Once installed, you can right-click on a JavaScript file and select the **JSLint** option. All the code violations are then flagged within the gutter of the JavaScript file as a warning triangle, as shown in the following screenshot; hovering the mouse over any of the violations provides a tooltip showing further details:

```
37        Expected 'function' at column 5, not column 1. (Column: 1)
          function minErr(module, ErrorConstructor) {
              ErrorConstructor = ErrorConstructor || Error;
              return function() {
```

# Summary

In this chapter, we started by looking at how to create web projects with NetBeans and saw the differences between NetBeans and Maven web applications. We saw how easy it is to add different components to web applications using NetBeans, and how we can easily change a web project's run options, including its context path.

After looking at Java EE web applications, we looked at creating Spring Web MVC applications, and saw how we can quickly create Spring Boot applications and start developing them within NetBeans using Spring Initializr.

Finally, we looked at some of the tools NetBeans offers for styling via CSS and CSS preprocessors. We also learned to add different JavaScript frameworks into our applications.

In the next chapter, we'll continue looking at web applications, but our focus will move onto web services, where we'll see how to create and consume web services from within NetBeans.

# 9
# Creating and Consuming Web Services

In the world of enterprise computing, communication between different servers has typically been used for data interchange so that clients can request services offered by third-party servers. With the mobile revolution, this transferring of information between computers and making remote requests for information has become common in the mobile world as well.

Consider the simple weather application on your mobile device. Typically, this will obtain its location as a latitude and longitude and will then invoke a remote server to obtain the weather information before displaying it to you. There's no way that your mobile device can forecast the weather for your current location, let alone for where you're vacationing next week. This is where web services come into play.

Originally, data interchange between client and server used proprietary technologies such as **Common Object Request Broker Architecture (CORBA)** or **Remote Method Invocation (RMI)**. These worked fine when everything was written in the same framework by the same team, but as data interchange became more common, it became clear that open standards were required. This gave birth to **Simple Object Access Protocol (SOAP)**.

SOAP defines a protocol for exchanging data using XML for the data format and typically HTTP for transport (although other transport mechanisms such as SMTP or JMS can also be used to implement SOAP). It is one of the dominant protocols for information exchange.

Around the year 2000, the RESTful architectural style was coined as a set of guidelines and best practices for creating scalable web services that would offer an alternative to SOAP. As with SOAP, **Representational State Transfer (REST)** typically operates via HTTP to transmit information between client and server devices. REST, however, is free to use whatever data format it likes, and typically, REST web services use either XML or JSON to transmit data. Transmitting JSON data via HTTP is now the de-facto standard for modern web applications due to the ease and popular modern JavaScript frameworks that can easily consume JSON data into native objects.

In this chapter, we'll be looking at both SOAP and REST web services. In particular, we'll look at:

- Creating SOAP web services from scratch
- Creating SOAP web services from WSDL
- Consuming SOAP web services
- Managing SOAP web services
- Creating RESTful web services

# Creating web services

As you'd expect, NetBeans provides a set of wizards allowing you to easily create and test SOAP-based web services. Since web services are typically available via the Internet, creating a web service requires a Java web application; this can be either a standard NetBeans web application or a Maven web application, depending upon your choice of technologies.

Once we have a web application, the NetBeans **New File** wizard provides several options for creating web services:

- **Web Service**: This option creates an empty Java EE (JSR-109) web service. This is the simplest way to create a new empty SOAP web service.
- **Web Service From WSDL**: This creates a SOAP web service based upon a supplied **Web Service Definition Language (WSDL)** file. WSDL allows us to easily define SOAP-based web services, including the transport and payload for method and information exchange.

- **RESTful Web Services from Entity Classes**: This creates RESTful web services from a set of one or more classes annotated with `@Entity`.

- **RESTful Web Services from Patterns**: This creates RESTful web services based upon the **Simple Root Resource**, **Container-Item**, or **Client-Controlled Container-Item** patterns, all using the Java API for RESTful services (JSR-311).

- **RESTful Web Services from Database**: This creates RESTful web services from a set of one or more tables in a relational database.

- **RESTful Java Client**: This creates a Java REST client from a REST service defined within a NetBeans project or defined as a NetBeans service.

- **RESTful JavaScript client**: This creates a RESTful web service client using JavaScript instead of Java.

- **Cross Origin Resource Sharing (CORS) Filter**: This creates a CORS filter, allowing resources from different domains to be accessed.

- **JAX RS 2.0 Filter**: This creates a JAX RS filter that has the ability to process or modify request and response headers.

- **JAX RS 2.0 Interceptor**: This creates a JAX RS interceptor that has the ability to process or modify request and response message bodies.

- **Web Service Client**: This creates a Java web service client.

- **Secure Token Service (STS)**: This creates a skeleton web service that can have a secured access.

- **Logical Handler**: This creates a logical handler that has the ability to process or modify the payload of a SOAP message.

- **Message Handler**: This creates a message handler that has the ability to process or modify the entire SOAP message.

We could fill an entire book describing in detail all of these different types of web services, so let's take a few of the more common and describe how NetBeans implements them.

# Creating a SOAP web service

NetBeans allows us to create a simple web service and a web service from a WSDL, but what exactly is the difference?

SOAP web services have an interface definition that is described by WSDL. If you're developing a set of SOAP-based web services to supply to a third party, it's useful to supply the definition of a web service, its WSDL, to the third party. This is like supplying a Java interface to your customers. They won't know how you've implemented the interface, but they'll have all the information they need to start developing against your service.

 For more information on WSDL, refer to `http://www.w3.org/TR/wsdl`.

When someone has access to WSDL, they can easily create client applications as they know the methods and payloads that a web service requires.

If, on the other hand, you're creating a web service internally for your own use, or you have some control over the web service's clients, creating a web service first (and not placing so much reliance on WSDL) may be a better option. It's a decision that needs to be made before implementing a web service—do I need to create WSDL first or last?

 Note that whenever you supply a WSDL to third parties (even to your other applications), you'll want to keep modifications to a web service's WSDL to a minimum so that your changes don't break client applications. If you need to change a WSDL, it's useful to add new services or methods and keep the existing methods constant. Consider creating different versions of a web service where you can phase out older versions over time. Remember, it's not usually feasible for all of your web service clients to be updated at the same time that you deploy a new version of a web service.

# Creating a SOAP web service from scratch

To create a SOAP-based web service from scratch, we use the **Web Service** type within the **New File** wizard:

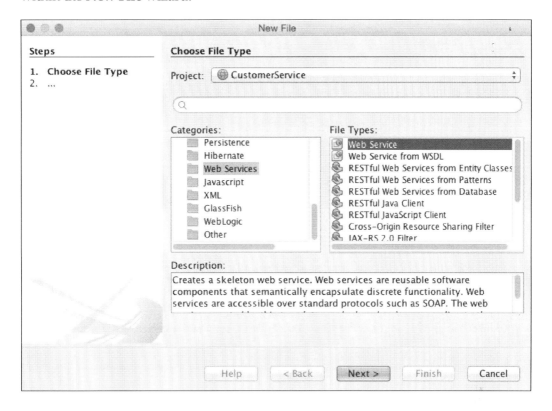

Upon selecting to create a web service, NetBeans displays the **Name and Location** page for the new web service.

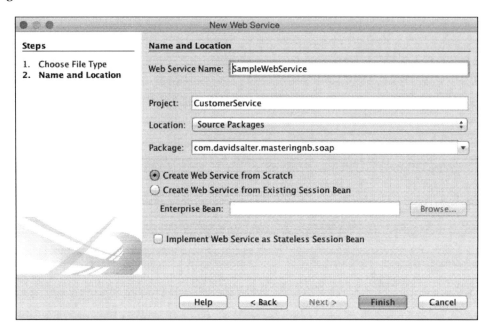

On this page, we can specify the new web service name along with the usual project, location, and package for the created Java source code. We then have several options for creating the web service:

- **Create Web Service from Scratch**
- **Create Web Service from Existing Session Bean**

For both these options, we also have the ability to implement the web service as a stateless session bean.

Taking the first option and creating a web service from scratch, NetBeans creates a simple Java class annotated with @WebService. A sample method is defined within the class to indicate how to declare web service operations within the class:

```
@WebService(serviceName = "SampleWebServiceFromScratch")
public class SampleWebServiceFromScratch {

    /**
     * This is a sample web service operation
     */
    @WebMethod(operationName = "hello")
    public String hello(@WebParam(name = "name") String txt) {
```

```
        return "Hello " + txt + " !";
    }
}
```

If the web service is created from scratch and we have configured it to be
implemented as a stateless session bean, NetBeans simply adds the @Stateless
annotation onto the class:

```
@WebService(serviceName = "SampleStatelessWebService")
@Stateless()
public class SampleStatelessWebService {
```

The second option for creating a web service is from an existing session bean. When
this option is selected, NetBeans displays a list of all the session beans within the
currently open projects, allowing one to be selected as the basis for the web service.

Upon selecting a bean, a web service class is created. Within the class, a reference to
the @EJB is stored and operations are created for each method on the EJB, as shown
in the following code fragment:

```
@WebService(serviceName = "SampleWebServiceFromEJB")
public class SampleWebServiceFromEJB {
    @EJB
    private WelcomeSessionBean ejbRef;

    @WebMethod(operationName = "sayHello")
    public String sayHello(@WebParam(name = "name") String name) {
        return ejbRef.sayHello(name);
    }
}
```

As with the simpler method of creating a web service from scratch, implementing the web service as a stateless session bean simply adds the `@Stateless` annotation onto the web service class.

Once we've created a web service, we need to add operations into it to make it useful to consumers. As can be seen from the previous examples, operations within a web service class are simply public methods annotated with the `@WebMethod` annotation whose parameters are annotated with `@WebParam`. As you'd expect, NetBeans provides help here to quickly add web service operations into a web service class.

Right-clicking within the body of a web service class and selecting the **Insert Code** option provides the **Add Web Service Operation...** facility.

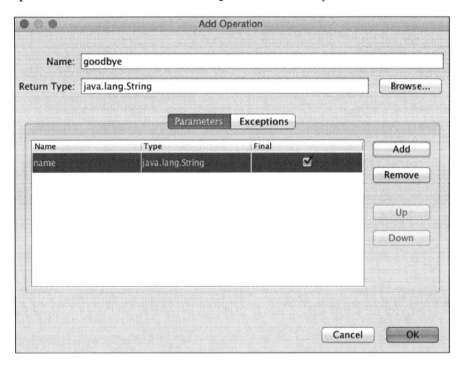

From within the **Add Operation** dialog, we can add new web service operations, specifying their names and return types. For each operation, we can define a set of parameters again, specifying their name and type, and also whether the parameter is declared as `final` or not. Finally, we can specify any exceptions that may be thrown from the operation. Upon completing the **Add Operation** dialog, an empty web service operation is added to the web service as defined:

```
@WebMethod(operationName = "goodbye")
public String goodbye(@WebParam(name = "name") final String name)
            throws UnsupportedOperationException {
```

```
    //TODO write your implementation code here:
    return null;
}
```

From here, completing the web service is a matter of implementing the relevant business logic within the newly created method.

# Creating a SOAP web service from WSDL

The final technique for creating a SOAP web service that we will discuss is creating a web service from WSDL. You'll remember from the previous section that we need to house standard web services within a web project. This is the same for web services that are created from WSDL. Once we've opened a web project, we can create a new web service from WSDL again with the **New File** wizard.

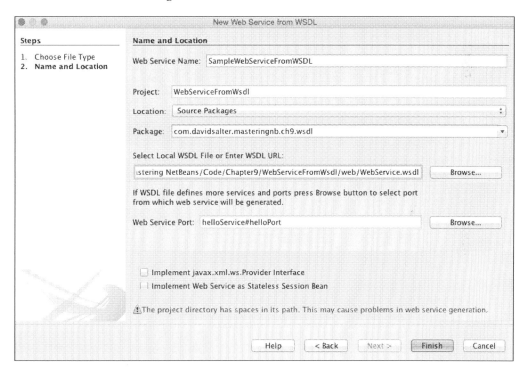

The web service name, project, location, and package are all defined in the same way as they were when creating a web service from scratch. In this case, however, we must specify a WSDL file as the basis of the web service. We can either enter or browse to a local WSDL file (this browses the local filesystem and not local projects) or enter the URL of a WSDL file located elsewhere. Upon entering a valid WSDL, NetBeans will parse the WSDL and select a web service port if only one is found within the WSDL file. If there are multiple web service ports defined, the appropriate **Browse** button can be used to select the required port.

Finally, there are two additional options that can be used to define the web service:

- **Implement javax.xml.ws.Provider Interface**: The generated web service is annotated with the `@WebServiceProvider` annotation, effectively providing a single input to all the web service operations. If this option is not selected, the web service is generated as a standard `@WebService` annotated class.

- **Implement Web Service as Stateless Session Bean**: If selected, annotates the class with the `@Stateless` annotation to declare it as a stateless session bean.

Upon completing the wizard, NetBeans parses the WSDL file and generates code artifacts to allow a web service to be created that exactly matches the WSDL file. For a simple WSDL, the generated code would look something similar to the following (the WSDL used to generate this code is included in the code bundle for this chapter):

```
@WebService(serviceName = "helloService",
  portName = "helloPort",
  endpointInterface =
   "com.davidsalter.helloservice.HelloPortType",
  targetNamespace =
   "http://www.davidsalter.com/HelloService/",
  wsdlLocation =
   "WEB-INF/wsdl/SampleWebServiceFromWSDL/WebService.wsdl")
  @BindingType(value =
   "http://java.sun.com/xml/ns/jaxws/2003/05/soap/bindings/HTTP/")
public class SampleWebServiceFromWSDL {

    public com.davidsalter.helloservice.HelloResponse greetings(
        com.davidsalter.helloservice.HelloRequest helloInputPart) {
        //TODO implement this method
        throw new UnsupportedOperationException("Not impl yet.");
    }
}
```

Since NetBeans is following the WSDL structure exactly, you will see that there are multiple artifacts created to reference the web service port, request, response, and so on. All of these artifacts are standard Java code that can be examined within NetBeans. Since you're not meant to edit these files, however (if you did, your implementation of the web service wouldn't match the WSDL), NetBeans places them outside of the standard **Source Packages** hierarchy in the **Projects** window and places them within a **Generated Sources (jax-ws)** hierarchy:

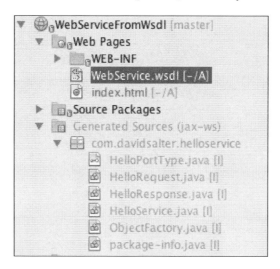

# Managing SOAP-based web services

So far, we've looked at creating SOAP-based web services. NetBeans provides many more tools to manage web services however. For example, while it's a good practice to create test harnesses and full test suites for all the code (including web service implementations), sometime we will want to quickly test a web service and see what parameters is takes and how it works. NetBeans provides tools to test, configure, and edit web services, all from within the project.

Within NetBeans, we can see and manage the web services that are available within a project by viewing the **Web Services** node of the project. Within this node, all of the web services defined within the project are displayed along with all the operations that each web service exposes.

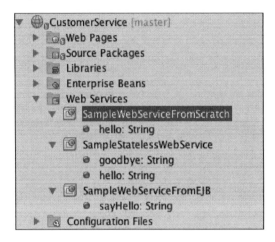

Right-clicking on a web service operation displays a pop-up menu, showing the different ways that the web service can be managed:

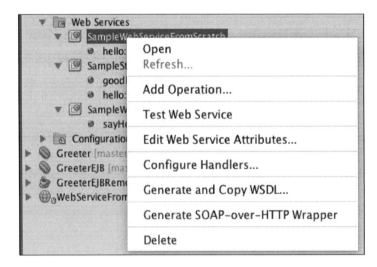

- **Open**: This opens the Java source code editor for the selected operation
- **Refresh...**: This refreshes the selected web service
- **Add Operation...**: This adds a new web service operation to the currently selected web service

- **Test Web Service**: This tests the web service
- **Edit Web Service Attributes…**: This configures the quality of service for the web service
- **Configure Handlers…**: This adds or removes message handlers to the selected web service
- **Generate and Copy WSDL…**: This generates WSDL for the selected web service and optionally places a copy of it within the project's structure at a user-selected location
- **Generate SOAP-over-HTTP Wrapper**: This generates a RESTful web service that wraps the SOAP web service
- **Delete**: This deletes the selected web service

Let's take a look at some of these options.

# Testing web services

Selecting the option to test a web service opens the system's default browser at a test page that lists all the operations in the selected web service. In the following screenshot, you can see that `SampleSatelessWebService` is being tested. This web service can be seen to have two operations—`hello` and `goodbye`.

 The NetBeans project for this web service is included with the code bundle for this book.

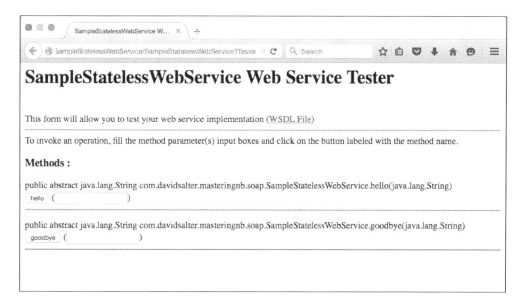

To test a method within the web service, simply enter the required parameters and click on the button corresponding to the web service operation. The web service is then invoked, and the SOAP request and SOAP response are displayed for diagnostic purposes.

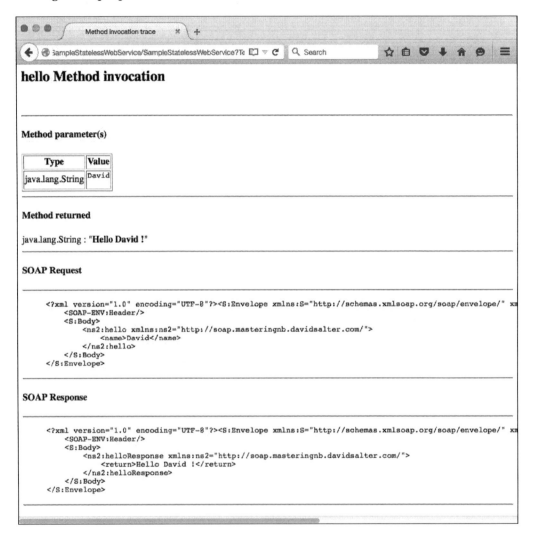

# Message handlers

As stated earlier, a logical handler can access the payload of a message, whereas a message handler can access the entire SOAP message. Message handlers can be created using the **New File** wizard and selecting either the **Logical Handler** or **Message Handler** options. To create a handler, no special options are required within the preceding wizard, other than specifying the package and name of the handler to create.

Upon creating a handler, the class is opened within NetBeans for editing:

```
public class LoggingMessageHandler implements
SOAPHandler<SOAPMessageContext> {

  public boolean handleMessage(SOAPMessageContext messageContext) {
   SOAPMessage msg = messageContext.getMessage();
   return true;
  }
  public Set<QName> getHeaders() {
   return Collections.EMPTY_SET;
  }
  public boolean handleFault(SOAPMessageContext messageContext) {
   return true;
  }
  public void close(MessageContext context) {
  }
}
```

Any required message handling is placed within the `handleMessage` method. The sample message handler illustrated here is included as part of the code bundle for this chapter. We're not going to go into any more detail about message handlers. Our purpose here is to show how they can be created and then configured against a web service within NetBeans.

For more information about message handlers, refer to `http://docs.oracle.com/cd/E13222_01/wls/docs103/webserv_adv/handlers.html`.

Once we've created a handler, we need to configure its use within the web service so that it is invoked correctly. To add the handler, select the **Add Handler** option from the right-click context menu within the **Web Services** node of the project as described previously. The **Configure Message Handlers** dialog will now be displayed.

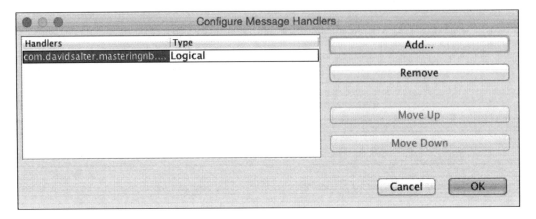

From this dialog, we can add and remove message handlers and modify the order of their invocation. Upon adding one or more handlers to a web service, we can go back to the Java source code for the web service and see that the @HandlerChain has been added onto the web service. This defines the handlers that are to be invoked for a web service within an XML file; in this example, it is SampleStatelessWebService_ handler.xml. This file is located within the same package as the web service itself:

```
@WebService(serviceName = "SampleStatelessWebService")
@Stateless()
@HandlerChain(file = "SampleStatelessWebService_handler.xml")
public class SampleStatelessWebService {
```

If we look at this XML file, we can see that it's a regular XML file that simply lists all of the handlers in the handler chain for the web service:

```
<?xml version="1.0" encoding="UTF-8"?>
<handler-chains xmlns="http://java.sun.com/xml/ns/javaee">
  <handler-chain>
    <handler>
      <handler-name>com.davidsalter.masteringnb.soap.handler.
LoggingLogicalHandler</handler-name>
      <handler-class>com.davidsalter.masteringnb.soap.handler.
LoggingLogicalHandler</handler-class>
    </handler>
  </handler-chain>
</handler-chains>
```

# Managing web services graphically

In addition to the management facilities we've seen so far for SOAP-based web services, NetBeans also provides a graphical editing facility for web services. At the top of a Java source code window for a web service class are the standard **Source** and **History** buttons to display the Java source code and the history of the file. For web services, there is also a **Design** button.

Selecting this button causes the design surface for the web service to be opened. From within this design surface, we can see a graphical representation of the operations available within the web service as well as the sample request and response objects. The functionality available here is the same as when right-clicking on a web service within the **Projects** window, however, the graphical representation makes it easier to see the details of the web service at a glance.

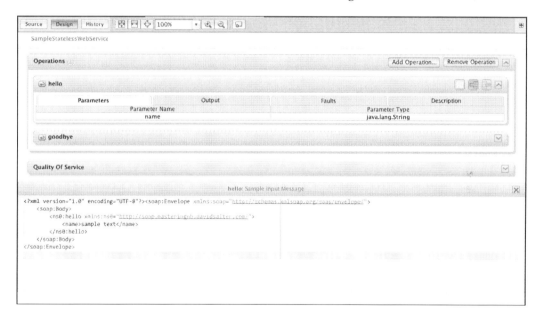

# Consuming SOAP web services

So far, we've looked at how to create SOAP-based web services. Let's now take a look at how we can consume those services from within NetBeans. Unlike web services, web service clients can be used in all sorts of applications whether they are standalone Java desktop applications, or running within an EJB framework, or anywhere in between. To invoke a web service, we first need to define a web service client. A web service client is configured with the WSDL for a web service and therefore, knows all of the web service operations and parameters.

To create a web service client, invoke the **New File** wizard and select **Web Service Client** from the list of **File Types** within the **Web Services** category.

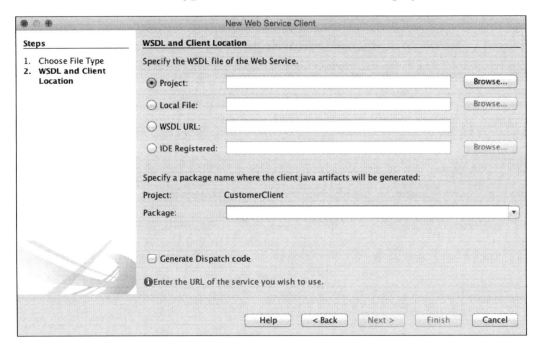

Within the **New Web Services** client dialog, we are provided with four different ways to select a WSDL file:

- **Project**: This allows a WSDL file to be selected by browsing through all of the WSDL files available within the currently open projects in NetBeans.
- **Local File**: This allows the local filesystem to be browsed for a WSDL file.

- **WSDL URL**: This allows a remote URL for a WSDL file to be specified.

- **IDE Registered**: This allows one of the WSDL files supplied with NetBeans to be specified. NetBeans is currently supplied with registered web services from Amazon, Delicious, Flickr, Google, StrikeIron, WeatherBug, Zillow, and Zvents.

 In order to increase your understanding of SOAP-based web services, it's recommended to experiment with public web services and see how they can be consumed from within NetBeans. A good source of public web services can be found at `http://www.webservicex.net` that includes WSDL for different services. For example, the GeoIP lookup service, which maps IP addresses to countries, has a WSDL located at `http://www.webservicex.net/geoipservice.asmx`. Please remember to check any usage conditions though before using any service.

Upon selecting a WSDL file, NetBeans parses the file in a similar fashion to when we created a web service from a WSDL. Here, NetBeans creates classes to be used by client applications though. For our `SampleStatelessWebService` created in the previous sections of this chapter, NetBeans creates several JAX-WS files, which are displayed within the **Generated Sources (jax-ws)** node of the project. As earlier, we're not expected to edit these files, so they are still included within the project, but are displayed separately from our main application classes.

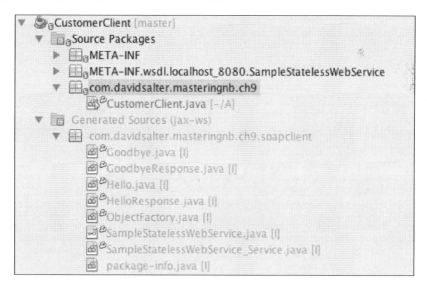

After creating a web service client, we are in a position to invoke the client and therefore, our requested web service. To add code to invoke a web service client, simply right-click within a Java method and select the **Insert Code** and then **Call Web Service Operation** options.

A list of all the operations available to invoke is then displayed within the **Select Operation to Invoke** dialog.

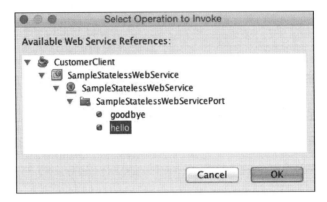

Upon selecting an operation, a new method is created within the currently open Java class. The new operation has the same name as the web service operation being invoked:

```
public class CustomerClient {

    public static void main(String[] args) {
        System.out.println(hello("David"));
    }

    private static String hello(java.lang.String name) {
com.davidsalter.masteringnb.ch9.soapclient.SampleStatelessWebService_
Service service = new com.davidsalter.masteringnb.ch9.soapclient.
SampleStatelessWebService_Service();
        com.davidsalter.masteringnb.ch9.soapclient.
SampleStatelessWebService port = service.
getSampleStatelessWebServicePort();
        return port.hello(name);
    }
}
```

# Creating RESTful web services

In addition to creating and consuming SOAP-based web services, NetBeans also provides sophisticated tools to create and consume RESTful web services. As with a SOAP-based web service, RESTful web services need to be deployed within a web application.

You'll remember from earlier in this chapter that for RESTful web services, we can choose to create from entity classes, patterns, and database tables. Creating RESTful web services is much simpler than SOAP-based web services as all that is required to create the RESTful service is the base entity or database table; we do not need to worry about WSDL file, we simply need to state the source of the data that we wish to expose as a RESTful web service.

Creating a RESTful service for an entity or database table is essentially the same procedure. For each of these cases, a set of @Entity or database tables is selected and then a set of RESTful web services are created to manage the lifecycle of the entities.

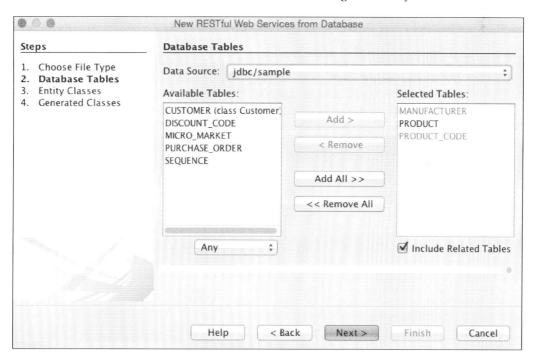

For each `@Entity` or database table, a corresponding ...FacadeREST class is created. For example, in the case of a `Customer` entity, a `CustomerFacadeREST` class is created:

```
@Stateless
@Path("com.davidsalter.masteringnb.rest.customer")
public class CustomerFacadeREST extends AbstractFacade<Customer> {
    @PersistenceContext(unitName = "CustomerRestServicePU")
    private EntityManager em;

    public CustomerFacadeREST() {
        super(Customer.class);
    }

    @POST
    @Override
    @Consumes({"application/xml", "application/json"})
    public void create(Customer entity) {
        super.create(entity);
    }
    // @PUT, @DELETE @GET methods omitted for brevity.
```

> The code supplied for this example is available with the code bundle for this chapter. It's recommended that you download this code and examine it while reading this section in order to understand the workings of the example and the techniques available within NetBeans.

Each of the REST verbs GET, PUT, POST, and DELETE are mapped to corresponding Java methods to expose all of the CRUD functionality for the selected objects via RESTful services.

> For more details on the RESTful approach to web services and the different uses of HTTP verbs, refer to http://en.wikipedia.org/wiki/Representational_state_transfer.

As with SOAP web services, NetBeans provides the ability to manage RESTful web services within a project. When a project contains RESTful web services, a **RESTful Web Services** node is displayed within the **Projects** window. Unlike SOAP-based web services, the number of management options here is limited to opening the Java class that implements the RESTful web service and testing the service. As with SOAP services, testing a RESTful web service causes a browser window to be displayed from within which the web service operations can be exercised.

When creating a RESTful web service from a pattern, we are given the choice of the pattern to use.

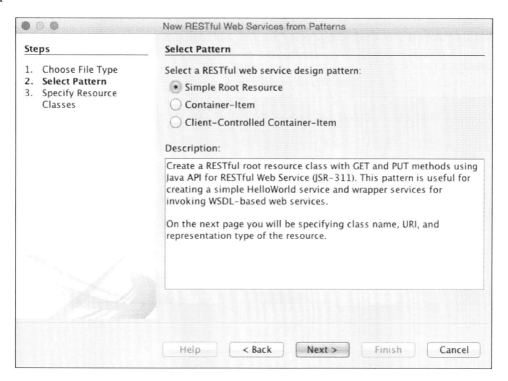

# The Simple Root Resource option

The **Simple Root Resource** option creates a simple REST-based web service where the path to the resource and class representing the resource can be specified along with the MIME type of the data returned to the client. The MIME type can be configured as either `application/xml`, `application/json`, `text/plain`, or `text/html`. For interaction with modern JavaScript web frameworks, `application/json` is probably the most relevant MIME type as JSON objects can be easily consumed by JavaScript as standard JavaScript objects.

This creates a very simple RESTful web service with GET and PUT methods available to clients.

# The Container-Item option

The **Container-Item** option creates a complete set of RESTful web services to access a resource and a collection of resources, for example, a singular customer and a collection of customers. As with the **Simple Root Resource** option, the MIME type can be specified to determine how data is returned to the client.

| | |
|---|---|
| Path: | {id} |
| Container Path: | /Items |
| MIME Type: | application/xml |
| Representation Class: | r.masteringnb.rest.Customer | Select... |
| Container Representation Class: | java.lang.String | Select... |

# The Client-Controlled Container-Item option

The **Client-Controlled Container-Item** option creates a complete set of RESTful web services to access a resource and a collection of resources similarly to the **Container-Item** pattern. With this pattern, however, there is no POST method on the resource, rather resources are created via the PUT method, thereby creating a client-controlled URI resource creation rather than a server controlled URI.

# Summary

In this chapter, we looked at both SOAP and RESTful web services. We saw how NetBeans provides support for creating SOAP-based web services from scratch and also from WSDL files. We saw that we can create RESTful web services from a set of @Entity classes or database tables, or through several patterns. With both SOAP and RESTful web services, we saw how NetBeans provides tools for creating and managing web services. We also learned how we can easily consume SOAP web services, and how JavaScript clients can easily consume RESTful web services.

In the next, final chapter of the book, we'll take a wider look at NetBeans and see how we can create NetBeans plugins and rich client platform applications.

# 10
# Extending NetBeans

NetBeans is developed as a suite of modules. This modular nature of NetBeans is one of the main features of the IDE in that it allows additional modules to be easily written that can provide extra functionality to developers. NetBeans provides a vast amount of functionality as standard; however, there is still a thriving ecosystem in third-party plugins that can provide additional functionality into the IDE. For example, there are plugins that allow NetBeans to interact with NoSQL databases such as MongoDB or modern web frameworks such as NodeJS.

The modular nature of NetBeans also means that NetBeans is ideally suited as a basis for developing desktop applications. The NetBeans IDE is after all a NetBeans Platform application that is tailored to developers' needs. All of the functionality that is required for a modern desktop application is provided by different modules that can equally be used by third-party developers to create standalone applications. You may be wondering though, who wants a desktop application that looks a lot like an IDE. NetBeans provides branding support for Platform applications so they don't need to look like the IDE. Fortunately, developers can tailor NetBeans Platform applications to their own demands — applications can have their own splash screens and about screens; they can have any number of windows in whatever layout is required and can use as much or as little of the framework as required.

In this chapter, we'll take a look at the features offered by NetBeans when creating new plugins and Platform applications. We'll cover the following topics:

- Creating NetBeans plugins
- Creating NetBeans Platform applications

# Creating NetBeans plugins

NetBeans is developed as a very modular IDE with all of the functionality provided by different modules or plugins. As mentioned previously, the majority of the functionality required for day-to-day use of the IDE is already provided with NetBeans, however, we can create additional functionality by creating new plugins. These plugins can then be installed into NetBeans via the Update Center.

To create a new NetBeans plugin, we need to invoke the **New Project** wizard and select the **Module** project type from within the **NetBeans Modules** category.

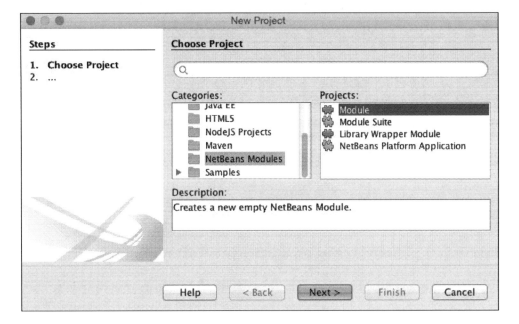

On the **Name and Location** page of the **New Module** wizard, we must specify the standard attributes of a NetBeans project: **Project Name**, **Project Location**, and **Project Folder**. We then have the choice of specifying whether the module is standalone or whether it should be added to a module suite.

A standalone module is a single plugin that can be installed into either the NetBeans IDE or into a NetBeans Platform application (we'll learn more about NetBeans Platform applications later in this chapter). For a standalone module, we must specify the NetBeans Platform that the module will be built against. The default option is to use the current development IDE, but other versions of the NetBeans Platform can be selected by pressing the **Manage...** button. A standalone module is typically used to provide a small piece of functionality that can be distributed on its own for clients to install into a larger application (or NetBeans itself).

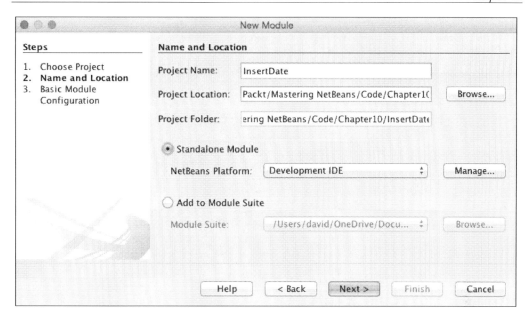

If we wish to develop a module for inclusion into a NetBeans Platform application, we must select the **Add to Module Suite** option. The **Module Suite** dropdown lists all of the module suites (including Platform applications) that are currently open within the IDE. Alternatively, we can browse for previously created module suites by clicking on the **Browse…** button.

The next page of the wizard is **Basic Module Configuration**:

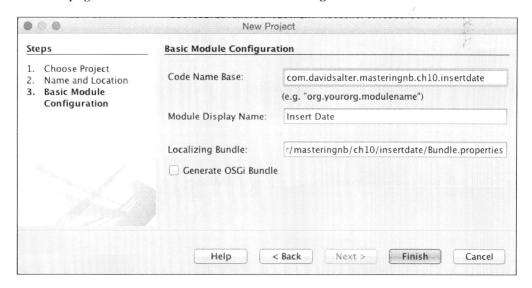

The code name base is a unique string that is used to name your module. As this has to be unique, it's a good idea to use a similar naming scheme as for classes by using a combination of reverse domain name and identifier for the module. For example, in the preceding screenshot, the reverse domain name of `com.davidsalter` is used together with the `masteringnb.ch10.insertdate` identifier.

Finally, we must choose the localization bundle along with, whether we want to create the module as an **open services gateway initiative (OSGi)** bundle or a standard NetBeans module.

> OSGi defines a modular packaging structure for Java modules. Unless you have a specific reason, creating standard NetBeans modules is the recommended approach when creating modules. For more information about OSGi, visit `http://www.osgi.org/Main/HomePage`.

Once we've created a standard NetBeans module, we can add functionality into it, such as code generators, windows, or actions. Using the **New File** wizard, we can create the following types of actions:

- **Action**: This creates an action. An action is something that can be invoked from a user action such as selecting a menu item or clicking on a toolbar button.

- **Window**: This creates a new window that is displayed within the main NetBeans windowing system. The location of the window and its attributes can be defined.

- **Wizard**: This creates a custom wizard that can be invoked from anywhere within the code in the application, or a **New File** wizard that can be invoked from the **New File** command.

- **Options Panel**: This creates a new options panel that is displayed within the **Options** window of the application.

- **File Type**: This creates a new file type by associating a MIME type and a file extension or XML root element so that custom file viewers can be created.

- **Update Center**: This creates a new Update Center for use with the application so that any custom modules used within the application can easily be updated.

- **Installer/Activator**: This creates a class that can install and uninstall the module.

- **Quick Search Provider**: This allows a class to be created that integrates into the NetBeans Platform's quick search functionality so that the search results can easily be provided within an application.

- **JavaHelp Help Set**: This creates a new JavaHelp Help set.

- **Project Template**: This defines a new template that can be added to the **New Project** wizard.

- **Java SE Library Descriptor**: This defines a new library for use within the **Library Manager** window.

- **Code Generator**: This creates a new option on the **Insert Code** pop-up dialog, allowing the code to be added quickly into a file.

- **XML Layer**: This allows the advanced customization of a module to be performed on modules that do not conform to the latest Platform APIs.

- **Java Hint**: This creates a popup Java hint that will be displayed with a Java code file.

- **Layout of Windows**: This allows the layout definition of an application to be modified.

Some of these file types (such as **JavaHelp Help Sets** or **Java SE Library Descriptors**) are more applicable as NetBeans IDE modules, whereas others such as **Actions** and **Windows** are applicable to both custom applications and the NetBeans IDE itself.

Let's take a look at the new **Code Generator** wizard.

 This source code for the `InsertDate` code generator, described in the next section, is available as a part of the code bundle for this chapter.

A **Code Generator** wizard allows us to easily insert snippets of code into a source code file using the **Insert Code** option (*Ctrl + I,* or *Cmd + I* on Mac OS).

When creating a code generator, we need to enter the class name and package that the generated class is to be defined within.

Next, we must specify MIME type. This specifies which files the code generator is applicable to. For Java source code files, MIME type is text/x-java.

Upon completing the wizard, NetBeans creates the required Java source code files and opens the newly created code generator class for editing.

When creating a code generator, we need to access the currently open Java source code to be able to modify it. To do this, we need to add module dependencies to the code generator (remember NetBeans is very modular, so there is naturally a module that allows us to modify the existing source code).

To add dependencies to the project, right-click on the project within the **Projects** window and select **Properties** and then select the **Libraries** category.

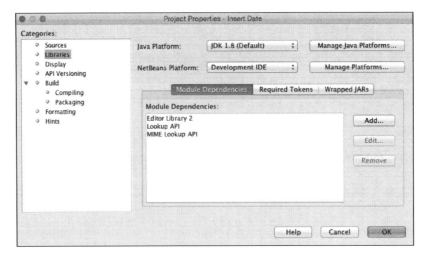

This properties page allows additional module dependencies to be specified. This is where all the dependencies are defined for other modules that provide required functionality for an application. When creating a code generator for modifying source code, we typically need to add dependencies on the Javac API Wrapper, Java Source, and Utilities API modules. Clicking on the **Add...** button displays the **Add Module Dependency** dialog from which dependencies can be browsed and selected.

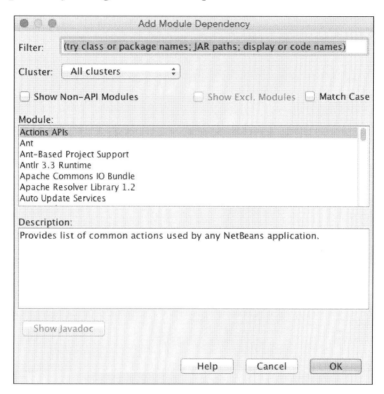

Within a code generator, there are two methods that need to be overwritten to provide functionality. The getDisplayName() method provides the name that is displayed to the user within the **Insert Code** popup:

```
public String getDisplayName() {
    return "Current Date";
}
```

The invoke() method needs to be implemented to perform the code modification. In the case of simply inserting a value, we can use the Swing APIs to insert any string we want. The following code shows how to insert the current date at the current caret location:

```
public void invoke() {
    Document doc = textComp.getDocument();
    try {
        Caret caret = textComp.getCaret();
        int dot = caret.getDot();
        doc.insertString(dot, new Date().toString(), null);
    } catch (BadLocationException ex) {
        Exceptions.printStackTrace(ex);
    }
}
```

If, however, we want to modify the actual Java source code, for example, adding new methods or variables, we can use the Java Source and Javac API Wrappers modules to correctly modify the source code.

For more information on modifying source code, refer to the API documentation at http://bits.netbeans.org/8.0/ javadoc/org-netbeans-modules-java-source/org/ netbeans/api/java/source/package-summary.html.

Upon creating a plugin, we can simply select the **Run** option on the project to open a new instance of NetBeans with the plugin preconfigured. The plugin functionality can then be exercised as required. Alternatively, we can create a .nbm file for the plugin by right-clicking on the project within the **Projects** window and selecting the **Create NBM** menu option. When this is selected, the project is built and a .nbm file is created that can be distributed to other developers.

 It's a good idea to never debug .nbm files within your development instance of NetBeans. If something goes wrong with your .nbm file, you want to keep a stable IDE to debug it; hence it's a good practice to always debug these types of modules in a separate instance of NetBeans.

# NetBeans rich client platform applications

In addition to extending NetBeans by developing custom functionality as plugins, NetBeans can also be used to develop **rich client platform** (**RCP**) applications.

You might be wondering why would you create an application using NetBeans as the foundations of your application, why not just develop it as a Swing application? NetBeans offers many advantages over building a standalone Swing application.

When you've developed desktop application, how many times have you had to write code to handle toolbars or menu items? How many times have you had to write code that allows you to manage windows and allows interaction between different windows? The NetBeans RCP provides all of this functionality and more.

NetBeans provides a basic structure for an application that allows you to get started quickly, so there's no more writing a main() method that creates a JFrame and then creates toolbars and menus and all the other components that you expect to see in a modern desktop application. Additionally, NetBeans provides a modular system where components can easily find and interact with other components. So, for example, you can create componentized functionality within your application, which can then be used by many different components. All of these components can be versioned, giving you a greater control over upgrading your application and ensuring that all the different components work together.

When all of these features are brought together, it's easy to see how much time can be saved by developing a NetBeans RCP application rather than a Swing-based application. That's not to say that you don't use Swing components in your RCP applications, but all of the mundane plumbing has already been written (and is being maintained) by someone else.

Now that we've seen some of the benefits of a NetBeans RCP application, let's see how to create a simple RCP application.

# Creating a NetBeans RCP application

A NetBeans RCP application is created using the **New Project** wizard in a similar fashion to creating many different NetBeans projects. After invoking the wizard, the option to create a **NetBeans Platform Application** project is provided within the **NetBeans Modules** category, as shown in the following screenshot:

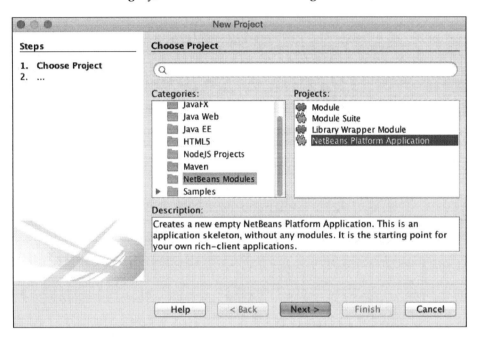

Upon clicking the **Next >** button, we are presented with the standard NetBeans options for specifying **Project Name**, **Project Location**, and **Project Folder**. What's different here, however, is that we can specify NetBeans Platform.

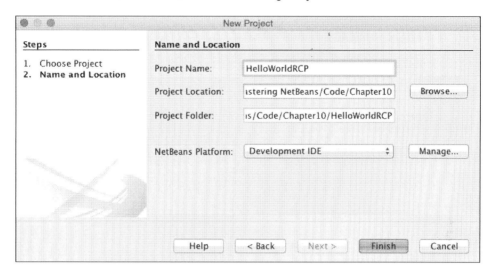

The NetBeans Platform dropdown initially contains only one entry—**Development IDE**. This is where the version of the NetBeans platform used as the basis for applications is defined. The **Development IDE** means the current version of NetBeans that the application is being developed with; this makes things easier as the version of NetBeans used for development is the same as the version running your application.

Selecting the **Manage...** button allows different platforms to be defined that can be used as the basis for RCP applications. Upon selecting the **Manage...** option, the **NetBeans Platform Manager** dialog is displayed, listing all the currently installed platforms. New platforms can be added and removed via the **Add Platform...** and **Remove** buttons. For each installed platform, the name of the platform (**Platform Label**) and location (**Platform Folder**) are displayed along with a list of **Modules**, **Sources**, **Javadoc**, and **Harnesses** used by the platform.

The list of modules shows all of the modules that are available to the platform. This includes things as Editors, the core windowing framework, and the embedded browser. When developing an RCP application, you will typically make use of one or more of these modules.

The source code for a particular platform can be registered along with the corresponding Javadoc in the **Sources** and **Javadoc** tabs. Since the Javadoc is included within the source code for a particular version of a platform, if you register the source code, it is not necessary to also register the Javadoc as this is already taken care of.

Finally, the **Harness** tab allows different build harnesses to be defined.

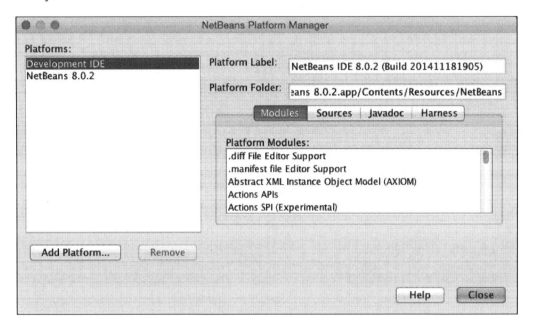

 When adding different platforms on the Mac, the platforms are located within the NetBeans<version>.app/Contents/Resources/ NetBeans folder. Simply browsing to the NetBeans<version>.app folder will not locate the required platform.

Upon creating a NetBeans Platform application, the project is automatically opened within the **Projects** window. Empty projects have no modules defined, but have several important files defined that specify how the project is built and any custom properties or internationalization used by the project.

 The sample application used within the following section is available as a part of the code bundle for this chapter.

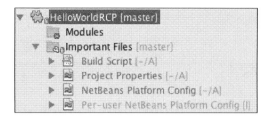

At this stage, we have a fully functional NetBeans Platform application. If we run the application, we see a splash screen (albeit the NetBeans splash screen) and then the application opens up, displaying a main frame with some of the more common menu items contained within it.

# Branding the application

The default settings for a NetBeans Platform application are to use the standard NetBeans splash screen and about screen along with the standard NetBeans icons. These can all be changed to any custom image using the project's branding. To access the project's branding, right-click on the project within the **Projects** window and select the **Branding** menu option.

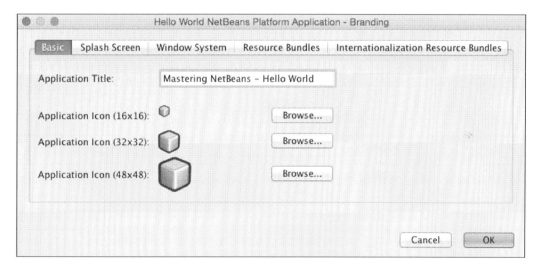

Within this dialog, we are presented with several tabs, on each of which we can set specific information about the application and its appearance.

On the **Basic** tab, we can set the application's title along with the application's icon.

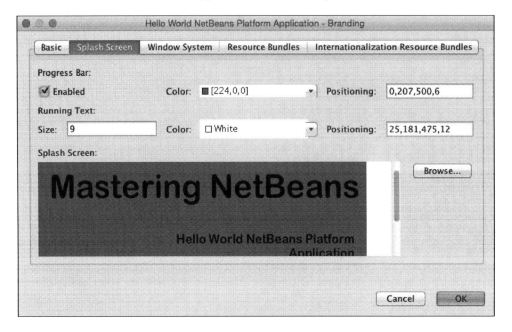

On the **Splash Screen** tab, we can specify whether a progress bar is to be used or not via the **Enabled** checkbox. The color of the progress bar is specified by the first **Color** field ([244, 0, 0] in the preceding screenshot), and its position is defined by the first **Positioning** edit box ([0,207,500,6] in the preceding screenshot). The values for the positioning are in the format: *x position, y position, width, height with the x position* starting from the left and increasing to the right and the y position starting from the top and increasing downward.

Along with a progress bar, messages are displayed showing the status of the application while it loads (for example, specifying that modules are loading or configuration files are being parsed). The size of this text is specified in the **Size** edit box. The color of the text is defined within the second **Color** edit box (**White** in the preceding screenshot) and its location is specified in the second **Positioning** edit box ([25,181,475,12] in the preceding screenshot).

The preceding screenshot illustrated how predefined colors can be used for the progress bar and text (for example, White), or custom colors can be defined by selecting the **Custom** entry from the **Color** dropdown.

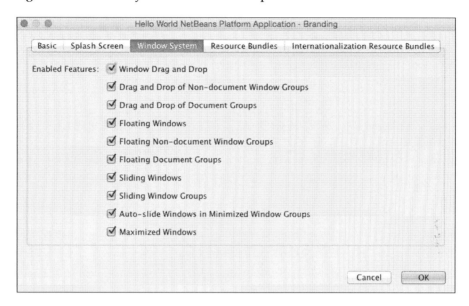

Next, is the **Window System** tab, which allows us to define the windows-specific features that are enabled within the application:

- **Window Drag and Drop**
- **Drag and Drop of Non-document window groups**
- **Drag and Drop of Document Groups**
- **Floating Windows**
- **Floating Non-document Window Groups**
- **Sliding Windows**
- **Sliding Window Groups**
- **Auto-slide Windows in Minimized Window Groups**
- **Maximized Windows**
- **Closing of Non-document Windows**
- **Closing of Document Windows**
- **Closing of Window Groups**
- **Window Resizing**
- **Respect Minimum Size When Resizing Windows**

The final two tabs, **Resource Bundles** and **Internationalization Resource Bundles**, allow us to configure the resource bundles used within an application and internationalize all the resources used within our application.

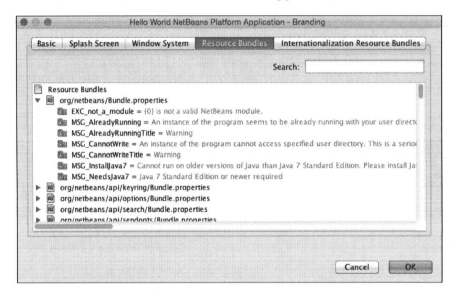

# Application properties

For each NetBeans Platform application, the **Project Properties** window allows us to define which modules are used by the application, how the application is distributed, and what hints are to be available to the application.

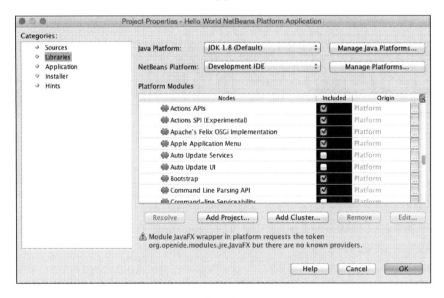

Let's take a look at the different categories of the project's properties:

- **Sources** : This category allows the different modules used by a NetBeans Platform application to be defined. Selecting the **Add** button allows module suites to be selected and configured for use within the current application. Modules that have been previously created as either **Module** or **Module Suite** project types within the **New File** wizard can be selected here.

- **Libraries**: Within this category, the Java platform and NetBeans platform can be specified. Initially, these are set to the current Java platform that is executing the current NetBeans development environment. Upon configuring the Java and NetBeans platforms, different modules that are to be used by the application can be specified. This lists all of the NetBeans modules that are available within the currently selected NetBeans platform. It is, however, possible to add modules from outside the currently selected platform using the **Add Project** and **Add Cluster** buttons.

>  A NetBeans cluster is essentially a directory on disk that contains a set of NetBeans modules.

- **Application**: Within this category, we can define whether a standalone application will be built from the project, or whether a collection of modules that can be loaded into an existing NetBeans Platform application will be built. If a standalone application is to be built, the name of the executable can be specified within the **Branding Name** edit box.

- **Installer**: When packaging an application, installers can be created for different platforms. The license for the application can be specified along with the platforms to create an installer for. Installers can be created for:
  - Windows
  - Linux
  - Max OS X
  - Solaris

- **Hints**: The final category of the project's properties allows us to define what hints are displayed within the source code of the application while it is being developed. This can be configured to use the IDE-wide hints, or a more project-specific set of hints.

# Creating platform application components

In the previous section, we saw how to create a NetBeans Platform application and configure the branding for it. An application isn't very useful though if all it has is a splash screen and some menus.

 The source code for the application illustrated in this section is available as part of the code bundle for this chapter.

As the NetBeans Platform is highly modular, to add components into an application, we need to create additional modules and add these modules into the application. To create a module and automatically add it into the current application, right-click on the modules node for the project and select the **Add New...** option.

Alternatively, selecting the **Add New Library...** option or the **Add Existing...** option will allow any previously created modules to be added as either a library or module.

Upon selecting to create a new module, the **New Module Project** dialog is displayed. As with most of the **New Project** wizards within NetBeans, a project name, location, and folder must be specified first. After specifying these, the **Basic Module Configuration** page is displayed.

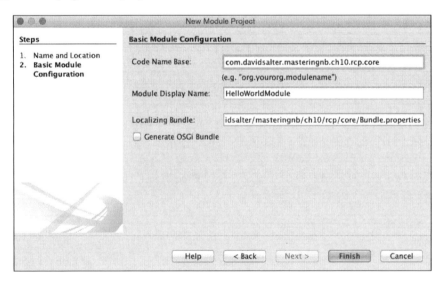

The **Code Name Base** field is used to uniquely identify a module, so typically a combination of package name and module name is used here to ensure that the name is unique. The **Module Display Name** field specifies how the module is displayed within NetBeans, for example, in the following screenshot, we can see that there is a module called **HelloWorldModule** that is being used within **Hello World NetBeans Platform Application**.

Finally, we can specify the localization bundle for the application along with whether we wish to create the bundle as an OSGi bundle or a standard NetBeans module.

Upon creating a module, different functionality can be added to the module using the **New File** wizard. The **Module Development** category allows us to add platform-specific items such as windows, wizards, or file types.

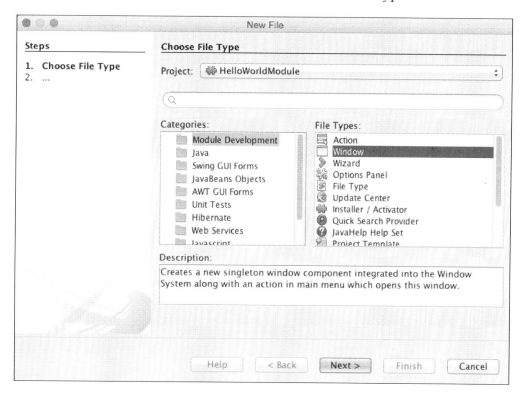

The different file types that we can create here are the same as when we create modules, as discussed earlier in this chapter. Again, some of them are more useful for standalone modules, whereas others are equally important to standalone and Platform application modules.

Let's take a look at the **Window** file type as this is one that is used within the majority of NetBeans Platform applications.

## Creating a NetBeans window

Upon selecting to create a window for a Platform application, the **New Window** dialog displays the **Basic Settings** page.

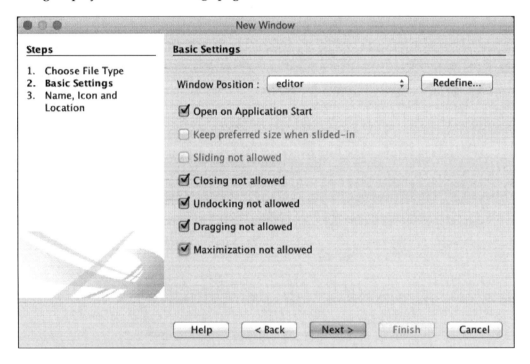

The first setting for a new window is the **Window Position**. This can take one of several values and defines where the window is initially displayed within NetBeans:

- **bottomSlidingSide**: This is displayed as a button at the bottom of the application window
- **editor**: This is displayed where the main editor windows are shown within NetBeans
- **explorer**: This is displayed where the explorer style windows are shown within NetBeans

- **leftSlidingSide**: This is displayed as a button on the left-hand side of the application window

- **output**: This is displayed where the main output window is shown within NetBeans

- **properties**: This is displayed where the properties windows are shown within NetBeans

- **rightSlidingSide**: This is displayed as a button on the right-hand side of the application window

- **topSlidingSide**: This is displayed as a button at the top of the application window

For each window location, several options are available to define the actions and abilities of a window:

- **Open on Application Start**
- **Keep preferred size when slided-in**
- **Sliding not allowed**
- **Closing not allowed**
- **Undocking not allowed**
- **Dragging not allowed**
- **Maximization not allowed**

The final page of the wizard allows the name, icon, and location of the class to be specified.

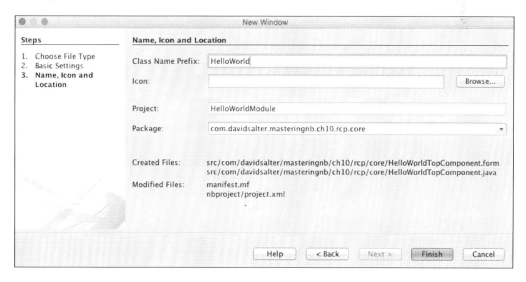

On this page, standard details such as a prefix for the class name, an icon for the window, and the package for the new Java class are specified.

Upon completing the wizard, the new window class is opened within the standard NetBeans GUI editor.

The code bundle for this chapter contains a simple NetBeans RCP application, as shown in the following screenshot:

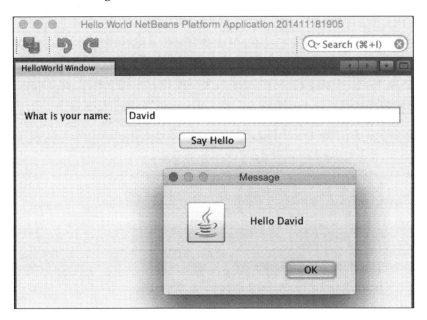

# Summary

In this chapter, we introduced the NetBeans modular system and saw the benefits that this can give us. We looked at creating standalone modules that can be installed into the NetBeans IDE, and saw how to create a NetBeans code generator. We then moved on and looked at the NetBeans Platform and saw all of the benefits it gives to application developers, notably the speed of development and the use of the vast array of NetBeans features. We looked at an example application and saw how to create different windows within a Platform application.

After reading all of the chapters in this book, you should now be familiar with the different functionality provided by NetBeans as both an IDE and a platform. With this knowledge, you will now be better equipped and better enabled to develop reliable applications using one of the best Java tools available. Congratulations, and happy developing!

# Index

## A

## O

**open services gateway initiative (OSGi)**
  about  300
  URL  300
**Oracle**
  URL  117
**Output window  37**

## P

**palette items**
  deleting  50, 51
  editing  52, 53
**Palette Manager  50, 51**
**Palette window**
  about  36
  code snippets  49, 50
**Payara Server**
  URL  125
**persistence.xml file**
  editing  142-144
**platform application components**
  creating  314-316
  NetBeans window, creating  316-318
**Platforms as a Service (PaaS)  111**
**properties, Swing forms**
  defining  168
  editing  169, 170
**Properties window  37**
**public web services**
  URL  291

## R

**Red-Green-Refactor cycle  106**
**remote application**
  URL  90
**Remote Method Invocation (RMI)  273**
**Representational State Transfer (REST)  274**
**RESTful web services**
  creating  293-295
  creating, with Client-Controlled
     Container-Item option  296
  creating, with Container-Item option  296
  creating, with Simple Root
     Resource option  295, 296
  reference link  294

**rich client platform (RCP) applications**
  about  305, 306
  branding  309-312
  creating  306-309
  properties  312, 313

## S

**SASS**
  configuring, in NetBeans  262, 263
  configuring, on project basis  264-267
  URL  261
**screen layout**
  about  28, 29
  explorer style windows  30
  Favorites window  31
  Navigator window  32
  Output window  37
  Palette window  36
  Properties window  37
  source code editor window  32, 33
  Window management  38-41
**session bean façade**
  creating, for entity classes  214-218
**session façade pattern**
  URL  214
**Sessions window  78, 79**
**Simple Object Access**
     Protocol (SOAP)  273, 274
**Simple Root Resource option**
  used, for creating RESTful
     web services  295, 296
**single-page applications (SPAs)  269**
**SOAP web service**
  consuming  290-292
  creating  276
  creating, from scratch  277-281
  creating, from WSDL  281-283
  managing  283-285
  message handlers  287, 288
  testing  285, 286
**source code editor window**
  about  32, 33
  History view  34, 35
**Sources window  80**
**Spring**
  URL  237

## Thank you for buying
# Mastering NetBeans

# About Packt Publishing

Packt, pronounced 'packed', published its first book, *Mastering phpMyAdmin for Effective MySQL Management*, in April 2004, and subsequently continued to specialize in publishing highly focused books on specific technologies and solutions.

Our books and publications share the experiences of your fellow IT professionals in adapting and customizing today's systems, applications, and frameworks. Our solution-based books give you the knowledge and power to customize the software and technologies you're using to get the job done. Packt books are more specific and less general than the IT books you have seen in the past. Our unique business model allows us to bring you more focused information, giving you more of what you need to know, and less of what you don't.

Packt is a modern yet unique publishing company that focuses on producing quality, cutting-edge books for communities of developers, administrators, and newbies alike. For more information, please visit our website at www.packtpub.com.

# About Packt Open Source

In 2010, Packt launched two new brands, Packt Open Source and Packt Enterprise, in order to continue its focus on specialization. This book is part of the Packt Open Source brand, home to books published on software built around open source licenses, and offering information to anybody from advanced developers to budding web designers. The Open Source brand also runs Packt's Open Source Royalty Scheme, by which Packt gives a royalty to each open source project about whose software a book is sold.

# Writing for Packt

We welcome all inquiries from people who are interested in authoring. Book proposals should be sent to author@packtpub.com. If your book idea is still at an early stage and you would like to discuss it first before writing a formal book proposal, then please contact us; one of our commissioning editors will get in touch with you.

We're not just looking for published authors; if you have strong technical skills but no writing experience, our experienced editors can help you develop a writing career, or simply get some additional reward for your expertise.

## NetBeans IDE 8 Cookbook

ISBN: 978-1-78216-776-1          Paperback: 386 pages

Over 75 practical recipes to maximize your
productivity with NetBeans

1. Increase developer productivity using features
   such as refactoring and code creation.

2. Test applications effectively using JUnit,
   TestNG, and Arquilian.

3. A recipe-based guide filled with practical
   examples to help you create robust applications
   using NetBeans.

## Java EE 7 Development with NetBeans 8

ISBN: 978-1-78398-352-0          Paperback: 364 pages

Develop professional enterprise Java EE applications
quickly and easily with this popular IDE

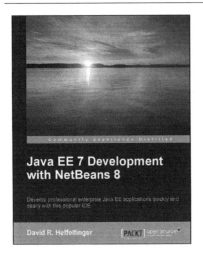

1. Use the features of the popular NetBeans
   IDE to accelerate your development of
   Java EE applications.

2. Covers the latest versions of the major Java EE
   APIs such as JSF 2.2, EJB 3.2, JPA 2.1, CDI 1.1,
   and JAX-RS 2.0.

3. Walks you through the development of
   applications utilizing popular JSF component
   libraries such as PrimeFaces, RichFaces,
   and ICEfaces.

Please check **www.PacktPub.com** for information on our titles

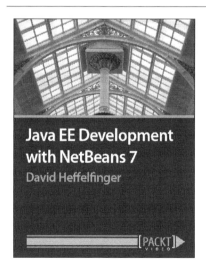

Made in the USA
San Bernardino, CA
24 April 2016